German Social Policy 1

Edited and introduced by
Lutz Leisering

German Social Policy
Edited and introduced by Lutz Leisering

The 5-volume series "German Social Policy" presents a unique multidisciplinary approach to the history of German social policy and is written by the doyens of their respective disciplines. The volumes expound the contribution of the German tradition to the rise of social policy in the Western world in the 19th and 20th centuries. Germany pioneered modern social policy in the 19th century when Bismarck introduced social insurance. After the Second World War, Germany's Social Market Economy became a model of social integration. The volumes cover the history of ideas (volume 1), the legal and political history before and after 1945 (volumes 2 and 3), the German Democratic Republic (1949-1990) and the impact of German reunification (1990) (volume 4). Volume 5 embeds the German case in a major comparative study of European welfare states, complemented by a study of the USA and the Soviet Union. The volumes also yield insights into general theoretical issues of social policy beyond the empirical case of Germany. Each volume has an introduction by the editor who summarizes the contribution made by the volumes and looks into the future of German social policy.

Volume 1:
F.-X. Kaufmann: Thinking About Social Policy – The German Tradition
2013. ISBN 978-3-642-19500-6

Volume 2:
M. Stolleis: Origins of the German Welfare State – Social Policy in Germany to 1945
2013. ISBN 978-3-642-22521-5

Volume 3:
H.F. Zacher: Social Policy in the Federal Republic of Germany – The Constitution of the Social
2013. ISBN 978-3-642-22524-6

Volume 4:
M.G. Schmidt and G.A. Ritter: The Rise and Fall of a Socialist Welfare State - The German Democratic Republic (1949 – 1990) and German Unification (1989 – 1994)
2013. ISBN 978-3-642-22527-7

Volume 5:
F.-X. Kaufmann: Variations of the Welfare State – Great Britain, Sweden, France and Germany Between Capitalism and Socialism
2013. ISBN 978-3-642-22548-2

Franz-Xaver Kaufmann

Thinking About Social Policy

The German Tradition

Translated from the German by Thomas Dunlap

Springer

Prof. em. Dr. oec. DDr. h.c. Franz-Xaver Kaufmann
Römerstraße 118
53117 Bonn
Germany
f.x.kaufmann@uni-bielefeld.de

Operative editors: Günter H. Ast, Lutz Leisering

Published with the financial support of:

VolkswagenStiftung

Federal Ministry of Labour and Social Affairs

Parts of this volume have been published previously in German in the following publication: Bundesministerium für Arbeit und Sozialordnung [Federal Ministry of Labour and Social Order] and Bundesarchiv [Federal Archive] (eds.): Geschichte der Sozialpolitik in Deutschland seit 1945, vol. 1 (of 11 volumes published 2001-2008): Grundlagen der Sozialpolitik, Baden-Baden, Nomos, 2001, ISBN 3-7890-7314-8

Kaufmann, F.-X.: Sozialpolitisches Denken, Suhrkamp: Frankfurt am Main, 2003. ISBN 978-3518123218

ISBN 978-3-642-19500-6 ISBN 978-3-642-19501-3 (eBook)
DOI 10.1007/978-3-642-19501-3
Springer Heidelberg New York Dordrecht London

Library of Congress Control Number: 2011939488

Printed on acid-free paper

Springer is part of Springer Science+Business Media (www.springer.com)

Preface to the Book Series "German Social Policy"

The welfare state originated as a project of nation states, with roots in the nineteenth century. This book is part of a book series about the German tradition of social policy, which is one of the three paradigmatical European traditions of social policy besides the British and the Swedish traditions. The book series covers modern social policy in Germany from its beginnings under the early modern state to its breakthrough in the nineteenth century to the present day, ranging from poor relief to Bismarckian social insurance to the post World War II "social market economy" and the current crisis. The series provides even more: it also locates Germany in the wider context of a comparative study of European welfare traditions, complemented by a study of the USA and the Soviet Union proposed to be non-welfare states (volume 5). Furthermore, volume 4 contrasts a democratic welfare state with a communist "welfare state", namely the Federal Republic of Germany with the German Democratic Republic which resided side by side 1949–1990, followed by an analysis of the transition to the new unified Germany in 1990.

Beyond the empirical case of Germany, the work yields insights into general issues of social policy which have been addressed in German discourses in-depth and at an early stage. This includes the distinction "state versus society" which is essential for a theoretical understanding of the welfare state; the meaning of "the social" and the "social question"; the identification of what a "welfare state" is compared to non-welfare states; and social policy issues arising during the transition from communism to democratic capitalism.

The unique quality of the book series derives from its authors. The grand old men of German scholarship on social policy, coming from diverse disciplines, have rendered their legacy to the scientific community and to politics: *Franz-Xaver Kaufmann* (sociology) writes on the history of the idea of "social policy" in German politics since the nineteenth century (volume 1); *Michael Stolleis* (legal history) presents an overview of social policy in Germany from the middle ages to 1945, with an emphasis on the years after 1871 (volume 2); *Hans F. Zacher* (constitutional law) investigates the history of the German post-war welfare state and its normative foundations (volume 3); *Manfred G. Schmidt* (political science) analyses communist East Germany, the German Democratic Republic (GDR, 1949–1990), followed by *Gerhard A. Ritter's* study of German unification (1989–1994) (volume 4); and *Franz-Xaver Kaufmann* provides an international comparison of welfare states (and some non-welfare states) (volume 5). All authors take a distinctly historical approach to their subject, elaborating the formative forces of social policy in Germany.

The book series is a translated, revised and up-dated version of the first of the 11 large volumes of the "History of Social Policy in Germany Since 1945".[1] While two contributions of the first volume have been left out, a study of German unification by Ritter (based on his award-winning study of the subject) has been added to the English version. The 11 volumes of the German work add up to the most ambitious and comprehensive study of the history of German social policy ever published. The work not just displays the state of the art but includes original studies which draw on historical sources that have not been accessible before. Especially for this work the government lifted confidentiality from many documents. Volume 1, which underlies this book series, provides a general framework for the more specific Vols. 2–11 that cover 17 fields of West and East German social policy chronologically. The work was initiated by Chancellor Kohl in 1994. The idea was to take stock of the German social policy tradition at a historical moment: the Iron Curtain over East Europe had fallen, the Treaty of Maastricht had created the "European Union" (1992/1993) and German politics had eventually realized that the "golden years" of the post war welfare state had come to a close. At the same time, the new challenges of globalization and demographic change had become apparent. In the early 1990s, German politics was only just beginning to face up to these challenges while the authors of Vol. 1 of the German work were already sensible of the inherent tensions and uncertainties of the advanced post war welfare state.

Translating, revising and extending the original German "History of Social Policy in Germany Since 1945" was not an easy task. It required a joint and protracted endeavour of a number of persons and a considerable sum of money. I am indebted to Richard Hauser for bringing up the idea of a translation (and joining, with Werner Abelshauser, my application for funding with the Volkswagen Foundation); to Franz-Xaver Kaufmann for continuously supporting the project in many ways and with verve; to Thomas Dunlap, David Antal and Ben Veghte who translated the demanding texts with admirable skill and care; to Günter H. Ast, formerly Federal Ministry of Labour and Social Affairs, who acted as operative editor of the texts with unceasing commitment and patience; to Werner A. Müller, Katharina Wetzel-Vandai, Irene Barrios-Kezic and Kay Stoll from Springer publishers who supported the project with diligence; and, last but not least, to the authors for their support and patience.

[1]Geschichte der Sozialpolitik in Deutschland seit 1945. Edited by the Federal Ministry of Labour and Social Affairs (*Bundesministerium für Arbeit und Soziales*) and the Federal Archive (*Bundesarchiv*). 11 volumes, Nomos publishers, Baden-Baden. 2001–2008. The book series is based on a translation of the first volume, *Grundlagen der Sozialpolitik*. (See footnote on p. 125).

I thank the Volkswagen Foundation, Hannover/(Germany), for generously funding the translation under their scheme "'Deutsch plus' – A Program for Multilingualism in Teaching and Research" (Az. II/83 610). I equally am indebted to the Federal Ministry of Labour and Social Affairs, Berlin/Bonn which co-funded the project, approved by the minister, Ursula von der Leyen, and processed by Thomas Biewer. I also thank the Ministry and the Federal Archive, Nomos publishers, Suhrkamp, C.H. Beck and VS publishers for granting permission to translate the German work. Sage gave permission to adopt passages for the introduction from an earlier article I wrote.[2] Finally, I am most indebted to my wife Maria who gave me time to finish this undertaking.

Lutz Leisering

[2]Leisering L (2003) Nation state and welfare state. An intellectual and political history. Journal of European Social Policy 13:175–185.

Contents

Nation State and Social Policy: An Ideational and Political History Introduction to the Book Series "German Social Policy" 1
Lutz Leisering
1 The Distinction "State Versus Society" 2
2 "The Social" 3
3 Variations of Modern Society: Distinguishing Welfare States and Non-Welfare States 6
4 Variations of the Welfare State: The Idiosyncrasy of National "State Traditions" 9
5 Post-War German Social Policy in Retrospect: The Genesis of a Welfare State 12
6 What Future for the Social? 14
References 20

Thinking About Social Policy: The German Tradition 23
Franz-Xaver Kaufmann
1 Introduction 23
2 Social Policy as Mediation Between "State" and "Civil Society" 26
2.1 Social – Socialism – Science of Society 26
2.2 Social Question – Social Reform – Social Policy 32
3 The Workers' Question and Social Policy (1863–1918) 42
3.1 Latency of the Term *Sozialpolitik* 42
3.2 The Influence of the *Verein für Socialpolitik* 47
3.3 First Conceptual Debates 54
3.4 The Influence of the First World War 63
4 The Crisis of Social Policy (1920–1945) 65
4.1 The Crisis Discussion and its Context 66
4.2 Social-Democratic Perspectives: Between Socialization and the Social *Rechtsstaat* (rule of law) 69

4.3 "Christian Social Reform" and the Failure of Corporatist Solutions to the Conflicts 78
4.4 Reactions from Scientific Social Policy 80
4.5 Social Policy Under National Socialism 89
5 Social Policy Since the Second World War 92
5.1 Normative Orientations 93
5.2 Social Policy as Social Science Between Tradition and new Orientations (1946–1966) 100
5.3 Social Policy Between "Quality of Life" and "Crisis of the Social State" (1967–1999) 113
6 Concluding Remarks 122
References 125

Index of Persons 155

Subject Index 161

Nation State and Social Policy: An Ideational and Political History

Introduction to the Book Series "German Social Policy"

Lutz Leisering

Advances in social policy were often related to processes of nation-building, like the introduction of social insurance by Chancellor Bismarck during the years 1883–1889 which contributed to the social integration of the new German Empire. The Empire had been created through the unification of the numerous German states in 1871. Critical periods in a country's history that went along with a renewal of the national spirit also propelled social reform, like the New Deal during the Great Depression in the 1930s and the creation of the British "welfare state" in the immediate aftermath of World War II. Today, the golden age of the welfare state, the decades after WW II, has passed. Domestic problems combine with the impact of globalisation. Some authors assume that globalisation makes nation states increasingly irrelevant. What, then, is a history of a national welfare state as presented in this book series good for in the contemporary debate?

Western welfare states have proved to be resilient amidst domestic and global crises. While welfare states are undergoing far-reaching change there is no sign that welfare statism is disappearing. To the contrary, the "social" and social policy have been spreading to the global South since the 1990s to become a key issue of global politics – "socialization of global politics" (Deacon 1997). Looking into the intellectual and political history of one of the great traditions of social policy, indeed the pioneer of modern social policy, Germany, may then shed light on key issues of social policy that continue to underlie political debates and conflicts. Stolleis (in volume 2 of the work) argues that the past is still present in current policies and institutions, like layers that have piled up in the course of history, including pre-Bismarckian social policies.

The analysis of the last 130 years of German social policy (plus earlier periods) as presented in this work uncovers key issues of social policy which are relevant beyond the German case: the disjunction "state versus society" to which social policy is seen as a response in the German intellectual tradition; the meaning of "the social", the "social question" and "social policy"; the meaning of "welfare state" as compared to non-welfare states; and social policy in different societal settings like monarchy, national socialism, communism, democracy and affluent society – and during periods of transition.

F.-X. Kaufmann, *Thinking About Social Policy*, German Social Policy 1,
DOI 10.1007/978-3-642-19501-3_1, © Springer-Verlag Berlin Heidelberg 2013

1 The Distinction "State Versus Society"

The history of social policy has been riddled with debates about individualism versus collectivism, about state versus market and related dichotomies. In current controversies about "globalisation", free marketeers quarrel with advocates of social and ecological regulation of global markets. While these are world-wide issues, Germany, more than any other country, has developed an intense political discourse on "the state" and on the distinction between "state" and "society" that goes back to the early nineteenth century and is worth looking at.

Franz-Xaver Kaufmann's *Thinking About Social Policy* (volume 1 of the book series) traces the political history of the concept of social policy. "Social policy" as a political and scholarly concept originated in Germany in the second half of the nineteenth century, to become more prominent only after World War II. In Britain, France and other countries it gained ascendance only in the 1970s. Kaufmann argues that "social policy" has emerged as a response to problems of societal integration which, from the point of view of Hegelian philosophy, arose from a disjunction between "state" and "society".

Kaufmann's point – which sets the theme for the whole book series – is that the history of social policy is the history of the changing relationship between state and society and of the ensuing problems of social integration. The German Philosopher Hegel (1770–1831), after first allusions by Montesquieu, diagnosed the disintegration of the ancient and early modern idea of a unitary, politically integrated society – the Lockean "political society" – into two heterogeneous spheres, "state" versus "society" or "public" versus "private". "It was here [in Hegel's philosophy – L.L.] that the political and the social appeared for the first time as two separate spheres dominated by *different* legal principles, and the *relationships* between them subsequently became the fundamental issue of 'social policy'" (Kaufmann, volume 1, p. 29). The problem, as the Hegelians saw it, was that "society", mainly the economy, was a source of uncontrollable dynamics and social problems.

The diagnosis of separate spheres was further developed in the twentieth century by the sociologists Talcott Parsons and Niklas Luhmann under the name "structural" or "functional" "differentiation" of society (Luhmann 1982). In their view, too, functional differentiation generated a problem, namely the necessity of enabling persons to participate in functional systems. Drawing on T.H. Marshall they referred to this requirement as the problem of "inclusion".

While Marx (1818–1883), who was a Hegelian, proposed communism as a solution, that is, a fusion of the Societal and the Political, his contemporary Lorenz von Stein (1815–1890), also a Hegelian, proposed a compromise solution (which today could be termed "social-liberal") which he called "social-policy". Social-policy was to link the Societal and the Political (through "social administration") while preserving a basic autonomy of the Societal (in modern terms: to intervene in the economy, family etc. in a non-totalitarian way). Lorenz von Stein, a lawyer and economist, was the intellectual father of the welfare state, precisely 100 years before Beveridge (von Stein 1842) and two years before Marx published his first concept of communism (not yet termed as such; see Marx 1978, first published in 1844) based on the same diagnosis of class conflict in industrial society as von Stein's. The distinction between "state" and "society" and the analysis of their precarious relationship has shaped the German tradition of thinking about the state and social policy ever since (Luhmann 1987).

Germany was a latecomer to industrialization and to nation-building but the pioneer of state welfare. Bismarck's social insurance was a means of integrating the new nation state and securing support by the laboring classes. German liberalism was weak and the "Manchester theory" had eventually fallen in disrepute after the economic crisis of 1873, as Stolleis points out in his *Origins of the German Welfare State – Social Policy in Germany to 1945* (volume 2 of the book series, p. 52). During those years the term social policy started its career in politics. Social policy set out as a comprehensive "workers policy" (*Arbeiterpolitik*) in a society divided by class. During the nineteenth and twentieth centuries the concept of "social policy" changed its meaning several times, mirroring new challenges of societal integration and new ideas of "the social".

After World War II, social policy expanded in an unprecedented way, connected to two new formulas designed to denote the place of social policy in post-war society. The first formula, "Social Market Economy", aimed to integrate the economic and the social. The second formula, "social state", the German version of "welfare state", was contained in the post-war constitution of the new Federal Republic of Germany 1949, the *Grundgesetz* (1949). (The year before, 1948, had witnessed the creation of the British "welfare state".) The year 1949 marked a "double state building" (Christoph Klessmann) which reflected the link between social policy and nation building. While the German Constitution of 1919 had already included articles on social welfare regulations, the West German Constitution of 1949 was the first to establish the "social state" as constitutive principle of the German polity, not to be changed even by a majority in Parliament. In the same year, the German Democratic Republic (GDR) was founded in East Germany under the influence of the Soviet Union. The GDR opted for "socialism", presented as an alternative to the West German social state (see below). The meaning of "Social Market Economy" and "social state" was indeterminate and contested. Political controversies during the 1950s generated some clarification but the two formulas continued to indicate the openness of the idea of the "social" in the development of the Federal Republic of Germany.

2 "The Social"

Out of the three components of "democratic welfare capitalism" – "the hyphenated society" (Marshall 1981) – the component "welfare (state)" has remained more contested than the other two, democracy and market. This hints at problems of identifying "the social". ". . . the systemic character of social policy is not nearly as evident as that of the market economy. What 'the social' means in distinction to the economic and the political . . . – to this day no clarity has emerged on this question" (Kaufmann, volume 1, p. 97f.). Nullmeier, in his political theory of the welfare state (2000, chapter VI, p. 2), points at the inferior legitimacy of social rights as compared to civil and political rights.

Like the distinction between state and society, the term "(the) social" is part of the German tradition. Hans F. Zacher, in his *Social Policy in the Federal Republic of Germany* (volume 3 of the book series): "The social is in a very special way part of Germany's national identity" (pp. 315). Germans call their welfare state a "social state". In France, the term "solidarity" has played a comparable role from the nineteenth century and still shapes present-day debates on social policy. The term "social" emanated in the 1830s in Germany, with influences from France, and soon fed into the term "social policy" and other nineteenth century semantics like the "social question". Unlike British and French usage, the word "social" assumed a strongly normative and critical connotation in the German language: the word was contrasted to "the individualistic" to denote something that was seen to be absent from civil society (*bürgerliche Gesellschaft*; Kaufmann, volume 1, p. 32). After World War II, the "social" became a common element of the political and scholarly language in Germany. In the British community of social policy researchers, the term "the social" figures less though increasingly. Remarkably, the term has recently even reached the global level, as indicated by novel semantics of global social policy like "social pensions", "social cash transfers", "corporate social responsibility" and "social sustainability".

". . . '*social*' has something to do with *equality* and *inequality*. '*Social*' *negates* a certain measure of *inequality* – or more precisely: certain constellations of inequality. . . . '*social*' is a mandate to distinguish unreasonable inequalities from reasonable or at least tolerable ones (or less important ones), and to eliminate, compensate for, or at least diminish the unreasonable ones" (Zacher, volume 3, p. 24). This implies that the meaning of the "social" may change, and that it varies across time and between social groups. In politics, the semantic field of the social encompasses ideas like social justice, individual social rights, protection and security. In the British debate, the social is often defined with reference to "need" but need is an equally fluid concept. Despite or rather just because of its vagueness, reference to the "social" may exert considerable political pressure on policy-makers. What appears to be a deficiency is in Zacher's view the very essence of the "social". He sees the openness and changeability of the "social" as an intrinsic feature of a welfare state in a free and democratic society, a feature that was lacking, e.g., in the German Democratic Republic.

The difficulty to pin down the meaning of social policy and the "social" indicates the compromise character and the historical changeability of social policy: "From the point of view of the great political doctrines of liberalism, socialism and conservatism, 'social policy' has evolved as a seemingly heterogeneous sequence of inconsistent compromises. By contrast, this analysis rests on the assumption that the history of social policy in Germany reflects an independent 'reformist' strand which developed against the backdrop of the three 'great ideologies' but has independent roots and points of view. The social-democratic, Christian-social, and social-liberal position appear not only as a more or less consistent compromise between liberal, socialist, and conservative ideas, but in many cases also as a productive synthesis with far-reaching positions of its own" (Kaufmann, volume 1, p. 26; for Christian Democracy and the welfare state see van Kersbergen 1995). Therefore, remarkably, unlike British textbooks on social policy, Kaufmann in his *Thinking About Social Policy* (volume 1) pays scant attention to liberal, socialist and conservative thought when tracing the history of the idea of social policy.

The great ideologies do not tell us a lot about questions of social development and institutional design in a complex and changing society. Esping-Andersen has used these ideologies to label two of his three welfare regime types, the liberal and the conservative regime. Kaufmann's alternative approach to comparative welfare state analysis (see below) shows that these labels are inadequate to distinguish between welfare states. In line with Kaufmann's interpretation of social policy as an ideological compromise, Schmidt's (2005) and Obinger and Wagschal's (1998) empirical analyses of the impact of political parties have shown that the German welfare state is more accurately characterised as "centrist" rather than "conservative" (see below).

In the post-war period, the social has been strongly associated with state welfare and the idea of the welfare state. In Germany, the term "social state" is preferred to "welfare state", the latter sounding egalitarian or even totalitarian to German ears, and makes some people think e.g. of Sweden.[1] Zacher (volume 3) challenges the social democratic orthodoxy of equating the social with "social" intervention by the government. Rather, Zacher defines "the social" by a "basic formula" which posits work and family as the primary sources of providing for human needs, with the law enabling, securing and compensating the operation of work and family. "Only the state and society together can adequately bring about the social" (Zacher, volume 3, p. 46). Zacher (volume 3, p. 43) also speaks of a "constant intermingling of private, societal-public, and state activities". In Zacher's view the actual ability of the welfare state to impact on the welfare of individuals is mostly overrated, by advocates and critics of the welfare state alike.

The *doyen* of German post-war social policy thinking, Hans Achinger (1979, first published 1958) also objected to equating the social with the welfare state. In his view, social policy cannot lay claim to representing unique "social" values. Achinger challenged the claim that the social constitutes an independent normative province: "the idea of an autonomous normative sphere of social policy is a delusion. Social policy relies on ideas of order stemming from other social spheres" (Achinger 1979, p. 7; transl. L.L.). In the British debate, Robert Pinker, in his critique of the Titmussian orthodoxy (Pinker 1971, 1979), similarly rejected the notion of a moral superiority

[1] In addition, "social state" is a term of German constitutional law denoting the "social" obligation of the state. Therefore, Kaufmann and Zacher (volumes 1, 3 and 5) use the term "social state" rather than "welfare state" when they refer to Germany. The other authors of the series mostly use the Anglo-Saxon term "welfare state", which is also used as a theoretical term by German scholars. See Ritter (volume 4, footnote 64) for further explications of the terms.

of the "social market" (Titmuss) over the economic market. Rather, "the social", "welfare" and social policy are pluralistic concepts. "Welfare state" always means "welfare state in a free society" ("liberal welfare state"; "*freiheitlicher Wohlfahrtsstaat*"; Zacher, volume 3, p. 45), that is, a state in a mixed society in which "the social" is not primarily promoted by the government. State provision is part of a wider welfare mix, and in Germany even "state" often means "intermediary" agencies like social insurance, which in Germany are non-state agencies with separate budgets, or voluntary welfare associations.

3 Variations of Modern Society: Distinguishing Welfare States and Non-Welfare States

Studies of the welfare state normally assume that every Western society is a welfare state. Franz-Xaver Kaufmann's *Variations of the Welfare State* (volume 5 of the series) questions that assumption. Cross-national comparisons which use the typological method, most prominently Esping-Andersen's work, often cannot distinguish between welfare states and non-welfare states. In Kaufmann's view, the instability of the classification of countries (noted by many commentators especially with regard to Esping-Andersen's original classification of 1990) indicates that the dimensions of comparison have been insufficiently worked out in theoretical terms. Esping-Andersen, from a political economy point of view, defines welfare statism by decommodification but his decommodification index has no cut off point that could distinguish between welfare states and non-welfare states. Other authors define "welfare state" in descriptive institutional terms, by a list of social services (common in the Anglo-Saxon literature), but then any country with a range of social services may appear as a welfare state.

By contrast, Kaufmann emphasizes the normative and cultural dimension of the welfare state by distinguishing two sides of the welfare state: the "*welfare sector*" as a range of social services and administrations and *welfare politics* as political action revolving around "social" issues. We can speak of a "welfare state" if and only if social services are linked to normative orientations: if political actors assume a collective responsibility for the well-being of the entire population (Kaufmann, volume 5, p. 35). Kaufmann subscribes to the definition by Harry Girvetz (1968, p. 512) which emphasizes law and normative orientations: "The welfare state is the institutional outcome of the assumption by a society of legal and therefore formal and explicit responsibility for the basic well-being of all of its members. Such a state emerges when a society or its decision-making groups become convinced that the welfare of the individual [. . .] is too important to be left to custom or to informal arrangements and private understandings and is therefore a concern of government." The core of a welfare state is the commitment to social rights (inclusion) embedded in a culture of social responsibility.

This ambitious definition of "welfare state" has methodological consequences. It implies a new approach to the comparative study of nation states that emphasizes norms, culture and history. Kaufmann elaborates such a socio-cultural approach (see the next section). It is a holistic and institutionalist approach which yields rich analyses of the *gestalt* of a welfare state and, if used comparatively, produces accounts of the "idiosyncrasy" (*Eigensinn;* Kaufmann, volume 5, p. 31) of each welfare state (Ginsburg 1992 and Castles 1993 are cited as kindred approaches). In this way, the variety of welfare states is exposed while avoiding a coarse typology.

Moreover, the socio-cultural approach enables Kaufmann to show, based on meticulous secondary studies of the USA and the former Soviet Union, that not all modern nation states are welfare states. Some are just "capitalism" – the USA –, some are "socialism" – the former Soviet Union –, and others, especially countries of the global South, may muster some social services for privileged groups mostly related to government or the military but lack a normative concern that defines a welfare state.

In this light, the (essentially West European) welfare state appears as a third way between capitalism and socialism. Anglo-Saxon researchers easily classify the USA as welfare state or welfare capitalism. The USA has not ratified the International Covenant on Economic, Social and Cultural Rights of 1966. During the war on poverty in the 1960s there "arose – perhaps the only time in US history – a political and public majority opinion that believed in the potential of social policy to shape society" (Kaufmann, volume 5, p. 84). The departure of the 1960s was triggered by a moral and civil crisis, not by an economic crisis as in the case of the New Deal of the 1930s.

In the burgeoning literature on welfare regimes and typologies Kaufmann's comparative approach that highlights the "idiosyncrasy" of welfare states offers a stimulating new perspective. By including and identifying non-welfare states Kaufmann also contributes to the more general debate on the "varieties of capitalism" opened up by David Soskice and others (for an overview see Hall and Soskice 2001). The "varieties of capitalism" debate concentrates on the economy, on industrial relations and the labor market while Kaufmann adds the fields of social security and personal social services and discusses them in conjunction with the economic fields.

Manfred G. Schmidt's *Social Policy in the German Democratic Republic* (GDR, communist East Germany; in volume 4 of the series) helps to put the distinction between welfare states and non-welfare states to the test. The welfare of the people was a major promise and source of legitimacy of the GDR. "All power serves the good of the people" (Constitution, article 4). "We are guaranteed social security and safety, full employment, equal educational opportunities for all children of the people" (Honecker in 1986, quoted by Schmidt, volume 4, p. 27). The right to work was seen as the showpiece of the GDR. The status of the GDR as an independent nation state beside the West German Federal Republic was always contested. Social rights and social security were meant to underpin the claim of the GDR to be a genuine socialist nation and the better alternative to West Germany. Again, social policy and nation building were closely linked. Schmidt's contribution aims to test the claim of the GDR to be superior in "social" terms.

Social policy was not seen as an original field of politics in the GDR till 1961. This was true to the original doctrine of communism, because "social policy" assumes a distinction between "state" and "society" while communism means a fusion of both spheres. The East German leaders opted for Marx, not for Lorenz von Stein. 1961–1971 under Ulbricht, the concept "socialist social policy" emerged though "the social" remained subordinated to the economic. The year 1961 when the Berlin Wall was erected was the true founding date of the GDR. Honecker (1971–1989) made the "unity of economic policy and social policy" a key formula of social development. The strategy was to increase consumption, to raise the motivation of the workers and to boost birth rates.

Social spending was low by international standards (around 15% of gross domestic product (GDP), measured by the International Labour Organization (ILO)) and social services offered not more than bare minimum standards or even less. However, if we take into account the cost of subsidies to basic consumption goods and the cost of securing full employment through unproductive work, social spending figures easily double. But the economy was too weak to sustain that degree of "security and safety". Schmidt's key thesis is that there was a grave, in fact excessive imbalance between the moderate economic performance and the high degree of social protection in the GDR. The sociologist M. Rainer Lepsius once remarked that the GDR in 1989 became "the first welfare state to collapse under the burden of its social services".

But was it really a welfare state? Did the GDR positively grant social rights? Schmidt's answer is negative. The GDR was "far removed" from all Western welfare regimes (Schmidt, volume 4, p. 131). The right to work, to education, to housing and to protection in case of illness, incapacity and old age was proclaimed but it was substantially qualified in its realisation (and subject to "societal requirements" even in the Constitution, article 24). The gap between the rights and the actual services was wide: the level of services was low (with an estimated 40% of pensioners living in poverty, measured by the 50% income threshold), benefits were increased irregularly by way of political discretion and the rights could not be claimed in court. The GDR was not a welfare state as defined by Kaufmann because the "social" was dominated by the political and the economic. Political considerations were paramount, with substantial legal privileges for state elites, e.g. with regard to old-age pensions, and discrimination of children from "bourgeois" or religious backgrounds in the educational system. In addition, social security was used for economic purpose. The GDR was more of a workfare state than the USA.

The GDR was neither a welfare state as defined by Zacher. A closed, static notion of social needs prevailed: the level of benefits met pre-war standards and provisions were not responsive to changing aspirations in an individualistic society that emerged in the 1980s even in the GDR. This was not an open and pluralistic concept of the social stipulated by Zacher as the core of a welfare state in a free society. The implicit formula of the GDR "social rights without civil and political rights" did not work out because social rights interlock with civil freedom and political participation. But central planning, not freedom, was the overriding concept of society. "It thus seemed possible even to plan individual and social consumption" (Schmidt, volume 4, p. 30). Work was not seen as a social but as a mere economic issue that had been resolved – the Ministry of Labour was dismantled in 1958, the labor exchanges even earlier (Kahlenberg and Hoffmann 2001, p. 181). Even family policy was reduced to boosting birth rates; the traditional gender arrangement was only half changed, with more women in employment but still doing the house work. This was not a welfare state. It was an "authoritarian, paternalistic work and welfare state" (Schmidt, volume 4, p. 131).

Gerhard A. Ritter's *The Politics of German Unification. Social, Economic, Financial, Constitutional and International Issues* (in volume 4 of the series) analyses the years from the eve of unification of West and East Germany in 1989 to the aftermath of unification (till 1994). The transition from communism to a new post-communist order in East European countries has been widely studied. East Germany was special since it had a Western counterpart. In this case transition meant merger with the Federal Republic of Germany. In some respects this made things easier compared to other Eastern countries that were left to fend for themselves even if international agencies offered some support. In other respects the transition was more difficult due to problems of making two worlds meet and of integrating a less modernized region into the Federal Republic of Germany.

German unification made the link between nation building and social policy explicit again. The "Social Union", that is, the integration of the two Germanys in social policy terms, turned out to be a critical strand of unification. The Social Union was initially contested. When planning for unification, three alternative strategies were considered: delaying the Social Union, that is, not (fully) transferring the generous West German social services and rights to the East in order to facilitate economic growth; transferring the West German system topped up by alleged or real "social achievements" of the GDR to be retained; and transferring the West German system without topping up. The latter solution prevailed as a compromise, turning the GDR into a modern welfare state in one day, at least legally. Failure to achieve a viable Social Union might have put the entire process at risk: "... in light of the economic problems and constellation of political forces, there was ultimately no alternative to extending the West German welfare state to the East. This is not to deny several grave errors in the social policy of unification" (Ritter, volume 4, p. 204).

4 Variations of the Welfare State: The Idiosyncrasy of National "State Traditions"

With his holistic cultural approach Kaufmann's *Variations of the Welfare State* (volume 5) analyses Britain, Sweden, France and Germany (besides the USA and the Soviet Union as non-welfare states). Each country is portrayed as a singular case with an "autonomous cosmology" (Kaufmann, volume 5, p. 33) rooted in history and culture. While this may sound rather vague and "soft", Kaufmann's analyses yield ample new and fascinating insights into the cultural and institutional diversity of a continent (Europe) which is moving towards political unity. Kaufmann also provides analytical categories that can be used by students of comparative politics to move beyond the standard ways of comparing welfare states. All country studies follow the same pattern (which is also applied in the analyses of the non-welfare states), with a focus on three themes:

1. The relationship between *"state" and "society"* in a country, that is, the historical "state tradition" (see also Dyson 1980) with regard to institutional patterns (government, public administration, courts; federal vs. unitary systems, central-local government relationships etc.) and ideas (about the proper scope of government, about ways and means of intervening or not intervening in the economy, family and "private" life). Germany, e.g., as explicated earlier, is imbued by the distinction between "state" and "society". Stolleis specifies the influence of the German state tradition in the historical situation of German unification after 1871. In the face of a weak liberal tradition, the legacy of the autocratic state and of the corporatist or "intermediary" structures of early modernity produced a "mixture of half-authoritarian and autonomous structures" (Stolleis, volume 2, p. 59) typical of German social policy ever since.
2. The *problem definition* prevalent in social politics: ". . . how the 'social question' is posed [in a country L.L.], that is, how the guiding problem of the respective social policy was articulated at the beginning of its development, will be postulated as a revealing key for understanding national developments of the welfare state" (Kaufmann, volume 5, p. 32f.). The guiding problem (*Bezugs-problem,* problem of reference) is assumed to influence both discourse and institutional practice even at much later stages in the development of social policy. The original "social question", the problem that has propelled social politics in Germany, was the "workers question", that is, the social risks and needs of the industrial worker to which Bismarck's social insurance was a response. The "workers question" was the key issue of social integration in the new German Empire founded in 1871: "National and social questions came together in a half-finished state structure and necessitated an intensive linkage of domestic and foreign policy" (Stolleis, volume 2, p. 57). By contrast, British social policy remained oriented towards the problem of poverty. The social question which permeates the Swedish system is the issue of inequality, which gave rise to universal services. In France the concern for family and population has been at the heart of social policy. These four different problem definitions (which do not follow a linear order) have left their traces in the institutional design of each welfare state. They define national welfare paths.
3. The *sectoral structure of social services* in a country. Kaufmann looks at three heterogeneous fields of social policy: production (labor law, industrial relations, labor market policy), (re-)distribution (income maintenance) and reproduction (personal social services, benefits in kind). The literature is mostly confined to one or two of these fields or even parts thereof, so balances and imbalances,

similarities and dissimilarities, between the three fields in one country cannot be identified (Esping-Andersen 1990, e.g., operationalizes "decommodification" only on the basis of cash benefits.) The relationship between the fields also reflects political problem definitions, indicating a national profile of a welfare state. Alber (1995) and Mayer (1997) also analyse the question of homogeneity and heterogeneity of social policy fields as a methodological challenge for welfare state analysis. Kaufmann (2012; chapter first published in German in 1982) earlier developed a theory of socio-political intervention that yields a distinction of four heterogeneous types of intervention akin to four policy fields. Similarly, Kasza (2002) diagnoses "a disjointed set of welfare policies" in most countries. As a consequence he rejects the concept of welfare 'regimes' altogether and calls for restricting comparative analyses to specific policy areas. But this conclusion is not necessary. Kaufmann takes differences between policy fields as part of the profile of a welfare state.

The German welfare state, e.g., is biased towards income maintenance whereas the British welfare state is stronger on services. Old-age pensions are the "sacred cow" in German politics, a role which in Britain is played by the National Health Service. Labor law is more important in Germany than in Britain. Kaufmann is interested in tracing incongruent normative patterns in different fields of social policy in one country, indicating "package solutions" (Kaufmann, volume 5, p. 32) that have proved viable as a political compromise. The British welfare state, e.g., combines full egalitarian health services with a poverty approach to income security in old age. This is one reason for the difficulty of classifying the British welfare state.

With these three dimensions of welfare states in mind, the profiles of the British, the Swedish and the French welfare states emerge more clearly. For *Britain*, the most basic finding is that the distinction state versus society is not even applicable because it is rooted in the Roman legal distinction between public and private law which is not part of British common law. Since the Glorious Revolution and John Locke, "government" (not "the state"!) has been seen as the trustee of "civil society", a term that retained the old meaning of *res publica*, of a unitary, politically integrated "political society": "Thus, the notion of society was *not* depoliticized and was not infused with the derogatory aftertaste it acquired so often in continental political thought as the embodiment of particularist and mostly economic private interests" (Ritter 1964, p. 30, quoted by Kaufmann, volume 5, p. 93). In a paradoxical way, the weak notion of state enabled Britain to develop a system of government with powers that are constitutionally less restricted than in Germany. The British state tradition also includes a late professionalization and bureaucratization of the civil service and a liberal-utilitarian justification of state intervention that follows the logic of Benthamite rational collectivism. British utilitarianism and German Hegelianism have consistently ignored each other. The British labor movement was much more concerned with the idea of self-help than the German labor movement, and it produced a political (Labour) party much later (1900; Germany: 1863/1869/1875) even though Germany was industrialised much later than Britain.

The *Swedish* state-society tradition represents a third, peculiar type. "In Sweden, ... similar to England, the tension between 'state' and 'society' hardly played any role, though for very different reasons" (Kaufmann, volume 5, p. 117): While Britain was a latecomer to modern state bureaucracy, Sweden (together with France) was a pioneer, even preceding Prussia, the dominant German state before German unification in 1871. But the evolving civil society in Sweden never really confronted the state as in Germany. On this basis, a modern interventionist state could develop which never became detached from "society" for a number of reasons, such as extensive participation of "societal" interests through associations and political parties, an efficient public administration with relative independence of government, strong local government, pragmatic rationalism, ethnic homogeneity and the tradition of a unitary state church.

France represents yet another singular type. The relationship between state and society is ambivalent. There is a tradition of a strong central state and public administration but the unity of the country is projected onto "society" as a whole, e.g. by the early sociologists Comte and Durkheim. The nation (not the state) as a cultural entity and the idea of "solidarity" constitute the social bond in society.

We can conclude that simple distinctions like strong vs. weak state or big vs. small government do not capture the complexity of the state and its role in a given society. This complexity needs to be taken into account in order to understand the diversity of national paths of welfare state development in Europe.

5 Post-War German Social Policy in Retrospect: The Genesis of a Welfare State

History is subject to continuity and discontinuity, to stability and change, and so is the history of social policy. National transitions of welfare are "path dependent", that is, departures from institutional structures established during the formative years require sustained efforts to materialize. Stolleis (volume 2, p. 23, 24f.) speaks of "layers of historical growth", including pre-Bismarckian sources, that linger in present-day systems of social welfare: "All forms of provisioning against risk and its consequences that we know and practice simultaneously can be assigned to specific chronological stages: from family and neighbourly help to co-operative self-help, the formation of foundations as the bearers of charitable institutions, the emergence of funds that are meant to ensure against conventional risks – all the way to the modern protection systems that encompass nearly the entire population. Some of these institutions go back to the early Middle Ages .... Others can be assigned to the period of the emerging cities, to the beginnings of trade, and the formation of the first large fortunes in the fifteenth and sixteenth centuries, such as urban hospitals, charitable foundations, or social housing projects like the 'Fuggerei' in Augsburg. Others are the products of the society-shaping powers of the churches in the early modern period and especially of the early-modern territorial state, which implemented a new notion of 'work," combated 'idleness', and created penitentiaries and workhouses." At the same time, the future of the historically grown institutional structure is uncertain. Twentieth century advanced Western societies with their extended systems of social protection remain "a historical experiment, in the same way that other cultures of world history have been experiments" (Stolleis, volume 2, p. 151).

Most authors agree that in the German welfare state change is difficult to achieve, due to the veto players in the political system, to the high degree of juridification and due to mentalities grounded in the strong state tradition. There have indeed been few path-breaking reforms in post-war Germany. Even under National Socialism (1933–1945), the institutional structure of public welfare had remained largely intact (Stolleis, volume 2, p. 155: "ruptures and continuity"). Still, there has been change after World War II, but largely in an evolutionary manner – "reformless change" (Czada 1999). The change was obscured by old semantics like "social insurance", "social state" and "social market economy" which were retained in public discourse despite substantial changes in institutional realities. These terms have become "semantics of continuity" (Leisering 2000a).

If we take stock of the changes in social policy during the post-war decades until the crisis of the welfare state was widely acknowledged in the 1990s, the change has been considerable. It was during that period that "social policy" fully turned into a "welfare state" (Kaufmann, volume 1), and German society became a mixed society, as indicated in T. H. Marshall's (1981) term "democratic welfare capitalism". Public welfare expanded dramatically in terms of spending, benefit schemes, levels of benefits, coverage of schemes and legal and bureaucratic apparatuses. New institutions were created which demarcated the sphere of social policy, like a consolidated Statute Book for social legislation (*Sozialgesetzbuch,* from 1976), specialized labor courts (established as independent branch of justice since 1953) and social courts (created in 1954) and mushrooming social reporting since the 1960s. Politically, social policy issues moved to centre stage, turning social policy into the main source of legitimacy of the state. Elections could be won and lost on social policy issues. The institutional structure also changed gradually but markedly. While the Bismarckian core, contribution-based financing of social security, remained, the segmentation of social provisioning typical for conservative welfare states was reduced. Separate institutions of social security were coordinated, integrated or even fused (such as the Statutory Pension Insurances for blue and white collar workers in 2005), and extensions to the core schemes rounded off the architecture of public welfare, resulting in a structured "quasi-universalism" of benefit systems (Leisering 2009).

The "welfare sector" grew, going along with the rise of social professions and semi-professions, of a new labor market sector for public welfare employees and of "welfare industries", that is, commercial providers which deliver services to public agencies or provide services themselves. The character of social policy changed. Social policy turned from "workers policy" into a growing, though less ambitious redistributive policy for the whole population. The focus of societal integration shifted (Kaufmann, volume 1, pp. 106–113): class politics gave way to politics geared to individual social rights and "social security", a term which came to define the welfare state (Kaufmann 2001). Old age insurance, for instance, turned into a question of relations between generations, not classes, and the delivery and implementation of social services became a prime focus of social policy beyond ideological controversies over the orientation of social policy. From the 1970s the emphasis of German social policy on cash transfers began to be gradually supplemented by expanding personal social services.

Regarding outcomes, welfare policies came to shape the every day life of most citizens, advancing the standard of living and promoting socio-cultural individualization but also juridifying and bureaucratizing life. Zacher (volume 3, p. 376) diagnoses a move to more equality, a "process by which inequalities have proliferated": ever new inequalities were discovered to be addressed by welfare policies. This refers to labor law, to inequalities of gender and between white collar and blue collar workers, to protective rights e.g. for tenants and consumers, and to allowances for various exigencies regarding family, housing, education and special needs. As a result, "welfare state generations" emerged whose lives have been shaped by the experience of extensive social services (Leisering 2000b). Much of the change just described could as well be observed in other Western countries. However, while numerous studies compare social spending or policies and policy outcomes cross-nationally, there is little comparative work on the institutional, social and cultural aspects of the post-war welfare state.

6 What Future for the Social?

Is the German welfare state facing up to the new challenges and crises since the 1990s? Is the welfare state changing? While Germany shares some of the challenges faced by other countries, some problems are specific to Germany. Globalization exerts particular pressures on the competitiveness of the German economy since Germany is one of the world's biggest export economies. Financing social benefits mostly by contributions rather than taxes makes the German benefit systems particularly vulnerable to crises in employment – and to competition by low-wage countries – because half of the contributions are paid by the employers as part of labor costs. Similarly, the design of social insurance as pay-as-you-go-systems rather than capital funding, in conjunction with high (if falling) replacement rates, exposes the system more directly to the effects of the ageing of the population, especially in the context of one of the world's lowest birth rates. Above all, German unification in 1990 "exacerbated decisively the latent crisis of the German welfare state" (Ritter, volume 4, p. 204): East Germany had a run-down economy with low productivity; unification generated a need for massive redistribution to the East; the cost of unification were largely passed on to the social insurance system (rather than to the tax system which would have spread the cost more widely; see Ritter, in volume 4); and the regional division East-west became a new social cleavage. In the early years after unification, social spending in the

East temporarily soared to two thirds of the Eastern gross domestic product, unprecedented in any country.

Regarding domestic problems, the 1990s confronted the Germans with a new – or newly perceived – world of social heterogeneity and social cleavage. This created new demands on social policy in view of integrating the nation state. First, there is the East/West divide since unification in 1990. Unemployment in the East is still higher than in the West, and economic growth is too slow. More than 20 years after unification, divisive resentments between East and West linger. Some Eastern regions are depopulated and racism has spread. Second, there is a problem of immigration and ethnic conflict. Germany has one of the highest proportions of immigrants in Europe but politicians have been slow in facing up to this fact. Between 1988 and 1996, 2.3 million "settlers" from Eastern Europe and the former Soviet Union (recognized as ethnic Germans) and c. two million asylum seekers came to Germany. The poverty rate among migrants is twice that of native citizens, just as the unemployment rate; some of the settlers are becoming marginalized. Some third generation immigrants are less integrated than their parents, and religious fundamentalism has grown, especially among persons of Turkish origin who are the biggest ethnic minority. For decades, Germany has facilitated the immigration of unskilled workers, without reaching out to highly qualified professionals as other countries have done. Third, a new low pay sector of the economy has produced a group of working poor, a problem hitherto unfamiliar to Germans. Fourth, both higher education and pre-school education are wanting, with a new problem referred to as "educational poverty" *(Bildungsarmut).*

To ascertain if the German welfare state has changed, we need to become clear what the German welfare state is. We discuss three conceptions of the welfare state in view of identifying the German welfare state and its recent changes: concepts from political economy (Esping-Andersen), from political science (M. G. Schmidt) and from sociology (as found in this book series, especially in Kaufmann, volumes 1 and 5, and in the related legal approach by Zacher, volume 3).

Following Esping-Andersen (1990), Germany is the epitomy of the *conservative welfare regime*: achieving a medium degree of decommodification (of enabling people to live independently of the market) by regulating labor markets and containing labor market participation; basing entitlements on occupational and social status, producing structured inequality; and upholding a conservative concept of society emphasizing family, traditional gender roles and intermediate social bodies such as churches, voluntary welfare associations and status groups. The conservative welfare regime contrasts with the Anglo-Saxon liberal regime and the Scandinavian social democratic regime. Studies agree that conservative or "*Bismarckian*" welfare regimes – Austria, France, the Netherlands, Luxembourg, Italy, Spain, Belgium, The Czech Republic, Poland, Slovakia and Hungary also come near this ideal-type (Palier 2010, p. 24) – are changing but they do not agree in which way (see Palier and Martin 2007; Palier 2010). Bismarckian regimes have adopted some of the new policies also found in other regimes, such as "activating" policies, deregulating labor markets and raising labor market participation (reducing "labor shedding"), cuts in benefits and social services, and marketization.

This brings Bismarckian welfare states closer to liberal regimes. In Germany, corporatism in industrial relations and closed arrangements of collective bargaining under the Statutory Health Insurance have opened up to a degree. By contrast, some authors diagnose a deepening of the divisions of Bismarckian regimes. Seeleib-Kaiser (2002) differentiates between policy areas, diagnosing a "dualization" of the German welfare state, that is, the traditional objective of status maintenance through insurance benefits weakens while family benefits and services are expanded. Models of gender and the family relations are being modernized. This brings Germany closer to a social democratic regime. Lessenich (2003) argued that the German welfare state has a hybrid, not just conservative character which allows flexible adaptation to new situations, even if in a gradual way. He depicted the opening of regional collective wage agreements and the creation of a statutory Long-Term Care Insurance in 1994/1995 – the fifth branch of social insurance, 111 years after Bismarck introduced the first branch – as cases in point.

Schmidt (e.g. 2005, 2010) also rejects the notion of a merely conservative German welfare state but in a different way and with more scepticism about the ability of the German welfare state to adapt than Lessenich. From a political science point of view, Schmidt argues that the German regime is "*centrist*" rather than conservative, shaped by a reformist centre/centre-right party (the Christian Democrats) in conjunction with a pragmatic, strong social democratic party (though mostly in opposition; the Social Democrats): "the policy of the middle way" (Schmidt 2010). Re-analysing Esping-Andersen's data, Obinger and Wagschal (1998) found that his conservative type actually falls into two types, a "centrist European social insurance state" (including Germany) and a type which really meets Esping-Andersen's criteria of conservatism (found in France, Italy and Austria). The policy of the middle way goes along with a pronounced consensus which underpinned the German welfare state well into the 1990s. Germany was and still is a country with two big welfare state parties.

However, the pressure to reach consensus has also acted as a check to major reforms. "Centrist" implied the aim of achieving high economic growth *and* generous social benefits (Schmidt 2010). Schmidt argues that the centrist model is still in operation but with increasing cost and side-effects. In fact, the performance of the German welfare state has diminished over the last 10 years, with more poverty and more inequality, even if this only means that among countries of the Organisation for Economic Co-operation and Development (OECD). Germany fell from a position better than average to an average position. At the same time, Germany is the biggest spender among Western welfare states, only topped by France and small countries like Sweden – medium performance at highest cost. At the beginning of the 2010s, Germany is caught between the old political middle ground (the carrier of the welfare state consensus) which acknowledges the need for change but shies away from distinct reforms, a new market liberalism which tends to break away from the welfare state consensus but is equally at a loss, and a new social populism.

Authors of this book series characterize the German welfare state in a more sociological way (than the authors just mentioned), conceiving of German social policy as the outcome of the idea of a precarious disjunction between "state" and "society". This idea has given rise to a strong concept of state and para-state institutions that "mediate" between state and society, tied to a strong notion of the "social" that permeates policies, law and mentalities. Has the German welfare state recently been changing with regard to these defining characteristics? The volumes in this series suggest a positive answer, though with qualifications.

The relationship between "*state*" *and* "*society*" has been changing since the 1990s. There are indications – in labor market policy and social assistance, in old-age security and (least) in education – that Germany is restructuring the state-society relationship, with more reliance on "society" and with new instruments of intervening in society. We maintain that Germany is moving from a provider state to an "*enabling state*" (Gilbert and Gilbert 1989; Gilbert 2002; Kaufmann 2012 [chapter first published in German in 1994]),[2] or from direct to indirect social policy. The new policies include:

- enabling persons to participate in non-state welfare production – this facet of the enabling state figures in the literature since the 1990s as "*activating*" *social policy,* especially in labor market policy and social assistance
- enabling non-state welfare systems like markets, voluntary organizations and families to operate – this facet is addressed by the more recent literature on the "*regulatory state*" in social security (see Leisering 2011a).
- Furthermore, the concept "*social investment*" policies could also be grouped under "enabling state" since these policies, especially education and family policies, aim to enable individuals to provide for themselves in the long run.

Activating social policy in social assistance started in Germany well before the "Hartz IV" reforms of 2005, undertaken by the municipalities since the mid 1990s (Leisering 2001). *Regulatory* policies became more important with the new Long-Term Care Insurance (1994/1995) which opened care markets to private providers, and with the major pension reforms of 2001 (the *Riester* reform) and 2004 which boosted occupational and personal pension plans as part of a new multi pillar model. In a way, this reversed Adenauer's reform of 1957 which had turned the Bismarckian pension insurance into a quasi mono pillar model. The regulation of private providers by the state also extends to other fields, e.g. job centres rely on private temporary employment agencies. In this way, new links between state and society and new intermediate forms – public-private hybrids like the new *Riester* pension – have emerged. Moves towards *social investment* policies are weaker, contrary to the rhetorics from all political parties, with departures in family benefits and services but less in education.

However, the diagnosis of a move towards enabling policies needs qualification. First, enabling is not new. Historically, the German tradition already harboured

[2] In 1994, Kaufmann devised the concept of "*Steuerungsstaat*" independently of the concept "enabling state" which Gilbert and Gilbert had introduced 5 years earlier. The two concepts are akin.

a potential for change in the state-society relationship since "state" in "social state" primarily refers to the social responsibility of the state while the institutional realization of this responsibility, the "welfare sector", need not be "state" but is mostly in the hands of "intermediary" agencies like social insurance with separate budgets or voluntary welfare associations. Thus, there is a tradition of the state reaching out to "society" and regulating non-state welfare production rather than providing welfare by itself. But the intermediary agencies often had a symbiotic relationship with the state, operating in closed quasi-corporatist circles. This made the overall arrangement rigid and inert. Still, the tradition of "old" regulation may have eased the rise of the "new regulatory state" (Leisering 2011a). Second, in contrast to Gilbert, Kaufmann conceives of the move towards an enabling state *(Steuerungsstaat)* as a change in the *discourse* on the state, not as institutional or policy change, although the discursive change may reflect or spur "real" changes. In a state-oriented country like Germany, the new regulatory state indicates the (re-) "discovery of society" in social policy (using a phrase coined by Polanyi) by exposing the dependence of the provider state on societal forces (Leisering 2011b). Any complex policy intervention is of a regulatory nature. The notion of the provider state was a fiction cherished during the golden age of the welfare state. The advent of the new regulatory state helps to expose fictions underlying the provider state during its heyday like the notion of a neat separation of public and private and of the capability of the state to steer societal processes (Berner 2009) – the "heroic state" (Rüb 2003).

The changes in the relationship between state and society entail changes in the "*social*". In a study of recent changes in old-age security in Europe I suggested that the social is undergoing three kinds of transformation: 'rationalization', that is, an increasing emphasis on rational models and expert knowledge; 'civilization', that is, blending social rights and civil rights; and internationalization, that is, an increased influence of international law and global forces on national social law. In the process, the social takes on new sides – socio-technological, civil and international. This transformation pertains to both public and publicly regulated welfare production. While elements of the three transformations can be traced in several Bismarckian or even some other welfare states, all three are particularly momentous in the German context.

Rationalization: The 'social' in European welfare states has historically been framed by ideologies or social *Weltanschauungen* like social democracy, social liberalism, conservatism or Christian social thought. By contrast, in the Anglo-Saxon tradition, especially in the USA, the social is often related to rationalized models of producing welfare goods based on science and social technologies (Janowitz 1976), such as New Public Management in the administration of social services or Disease Management Programmes (DMP) and Diagnosis-Related Groups (DRG) in medical services. The rationalist approach implies a redefinition of the social. Efficiency, quality of services and "choice" hitherto associated with private provision become criteria of social policy-making. While social policy in Germany has been strongly framed in terms of ideologies, combined with a romantic distrust or even ignorance of scientific and technological approaches to the social, the pressure to restructure the welfare state has eventually led Germany to develop a more rationalist approach, often with imports from Anglo-Saxon countries. A "managerial state" has entered the social policy arena (Rüb 2003).

Civilization: Enabling policies – activation, regulation and social investment – aim to influence access, processes and procedures in social welfare rather than welfare outcomes. Rights of access to public and private social services, consumer rights and, e.g., "financial capability" in private pension markets become new objectives of policy. Organization-related norms include transparency of providers, procedural security, accountability and participation. In terms of rights, conventional social rights give way to civil rights set in a social context. Is this still a "social" state? The consequences of the civilization of the social are ambivalent: The substance of the social is attenuated as compared to the golden age of the welfare state, since the social refers only indirectly to welfare outcomes and redistribution. At the same time, the province of the social is extended beyond conventional domains of public welfare, to markets and civil society. Markets become socially regulated welfare markets. For Germany, with its history of distrust in "civil society", the new civil interpretation of the social is difficult to swallow.

Internationalization: While social policy originated as a project of nation states, social policy is increasingly embedded in international social policy contexts: regional associations like the European Union (EU), international organisations like the United Nations (UN), the World Bank and the ILO, global non-governmental organizations (NGOs) and international legal conventions and treaties have emerged as increasingly "social" regimes. Although ultimately based in nation states, these regimes have turned into a world *sui generis*, developing independent "social" ideas. In Zacher's view (volume 3), the internationalization of social policy generates new social ideas, in line with the openness of the concept of the "social". For example, in global discourses, the social and the ecological are often linked in semantics like "social and economic sustainability". This link has not been made in national welfare states. Being a large country with a distinct national tradition of social policy, Germany has been inward-looking and reserved about external influences. It was the European Court of Justice of the EU which had, e.g., to force gender equality on German labor law and social security law. But as a country situated in the centre of Europe, Germany is liable to migration and external influences. The "social state of the Federal Republic of Germany was never simply a nation state" (Zacher, volume 3, p. 315).

The message of the book series is that "the social" is a continuous subject of public deliberation and political struggle. It is constantly changing, it comes in many varieties, and its change is not linear. Some of the recent changes in German social policy in a way lead back to Bismarck, especially the increased emphasis on private provision by markets and families. Bismarck had conceived of social insurance benefits only as a supplement to other sources of income. In some ways, the current German welfare state even goes back to the time before Bismarck.

Bismarck's legislation established a distinction between policy for workers *(Arbeiterpolitik)*, above all social insurance, and policy for the poor (*Armenpolitik*), above all the poor law. The new German job seekers allowance created in 2005 ("*Hartz IV*") has blurred the distinction between the two policies by merging the former Unemployment Aid (the lower echelon of unemployment benefit) with social assistance. In this and other instances, Germany is making a step from an insurance state towards a social assistance state. In the wake of *Hartz IV*, more than 10% of the population are in receipt of social assistance, up from 1.2% in 1970.

Lockwood (1964) distinguished "social integration" and "system integration". From the onset, modern social policy was not only a response to problems of social integration in the process of nation building but also to problems of system integration, above all to problems of economic development. Without positive effects on the economy, the historical rise of social would have been inconceivable. But with the expansion of the welfare state, positive effects cannot be taken for granted. Imbalances between social concerns and economic development may even contribute to the breakdown of a society as experienced by Communist East Germany. The German distrust in "society" makes it difficult for Germans to acknowledge the societal functions of the entrepreneur. "... the political form of the state that guarantees rights of liberty and rights of participation acquires its social quality only on the basis of an efficient economic system. The greatest possible synergy of economic and social policy is therefore the prerequisite for the success of the policies of the welfare state" (Kaufmann, volume 1, p. 125). Against the backdrop of economic globalization, the need to adjust the social and the economic has assumed a new quality. Still, the volumes of this book series testify to the resilience of national welfare states, sustained by institutional and ideational traditions. Nation states continue to be "societal communities" (Talcott Parsons). The future of the welfare state depends on the future of the nation state, on new synergies between state, economy and civil society and on the availability of cultural ideas that mobilize people towards the "social". We are 130 years away from Bismarck's creation of social insurance. The next 130 years may bring less national and more trans-national social ideas and institutions but the "social" does not appear to be in retreat.

References

Achinger H (1979) Sozialpolitik als Gesellschaftspolitik. Von der Arbeiterfrage zum Wohlfahrtsstaat. 3rd edn (1st edn 1958). Eigenverlag des Deutschen Vereins für öffentliche und private Fürsorge. Frankfurt am Main New York

Alber J (1995) A framework for the comparative study of social services. Journal of European Social Policy 5:131–149

Berner F (2009) Der hybride Sozialstaat. Die Neuordnung von öffentlich und privat in der sozialen Sicherung. Frankfurt am Main New York

Castles FG (ed) (1993) Families of nations. Patterns of public policy in western democraties. Aldershot

Czada R (1999) Reformloser Wandel. Stabilität und Anpassung im politischen Akteursystem der Bundesrepublik. In: Ellwein T, Holtmann E (eds) 50 Jahre Bundesrepublik Deutschland. Politische Vierteljahresschrift, special issue 30/1999. Opladen, Wiesbaden: 397–412
Deacon B, with Hulse M, Stubbs P (1997) Global social policy. International organizations and the future of welfare. London
Dyson K (1980) The state tradition in Western Europe. Oxford
Esping-Andersen G (1990) The three worlds of welfare capitalism. Princeton
Gilbert N (2002) Transformation of the welfare state. The silent surrender of public responsibility. Oxford New York
Gilbert N, Gilbert B (1989) The enabling state. Modern welfare capitalism in America. Oxford New York
Ginsburg N (1992) Divisions of welfare. A critical introduction to comparative social policy. London Thousand Oaks New Delhi
Girvetz HK (1968) Welfare state. In: Sills DL (ed) International encyclopedia of the social sciences, vol 16. New York, pp 512–521
Hall PA, Soskice D (eds) (2001) Varieties of capitalism. The institutional foundations of comparative advantage. Oxford
Janowitz M (1976) Social control of the welfare state. New York
Kahlenberg FP, Hoffmann D (2001) Sozialpolitik als Aufgabe zentraler Verwaltungen in Deutschland – Ein verwaltungsgeschichtlicher Überblick. In: Bundesministerium für Arbeit und Sozialordnung and Bundesarchiv (eds) Geschichte der Sozialpolitik in Deutschland seit 1945, vol 1. Baden Baden, pp 103–182
Kasza GJ (2002) The illusion of welfare 'regimes'. Journal of Social Policy 31:271–287
Kaufmann F-X (2001) Social security. In: Smelser NJ, Baltes PB (eds) International encyclopedia of the social and behavioral sciences, vol 21. Amsterdam, pp 14435–14439
Kaufmann F-X (2012) European foundations of the welfare state. Bergholm New York Oxford
Leisering L (2000a) Kontinuitätssemantiken. Die evolutionäre Transformation des Sozialstaates im Nachkriegsdeutschland. In: Leibfried S, Wagschal U (eds) Der deutsche Sozialstaat: Bilanzen – Reformen – Perspektiven. Frankfurt am Main New York, pp 91–114
Leisering L (2000b) Wohlfahrtsstaatliche Generationen. In: Kohli M, Szydlik M (eds) Generationen in Familie und Gesellschaft. Opladen, pp 59–76
Leisering L (2001) Strategien des Umbaus im lokalen Sozialstaat. Chancen und Risiken der kommunalen Sozialhilfereformen (Hilfe zum Lebensunterhalt) unter besonderer Berücksichtigung neuer Informationssysteme. Final report of the research project 98-53-4 of the Hans-Böckler-Stiftung (with Bernhard Hilkert et al.). Manuscript. Bielefeld
Leisering L (2009) Germany: a centrist welfare state at the crossroads. In: Alcock P, Craig G (eds) International social policy: welfare regimes in the developed world, 2nd edn. Houndmills Basingstoke, pp 148–170
Leisering L (ed) (2011a) The new regulatory state. Regulating pensions in Germany and the UK. Houndmills Basingstoke
Leisering L (2011b) Afterword: rethinking the nation state. In: Leisering L (ed) The new regulatory state. Regulating pensions in Germany and the UK. Basingstoke, pp 289–312
Lessenich S (2003) Dynamischer Immobilismus. Kontinuität und Wandel im deutschen Sozialmodell. Frankfurt am Main New York
Lockwood D (1964) Social integration and system integration. In: Zollschan GK, Hirsch W (eds) Explorations in social change. London, pp 244–257
Luhmann N (1982) The differentiation of society. New York
Luhmann N (1987) Die Unterscheidung von Staat und Gesellschaft. In: Luhmann N (ed) Soziologische Aufklärung, vol 4. Opladen, pp 67–73
Marshall TH (1981) Value problems of welfare-capitalism. With afterthought – the 'hyphenated society'. In: Marshall TH, The right to welfare and other essays. London, pp 104–136 (article first published 1972)

Marx K (1978) On the Jewish question. In: Tucker RC (ed) The Marx-Engels reader, 2nd edn. New York, pp 26–52 (German 1844)
Mayer KU (1997) Notes on a comparative political economy of life courses. Comparative Social Research 16:203–226
Nullmeier F (2000) Politische Theorie des Sozialstaats. Frankfurt am Main New York
Obinger H, Wagschal U (1998) Drei Welten des Wohlfahrtsstaates? Das Stratifizierungskonzept in der clusteranalytischen Überprüfung. In: Lessenich S, Ostner I (eds) Welten des Wohlfahrtskapitalismus. Der Sozialstaat in vergleichender Perspektive. Frankfurt am Main New York, pp 109–135
Palier B (ed) (2010) A long goodbye to Bismarck. The politics of welfare reform in Continental Europe. Amsterdam
Palier B, Martin C (eds) (2007) Reforming the Bismarckian welfare systems. Social Policy and Administration 41(6) (special issue). Oxford
Pinker R (1971) Social theory and social policy. London
Pinker R (1979) The idea of welfare. London
Ritter GA (1964) Nation und Gesellschaft in England. Historische Zeitschrift 198:24–32
Rüb FW (2003) Vom Wohlfahrtsstaat zum "manageriellen" Staat? Zum Wandel des Verhältnisses von Markt und Staat in der deutschen Sozialpolitik. In: Czada R, Zintl R (eds) Politik und Markt. Politische Vierteljahresschrift, special issue 34. Wiesbaden: 256–299
Schmidt MG (2005) Sozialpolitik in Deutschland. Historische Entwicklung und internationaler Vergleich, 3rd edn. Wiesbaden
Schmidt MG (2010) The policy of the middle way: Germany since 1990. In: Bulmer S, Jeffery C, Padgett S (eds) Rethinking Germany and Europe. Democracy and diplomacy in a semi-sovereign state. Houndmills Basingstoke, pp 73–84
Seeleib-Kaiser M (2002) A dual transformation of the German welfare state. West European Politics 25:25–48
van Kersbergen K (1995) Social capitalism: a study of Christian democracy and the welfare state. London
von Stein L (1842) Der Socialismus und Communismus des heutigen Frankreich. Leipzig

Thinking About Social Policy: The German Tradition

Franz-Xaver Kaufmann

1 Introduction

Social policy [*Sozialpolitik*] is a scholarly term that has had a career in practical politics. It arose first in the German-speaking realm, within the horizon of the Hegelian distinction between state and civil society. It was gradually codified academically by scholars belonging to the *Verein für Socialpolitik* [Association for Social Policy], which was founded in 1873. Its institutional career began with Bismarck's social reforms, though it took quite some time before it won out over competing German as well as international terms. Until the end of the Weimar Republic, social policy remained chiefly an academic term for the institutional developments taking place under different names. Its introduction into practical affairs took place gradually and especially after the Second World War. The international career of the term dates only to the last three decades.

Unlike the term itself, the subject matter of social policy did not originate in the German-speaking realm. Already the radical constitution of the French Revolution in 1793 postulated the equality of employers and workers, as well as the obligation of the state to provide education to everyone, and to support citizens who had fallen into destitution. This was, in other words, the program of a welfare state, which was swept into oblivion by the terror of the guillotine that followed.

The first legal regulations of poor relief were enacted by Queen Elizabeth I around 1600. This "old poor law" was reformed in 1834 in the spirit of Jeremy Bentham and made harsher for the able-bodied so as to serve as a deterrent; for those unable to work, however, health relief was introduced, which subsequently gave rise to a developed public health system. Around the same time (1833), the British Parliament passed the first factory laws to regulate child labor and created the Institute of Factory Inspectors.

Occupational safety and factory legislation began even earlier in Switzerland: the earliest ordinance to protect working children was passed by the Canton of Zurich in 1799. In the Canton of Glarus, a limit on working hours for adults was enacted as early as 1848 and a comprehensive factory law in 1864, which was followed by

F.-X. Kaufmann, *Thinking About Social Policy*, German Social Policy 1,
DOI 10.1007/978-3-642-19501-3_2, © Springer-Verlag Berlin Heidelberg 2013

comprehensive factory legislation on the federal level in 1877 and 1881. Prussia became the leader in the area of state-sponsored national education and regulated relief funds; this was followed, with Bismarck's social legislation (1883–1889), by the breakthrough to social insurance for workers on the national level. Between 1891 and 1907, Denmark, which had introduced health insurance as early as 1862, created a system of need-based minimum insurance that protected nearly the entire population against poverty, work-related accidents, unemployment, and sickness.

Around 1900, the arsenal of what we today would call social policies or welfare state measures to solve the "social question" had thus essentially already been devised. But there existed no term that would have grouped the many measures together conceptually – with the exception of the German term *Sozialpolitik* ["social policy"]. This circumstance justifies a study that traces the emergence and transformation of this term. As we shall see, such an inquiry leads into core areas of the emerging social sciences, and it can therefore be seen as a contribution to international scholarship on the history of the welfare state, and to the history of the social sciences in Germany.

The term "social policy" postulates a conceptual unity of specific institutional developments which is not by any means self-evident, and as will be seen, the criteria of what constitutes such a unity have changed over time. The idea and conceptualization of social policy are the historical result of ethical ideas, the diagnoses of social problems, political postulates, and scholarly constructs. This study traces the emergence and standardization of the subject matter, for two reasons: first, to illuminate the substantive reach of the institutional understanding of social policy; second, to demonstrate the limits of the term and clarify its replacement in recent times by the concept of the social or welfare state. The German term *Sozialpolitik* can also refer to matters of different categories: the political struggle over measures and laws (social politics), the implementation of state-initiated measures (social policies), in Germany not only through public administration but also through autonomous bodies or even private agents; and, finally, the intellectual debate over the definition of social and political problems and the criticism of socio-political practices, especially by the legal, economic, and social sciences (socio-political ideas). These three spheres are of course subject to reciprocal interactions, though the latter become clear only from the third, scientific perspective that stands at the center of this study.

The differences between and convergence of theoretical and practical-political conceptions of "social policy" remain historically quite contingent and can therefore be mentioned only in passing.[1] Instead, my focus here is on the *conceptual*

[1] Surveys of the history of practical social policy in Germany since its beginnings are given by: Syrup and Neuloh (1957), Gladen (1974), Hentschel (1983), Frerich and Frey (1996), Lampert (1998, pp. 17–155), Schmidt (1998, pp. 21–173), Hockerts (1998b), Stolleis (2013, German Social Policy, vol. 2). An extensive history of social policy in Germany since 1945, covering until 1989 both German states, including source materials, has been published by the German Ministry of Labour and Social Affairs and the Federal Archive in 11 volumes (Bundesministerium für Arbeit und Soziales 2001–2008). (See footnote on page 125).

history of social policy ["Sozialpolitik"] in Germany and its intellectual context. I trace the emergence of the term social policy and shed light on the problems it referenced and by means of which the unity of the subject matter was constructed, while at the same time including competing terms in the discussion. That is also why no complete survey of linguistic usage is intended; rather, I will highlight meanings that the term was given in German scholarly language.[2] The source material therefore consists largely of academic texts, not documents from practical politics. To be sure, many of these texts were composed also with a political intent or at least within the horizon of certain political orientations; indeed, it is characteristic of the topic under discussion that normative and descriptive connotations are interwoven in a way that is difficult to disentangle, as is usual in political rhetoric. Still, we will be dealing typically with statements from *scholars*, not politicians or administrators. However, wherever they can be identified, I will mark points where scholarship and politics met, where, in other words, transfers from one direction or the other contributed to the historical constitution of the subject matter.

An examination focused purely on conceptual history[3] does not expose the real historical contexts behind the conceptual changes.[4] Academic discussions of social policy also referenced a concrete social and political situation, however, which formed the backdrop. But since this does not usually find expression in the conceptual analysis, real historical connections will occasionally be made, though in a very summary form. Even if the real political processes remain underexposed, the present study sees itself also as a contribution to a historical sociology of social policy. For like most of the "great" topics of sociology, social policy exists for us only as a historical object and in conceptual form.[5]

One final preliminary remark: from the vantage point of the great political currents of the nineteenth and twentieth centuries, namely, liberalism, socialism, and conservatism, social policy developed as a seemingly heterogeneous series of inconsistent compromises. By contrast, this study is based on the notion that the history of social policy in Germany is the expression of an autonomous "reformist" current, one that did develop within the field of tension created by these three

[2] I will pass over the rare attempts to make "social policy" into a universal historical concept; see e.g. Molitor (1990). Nor can the approach be to retrace the totality of the ideas and scientific notions and debates concerning the problems that were occasionally assigned to the term social policy. For the older period see von Philippovich and Heimann (1924), Keller (1955), Scheer (1975), G. A. Ritter (1996b).

[3] On the tasks and methods of conceptual history see Meier (1971), Gadamer (1971), Koselleck (1978), Koselleck (1986).

[4] This was rightly pointed out by Dipper (1992, p. 324f.). That study on the very closely related concept of *Sozialreform* [social reform] proved especially helpful. The numerous, mostly older, studies on the concept of social policy lack the methodology of conceptual history. Still very insightful is von Philippovich (1908).

[5] The frequent absence of this historical sense in contemporary German sociology was pointed out by Wehler (2000, pp. 113–121). For a historical account see Raphael (1996).

"major ideologies," but which definitely has roots of its own (especially within the ethical system of the two large Christian confessions[6]) and distinct ideological positions. In the process, the social-democratic, Christian-social, and social-liberal position appear not only as a more or less consistent compromise between liberal, socialist, and conservative ideas, but in many cases also as a productive synthesis with far-reaching positions of its own. I hope this makes clear why "pure-bred" liberal, socialist, and conservative positions receive less attention in this study.

2 Social Policy as Mediation Between "State" and "Civil Society"

Since the word "*sozial*" ["social"] appeared in the German language only in the 1830s, there is no need to trace the archaeology of our term back any further.[7] In the 1840s the spelling "*social*" quickly established itself[8] and prompted the emergence of a multitude of composites and related words, the most important among which, for our purposes, were "*soziale Frage*" ["social question"], "*soziale Bewegung*" ["social movement"], "*Sozialismus*" ["Socialism"], "*Sozialwissenschaft*" ["social science"], "*soziale Reform*" ["social reform"], "*Sozialstaat*" ["social state"], and "*soziale Politik*" (or "*sozialpolitisch*") ["social policy" or "socio-political"].[9] These terms, which arose largely independent of each other, converged in the 1850s and 1860s into a semantic field whose specific quality was identified by the adjective *sozial*, and it thus forms the starting point for a reconstruction of conceptual history.

2.1 Social – Socialism – Science of Society

The tension between the fading era of agrarian feudalism and the emerging era of liberalization and industrialization in Europe reached its high point in the 1840s. Famines, workers' uprisings, attempted revolutions, and civil wars formed the emotional foundation for scholarly attempts to interpret the events and the clashes

---

[6] Moenning (1927), Bredendiek (1953), Liebersohn (1980), Kaufmann (1988a), Kaiser and Loth (1997). One must also not forget the considerable scholarly and practical contributions to German social policy down to 1933 from the Jewish intelligentsia. So far these have been examined only for the health care system: Tennstedt and Leibfried (1979).

[7] References in Geck (1963). Here I should mention at least the oldest attestation of the phrase in L. F. Langemarck, Das allgemeine gesellschaftliche Recht nebst der Politik (Berlin 1745): "die gesellschaftliche Politik oder Sittenlehre (Prudentiam, Politicam socialem)," quoted in Geck (1963, p. 21f.).

[8] The spelling "*sozial*" did not generally prevail until around 1900.

[9] The connections between these terms was brought out by Pankoke (1970).

of political ideas at the time. In the process, political problems (nationalism and constitutionalism) and social problems (pauperism, urbanization, the impoverishment of the workers) remained closely intertwined. The emerging social-scientific thinking was accordingly subject to the various currents of the zeitgeist. That is especially true of England and France, the countries that experienced the most profound social changes (Pinker 1971; Metz 1985; Donzelot 1984; Castel 1995). The German-speaking realm was not yet unified politically and also lagged behind with respect to industrialization. As a result, German social scientists preferred to ponder conditions in England and France, and this gave them a more distanced perspective on the new conditions, which was helpful to the emergence of a separate science of society. When it came to social-scientific thinking, the German-speaking realm was the leader, and this circumstance justifies a detailed account of these early developments.

2.1.1 The "Social" as an Expression of Secularization

"Social" goes back to the Latin *socialis*, which already in Antiquity had been linked to social theory by Seneca, who translated the Aristotelian *zoon politicon* as *animal sociale*. Thereafter, the Latin word *socialis* served to describe the specifically political or social condition of mankind. This conceptualization was theologically transfigured by Medieval philosophy: here, human cohabitation resulted from God's gift of reason to humanity, which had the ability to understand what was right by nature. In the seventeenth century this Christian meaning was then challenged by the early modern doctrine of natural law. In this intellectual tradition, founded by Hugo Grotius and Samuel Pufendorf, the term *socialis* and the nouns *socialitas* and *sociabilitas* derived from it took on a categorial quality to describe human coexistence and the question about its foundations (Schieder 1984, p. 924; Müller 1967, pp. 23–46). In keeping with the secularizing conception of the world, the human inclination to live together and to bond politically was no longer grounded in a shared human reason derived from divine wisdom, but *required a specific justification*. The burden of justification grew, the more thinking in terms of natural law joined hands with the ideas of Enlightenment individualism.[10]

From the end of the eighteenth century, "the term '*Socialisten*,' taken over into German as a foreign word, is found as the quite value-neutral designation of the natural-law social philosophy of the school of Grotius and Pufendorf" (Schieder 1984, p. 930). Thus, socialists were initially those philosophers who addressed the question about the order of human social life from purely worldly premises. In the beginning that was still done from a primarily *political* perspective. The thinkers who were grouped under the name "Socialists" from the mid-1830s, especially

[10] This problem of justification gave rise not only to modern political philosophy, but also to sociology. Niklas Luhmann described "the insecure possibility of sociability as such" as "the problem that constitutes the discipline." (1993b, p. 195).

Robert Owen, de Saint-Simon, and Fourier, differed chiefly in that they no longer expected a solution to the problems of human society to come from political reforms or revolution, but from "societal" changes, especially a transformation of *property relations*. This shift in the awareness of the problem is closely related to the emergence of an independent "*science of society*" divorced from political and legal philosophy.

On occasion the German word "*social*" is already found around 1800, but its use did not become established yet (Geck 1963, p. 25ff.; Geck 1961). *Socialis* was usually translated as "societal" [*gesellschaftlich*] or with terms that have by now become obsolete. By contrast, in French, *social* had found widespread use around the turn of the nineteenth century, beginning with Rousseau's *Contrat social* (1762). Considering that only the German language has both "*sozial*" and "*gesellschaftlich*" as translations of *socialis* or *social*, this doubling calls for an explanation. The fact that no clear differentiation in meaning has taken hold in everyday language to this day may be one reason why this question has been hardly addressed in the literature on conceptual history.

"*Social*" established itself in German in the wake of a re-codification of the term "*Gesellschaft*" [society], which must be briefly recalled here (Riedel 1979a, b). Until the turn of the nineteenth century, use of the word *Gesellschaft* as the predominant translation of the Latin *societas* remained multi-faceted and covered nearly all forms of human coexistence. More specific in meaning was the phrase "*bürgerliche Gesellschaft*" (*societas civilis*) [civic society], which, following the Aristotelian concept, referred to the *political form of social formation*. Civic society was thus understood as an association of unequals, i.e. of political dominion, whereby in the wake of early modern ideas of natural law, the foundation of the legitimacy of political power merely shifted from a theological justification to one based on contractual theory.

Older forms of power must always be understood as a combination of household lordship and political authority; the only "citizens" bearing full legal rights in pre-revolutionary "society" (*societas civilis cum imperio*) were thus "masters of the house," who in turn had rights of authority over members of the household who had no rights in the political sense. This *intermediary structure* remained characteristic for the political-social relations in large parts of Europe from antiquity to the French Revolution, notwithstanding a multitude of changes in the power relationships between political overlords (kings, princes, magistrates) and masters of the household as well as their organizations (estates, corporations). In political terms, what was revolutionary about the events of 1789 was precisely the elimination of all *corps intermediaires* and the grant of civic rights to all people. But even here, women and dependent domestics continued to be excluded from the rights of political participation. And with the restoration of the monarchy in 1814, suffrage was limited to the wealthiest citizens.

The granting of *civil rights*, and with it the abolition of old duties of protection and obedience, occurred rapidly throughout Europe – not least as a result of the Napoleonic wars. By contrast, the generalization of the *rights to political participation* to include the population groups below the bourgeoisie and women was some time off and formed a central theme of political controversies until the First World War.

But the fight against political inequality was soon joined by that against social inequality, whereby the relationship between these two forms of inequality was seen in very different ways, depending on the commentator's political vantage point. In many cases this difference in perspectives was conceptually articulated in the relationship between "political" and "social reform" (Dipper 1992, p. 326ff.). The diagnosis put forth by advocates of *social* reform was clearly articulated by the Baden parliamentarian von Buß as early as 1837: "Since the uncertain legal and political status of the workers is rooted primarily in their unfavorable economic situation, in legal and political terms, as well, help must be expected to come from the improvement in the economic situation of the workers."[11] Or more graphically: "What does the constitution give to the people? Rights, but no bread, no work, no education. Rights are stones, and these stones are not given to everyone; those who, in the lowest case, do no pay taxes of 20 gulden, that is, those who do not already have bread, are not even given the stones of the law" (Grün 1845, p. 19).

2.1.2 The Differentiation Between the Political and the Social: G. W. F. Hegel

While the conceptual differentiation between "state" and "(civil) society" (*societas civilis sine imperio*), or between the "political" and the "social" had begun to emerge among the critics of absolutism since Montesquieu,[12] it reached a clear articulation only in Hegel's philosophy of right. It was here that the political and the social appeared for the first time as two separate spheres dominated by *different* legal principles, and the *relationships* between them subsequently became the fundamental issue of "social policy."

The new idea of the emerging "science of society" was the *inherent dynamic of the social*. The circumstance that political power was bound to the rules of the law and constrained by the rights of liberty in the constitution, while the individual was simultaneously released into freedom through the abolition of feudal ties and forced to compete, produced a dynamic that could no longer be controlled politically, nor should it be according to the liberal tenets of the self-limitation of the state. This dynamic expressed itself in multifarious ways: the spread of economic competition, a rural exodus and urbanization, the diffusion of industry and the destruction of proto-industrial outwork, and a general population growth, which was promoted by both the decline in mortality and the abolition of the marriage permit. The result was a surge in the number of job seekers, many of whom also had no permanent domicile. This change in living conditions taking place for all to see was discussed

[11] Franz Josef von Buß, "Begründung seiner Motion betreffend die Fabrikgesetzgebung im badischen Landtag" (1837), quoted here from Kuczynski (1960, p. 248). von Buß's motion is today seen as the first "social-political" initiative on German soil.

[12] See especially Montesquieu (1745, book 26, Chaps. 15–19).

in the 1820s and 1830s primarily under the heading of 'pauperism;' from 1840, however, a new term established itself: the "social question" [*soziale Frage*].[13] This renaming points to a new awareness of the problem: the issue was now no longer merely the treatment of the poor, but the relationship between "estates" or "classes," a question of *social structure*.

The content of the new theory of "society" remained contested throughout the nineteenth century, as did the subject of the emerging science of society or social science (Pankoke 1991; Jonas 1976). Of importance for our purposes are only the intellectual traditions that systematically reflected the *distinction between state and society*.

The dissolution of the 1,000 year-old notion of a social unity constituted by political authority into the *difference* between state, civil society, and family by *Hegel* represents the beginning of a *theory of the functional differentiation of modern societies*, which has become one of the most important paradigms of modern social theory especially through the work of Talcott Parsons (1971) and Niklas Luhmann (Luhmann 1982; 1993a). Hegel's concept of civil society was oriented toward the economic subsystem of society (to use modern terminology), whose conceptualization as an autonomous dynamic system of a market-driven division of labor had already been advanced by Adam Smith, Jean Baptiste Say, and David Ricardo. While human liberty in the state expressed itself, according to Hegel, as the free affirmation of a legal order that secured the liberty also of one's fellow men and found within the family the moral conditions of its realization, in civil society it expressed itself as the unconstrained will to satisfy needs. This will realized itself as work, which, under the conditions of civil society, becomes chiefly work to satisfy the needs of others as the condition for satisfying one's own.[14] *In contrast to economic theory, Hegel thus conceptualized the economic conditions not as processes of exchange mediated through market prices, but as relations between individuals.* It is not goods that form the starting point of this thinking, but the needs of the economic man and his labor. However, those needs do not by themselves lead to a "system of needs" as represented by *civil society*. Rather, the mutual benefit of the "mediation of need" is established only by the guarantee of private property and the legal security of contractual relationships, in other words, by *accomplishments on the part of the state* (Hegel 1821, §188). Hegel regarded the juridification of political rule, that is, the emergence of the constitutional state, as the historical realization of reason (Siep 1992). In Hegel's

[13] First as a translation of the French *question sociale* (e.g. Heinrich Heine from 1840); in fact, the early use of *sozial* and its composite terms and phrases generally points to French influences. See Geck (1961, p. 303f.); also Pankoke (1995a).

[14] For Hegel's theory of society see the excellent summary in Jonas (1976, pp. 144–163); for Hegel's concept of civil society see also Pankoke (1991, pp. 288–304 = §§ 182–207 from Hegel 1821) and Pankoke's commentary (ibid., pp. 1046–1064).

theory of society, the individual thus becomes a citizen in a twofold sense: as *citoyen* in the state, and as *bourgeois* in civil society.[15]

Hegel emphasized the "arbitrariness and randomness" of conditions within civil society. The latter was not a natural state of affairs, but the result of the pursuit of self-interest on the part of individuals acting as they saw fit. In contrast to the fundamentally equal rights of the citizen in the constitutional state, in civil society the "inequality in ability, wealth, and even in intellectual and moral education" among individuals resulted in "an inequality of men . . . inherent in the idea . . . and holding up (to it) the demand for *equality* is feeble-minded" (Hegel 1821, § 200). For Hegel, the *social inequality* of persons is thus a *constitutive* element of civil society.[16] This idea was subsequently picked up by Karl Marx and Lorenz von Stein from the perspective of class theory and combined in various ways with the diagnoses of the early Socialists.

What must be noted for now is that the Hegelian theory of society for the first time conceptualized essential characteristics of modern, industrial-capitalist society and thereby also the implicit tensions that exist between the ideal of political equality and socio-economic inequality. Through Hegel, "society" comes into its own, so to speak. In the concept of the *social question*, the civic public for the first time addressed the tension between the political ideals of civic equality and the de facto social development, which erupted repeatedly in violent clashes, especially in France. But in the German-speaking realm, as well, it was the uprisings of Bohemian and Silesian weavers (1844) that gave the social question public resonance and thus stimulated the interest in a better understanding of modern society.[17]

In contrast to the largely descriptive use of *social* in French and English, the word *sozial* in the German-speaking realm often carries a normative connotation - at times positive, at times critical. In the process, its meaning was initially closely

---

[15] For the interpretation of Hegel postulated here, centered on the theory of differentiation, which remains strangely underexposed in Luhmann, see Horstmann (1997); a systematic interpretation of Hegel's economic statements in Priddat (1990).

[16] Hegel did not overlook the problematic aspects of contemporary pauperization, though it found far less expression in his Philosophy of Right (1821, § 243f.) than in the notes of his lectures: "The appearance of poverty is in fact a consequence of the civil society, and on the whole it emerges by necessity out of it. In this way, wealth without measure and limit accumulates on one side, and misery and hardship on the other. The increase in wealth and poverty marches in tandem. The necessity for this phenomenon lies in the fact that the work to satisfy needs is becoming more abstract . . . The place of abstract work is taken, as we have seen, by the machine. In this way, the effects of abstract labor are multiplied further; . . . in all this, misery and poverty grows. At the same time, individuals are becoming increasingly dependent through the division of labor." From this diagnosis, Hegel already derived sociopolitical consequences (though without using that term): "This is the greater worry that rests upon the administration. It must see to it that individuals are given the opportunity to earn theirs through work. If there are jobless people, they have a right to demand that work be procured for them." Hegel (1983, p. 192ff.); quoted in Pankoke (1991, p. 1050f.).

[17] Dipper (1992, p. 326f.). However, just how much these efforts were impeded by a paternalistic state administration has been shown by Reulecke (1983).

tied to the poverty question and later to the worker question (Müller 1967, pp. 119ff., 192f.). Even if the general linguistic usage of the time lacked a clear distinction between "*gesellschaftlich*" [societal] and "*sozial*" [social], the specific difference in the connotations can be articulated as the relationship between a descriptive (societal) and a normative or critical sense (social).[18] In the process the social was often juxtaposed to the individualistic and then appears as that which the individualistic civil society in the liberal sense *is lacking*.[19] However, this lack does not appear as a constitutive defect of capitalism, as it does in Karl Marx, but as *remediable* through "social reform" or "social policy." However, this specific linguistic usage presupposes not only the distinction between "political" and "social," but also that between "social" and "economic." This latter distinction is not yet contained in Hegel's concept of the civil society. It was only Robert von Mohl who introduced into the debate the theme of a specific "science of society" that set itself apart in equal measure from "political science" (*Staatswissenschaft*) and from "economics" (*Nationalökonomie* or *Volkswirtschaftslehre*). Von Mohl criticized that the theories of society of his day, following the fictions of the French Revolution, conceived of society as too individualistic. Instead, he postulated the entire realm of the *intermediary corporations and associations* between the individual and the state as the topic of his "science of society" (von Mohl 1851; 1855, p. 72). This approach foreshadows the class-theoretical and the corporatist conceptions of society, both of which have exerted lasting influence on socio-political thinking.

The close connection between "*sozial*" and "*Sozialismus*" [Socialism] is explained by the fact that until the end of the nineteenth century, the latter was by no means fixated on the Marx-Engels edifice of ideas. Rather, it served sometimes as a collective term, sometimes as a term of differentiation for the various currents of the "social movement" and "social reform," but also for their intellectual "social-scientific" foundation (Müller 1967, pp. 131–156; Schieder 1984, pp. 949–952). In this link between social-scientific thinking and political engagement, which was often equated with "Socialism," lies also the enduring context for the emergence of "social policy."

2.2 *Social Question – Social Reform – Social Policy*

From the 1840s to the First World War, the term "social question" [*soziale Frage*] constituted the dominant problem addressed by "social reform" or "social policy."[20] In the process, with reference to German conditions, the social question

[18] On the sphere of meaning of "*sozial*," especially also with respect to the expression of the "social state" (*sozialer Staat*), see Benda (1966, pp. 89–103), Zacher (1980, pp. 18–22, 684–706).

[19] This was also the line of argumentation in the important tractate of Gurvitch (1972, first 1932): The "social" law – from Hugo Grotius to Maurice Hauriou – distinguishes itself from the prevailing, individualistic conception of the law by the emphasis on its trans-individual origins.

[20] In the literature of the 1840s, one finds, following von Stein (1842), above all the phrase "*sociale Reform*." – On the literature about social policy *avant la lettre* see von Philippovich (1908, pp. 2–47), Reidegeld (1996, pp. 65–150).

was identified until about 1850 with the problem of pauperism, while with respect to conditions in England and France, the problems of industrial workers were already coming into view. The earliest German linkage of the problems of the industrial proletariat with the semantics of the social is found in Franz von Baader (1835).

2.2.1 Science of Society and Social Reform: Lorenz von Stein

The writings of Lorenz von Stein were crucial to the emergence of a tight link between the worker question, social science, and the demands for social reform in Germany.[21] Von Stein combined the social diagnoses of the French socialists who were critical of capitalism with Hegel's social theory. In so doing, he arrived at diagnoses that were strikingly similar to – and preceded – those of Karl Max and Friedrich Engels about the inevitability of class struggle under the conditions of liberal capitalism. But he differed from them with respect to possible ways out of this situation: for von Stein, the solution to the misery of the proletariat was not a revolutionary change in the conditions of ownership, but "social reform" under the aegis of a "neutral" state that rose above the clash of classes.

Von Stein's intellectual advance over Hegel's thinking in terms of differentiation is evident in the articulation of the *tension between the "pure" concepts* of state and society, on the one hand, and their *real relationship*, on the other. Conceptually, the *state* in von Stein is the guardian of the overall interests of a people, and this guardianship takes place as representation in the person of the prince, and as work in the form of the administration. Conceptually juxtaposed to it is *society* as a moral order and the place where the person and his or her interests can develop under the given property relations. While state and society are clearly distinct as ideas, in historical reality they continuously interpenetrate one another and in this way give rise to different forms of society.[22]

Another intellectual advance by von Stein lay in the *dynamic conception* of the distinction between state and society, which had become reality with the French revolutionary constitution of 1789. The universalization of civic rights brings forth the "society of citizens," in which social inequality rests no longer on a distinction of rights, but only on that of property. *As a result, property takes on far greater*

---

[21] In 1848, von Stein republished his path-breaking work *Der Socialismus and Communismus des heutigen Frankreich* [Socialism and Communism in France] (1842) in an expanded, two-volume edition, and then issued it in a definitive, three-volume edition under the title *Die Geschichte der sozialen Bewegungen in Frankreich von 1789 bis auf unsere Tage* [History of Social Movements from 1789 until the Present Days] (Leipzig 1850). For an abridged English version see von Stein (1964). Interpretations of von Stein's work that appreciate its social theory element can be found in Böckenförde (1976a), Quesel (1989), Koslowski (1989) and in English by Roth (1968).

[22] For a concise statement see von Stein (1856, p. 22ff.).

importance for individuals and their community, it becomes the central characteristic of their social status. Work and property now become the structural characteristics of the "economic society," which developed on the basis of the legal equality of all (von Stein 1850, vol. 1, p. 451ff.). *Ideally*, this society opens the chance of social advancement and the acquisition of wealth to all, but the *de facto* effect of the universalized competition and the prevailing property differences lead to the solidification of social classes and thus to "industrial society," that is, to capitalism in the sense of Karl Marx (von Stein 1850, vol. 2, p. 55ff.; Hegner 1976).

The goal of von Stein's social theory was, first, to elaborate on the formation of the proletariat as a class and the inherently insoluble class conflict of industrial society, which – as von Stein demonstrated through his analysis of conditions in France – tended toward civil war. Next, it wanted to show that a constructive way out was possible, namely by mediating between the clashing, yet at the same time mutually interdependent, class interests of labor and capital with the help of a neutral third party. Von Stein initially referred to it as the "monarchy of social reform"; his central concern, however, was the "realization of the state principle."[23] To be sure, von Stein – following Hegel in this regard – had major reservations about the forms of democracy known to him at the time, since he feared that in this form of government the class struggle would be carried into politics and thereby destroy the necessary neutrality of the state. However, central for him was not the form the state took but the *success of the productive class compromise*, which von Stein believed he could discern in the constitutional guarantee of the right to private property for the property-owning classes, on the one hand, and in the promotion of the social and – flowing from it – the political emancipation of the working class through free associations ("social movement") and "social administration," on the other.[24]

Von Stein remained faithful to his idea of "social reform" also in his administrative doctrine that dominated his later work. He now focused on the sub-problem of "social administration," though here he ran into a problem that would become central to the subsequent conceptual history of "social policy": is "social administration" a *specific field* of public administration? Or is it a *particular intention or*

[23] Böckenförde (1976a, p. 162). On this see also Huber (1972). By contrast, Scheer (1975, pp. 174–203) rightly points out that the immediate effect of von Stein's analyses led in Germany to the goals of the "social monarchy." On this see Blasius (1971).

[24] "If, however, the propertied class exercises the administration of the state in the spirit of the non-propertied classes to alleviate the lot of the workers, provides for their education, and offers the possibility to acquire capital, even if only slowly, this class will be *to that extent more indifferent toward the form of the constitution as its interests are being more strongly promoted.* Under such an administration monarchy, dictatorship, aristocracy, and democracy are equally possible, for the reason, namely, *that the acquired property in the end makes unfreedom impossible*, and because the *promotion of its acquisition* becomes the *promotion of liberty*. . . The transition of democracy to that new form is already indicated in the slogan of 'social democracy'. As of yet the content of that idea is unclear. If it does not emerge from its lack of clarity, it will vanish. If it wants to escape from it, it must become a *science of society. Then the future will belong to it.*" Von Stein (1850/1972, vol. 3, p. 207).

direction of the state's intervention in societal conditions? In the 1876 edition of his *Handbuch der Verwaltungslehre* [Handbook of Administrative Doctrine], he tried to capture this difference with the distinction between "Administration of Society" [*Gesellschaftliche Verwaltung*] versus "Social Administration" [*Soziale Verwaltung*]. In the 1887/1888 edition, by contrast, the "social administration" appeared alongside the legal and economic administration as a specific field whose obligation it was, in conjunction with the relevant judicature, "to determine the relationship between capital and labor in such a way that, in addition to the preservation of the acquired capital, the capital-forming power of labor is simultaneously preserved." Consequently, he distinguished between "general social administration" and "social administration proper." The former referred to the administration overall, to the extent that is pursued the goal of promoting the "capital-forming power of labor." The latter, by contrast, had the task of defusing the conflict of interests between capital and labor (von Stein 1888, part 3, p. 35f.).

The term "*Sozialpolitik*" does not appear in von Stein until the edition of 1888, namely as a sub-category of "general social administration" and on par with "*Sozialpolizei*" [social police]. "*Sozialpolitk* – and here, too, the name does not matter (!) – arises where the general principle of social administration is brought to bear in the *individual* fields of administration, that is, in the *specialized* administrations and ministries. It embraces the totality of those measures through which it makes possible to the *individual* parts of the administrative organism the free and equal development of the labor power of all, *without* consideration of capital and income" (von Stein 1888, part 3, p. 46). Social police, by contrast, deals with the protection of property relations, though von Stein explicitly rejected a special law for this protection along the lines of the Bismarckian Socialist Laws.[25]

Von Stein was the first to take a theoretical position that corresponds to the now prevailing public policy conception of the social or welfare state. His "social state" has the task of simultaneously guaranteeing the conditions of private property and thus the development of an independent entrepreneurial function, and improving the working and living conditions of workers. This position also asserts a self-limitation of the state's activities in line with the principle of subsidiarity, though it is less restrictive than under the liberal views:

> The state, through its administration, should never and under any circumstances do more than create the conditions of personal, economic, and social development that the individual cannot create for himself, and then leave it to the individual and his free, autonomous act to fashion and develop a life of his own from the use of these conditions (von Stein 1866, p. 59).

In von Stein, "*Sozialpoli*tik" thus meant a certain *intention of the "working state,"* that is, public administration. It did not refer to the political process by which social

---

[25] "The real social danger within civic society lies therefore not in socialistic doctrines, but in the unemployment of labor. Thus the police persecution of socialist doctrines and beliefs of every kind is based on a misunderstanding of the nature of the social threat and the task of the police, as long as there is not direct *appeal* for the use of physical force against the existing order." Von Stein (1888, part 3, p. 75).

reforms were initiated. That process remained generally underexposed in von Stein's reflections. The recognition of the necessity of social reforms by the state, that is, the *authorities*, seems to have been sufficient for him as a historical driving force. And it was one of von Stein's central concerns to disseminate argument for recognizing the necessity of social reform, However, apart from this shortcoming with respect to democratic politics (though his view *was* accurate with respect to the reality of Habsburg and Hohenzollern social policy), we already find in von Stein most of the insights that are important to a modern justification of social policy, especially the theoretical insight regarding human capital and the argument for social order.

2.2.2 The Emergence of the Term *Sozialpolitik*

Pairings of the words "political" [*politisch*] and "social" [*social*] can be found from the middle of the 1840s, but the breakthrough came only in connection with the revolutionary year 1848. French influence was critical also for these word combinations,[26] as the semantics of the social was often transported into the German language by Germans who had emigrated to France or Belgium.[27]

Notable for the emergence of the German word pair is a study by the radical democrat Julius Fröbel.[28] Expelled from Prussia and living in Zurich as an émigré, he published this study first in 1846 under the pseudonym of *Junius C.* and with the title *Neue Politik* [New Politics], but then renamed the second edition *System der socialen Politik* [System of Social Politics] (Fröbel 1850).[29] In terms of content it was a broad philosophical justification – inspired by, among other things, conditions in his country of exile – of a republic with a federal structure and governed by a mixture of direct and representative democracy. This republic already envisioned such things as the constitutionally guaranteed formation of political parties, the right to vote for both men and women from the age of 20, and measures for the socio-economic equality of women. To that extent it was first and foremost a *political* reform tract, though it also addressed itself explicitly to questions of the economic order. Fröbel was as critical of unbridled liberal

[26] See, for example, the title of the book by Jules Lechevalier from the circle of the de Saint-Simonists: Question sociale. De la réforme industrielle, considérée comme problème fondamentale de la politique positive (Paris 1833), quoted in Geck (1950), who gives additional references to the early linguistic usage surrounding *Sozialpolitik*.

[27] See, for example, Grün (1845), which also contains what is to my knowledge the earliest instance of the German word pairing "*soziale Politik*": "Dezarmy [the "Communist" author of the *Code de la Communauté* (1843)] retains the word *Politik*, but he has a sensible explanation; he says *soziale Politik* is nothing other than the guidance of work and the repartition of the products" (p. 394).

[28] On Fröbel's life see Allgemeine Deutsche Biographie, vol. 49 (Berlin 1904, pp. 163–172); on his political theory see Koch (1978).

[29] There is also a Mannheim edition from 1847, which forms the basis of the reprint with introduction by Rainer Koch (Fröbel 1975).

acquisitiveness as he was of the socialist demand for a right to work: "The imbalance between needs and capacities is precisely the source of all injustices and the whole problem in the task of a just organization of property and work." That is why – 2 years before the Communist Manifesto – he advocated the following principle: "To each, work according to his capacities and the goods for his needs" (Junius 1847, II, p. 336). In contrast to the Socialists, however, he did not argue simply for common property, but for a "national economy" [*Volkswirtschaft*] that functioned in accordance with the principles of economic liberty, though "where it leads to defective conditions of society, the state economy must form the corrective for the deficient course of the national economy" (Junius 1847, II, p. 402). Fröbel derived the justification for this doubling of the economic system, which roughly follows the boundaries between production and redistribution, from a doubling of the concept of property as both private and communal property: qualified individuals would receive lifetime property titles in tenure from the political bodies, but would not be able to pass them on.

The text of the study is identical in the two editions and contains only sporadic use of the word "*sozial*" with reference to "*politisch*." However, in the preface to the second edition, the word pair is used quite matter-of-factly:

> For all social and political problems – including economic ones – there is only one decision-making basis, namely the ethical one ... and if the world is to take on a new political-social form, it must first make the advances in ethical awareness on which the new form depends ... the advances must be brought to full clarity within their contexts if work is to be done consciously constructing a better political-social order. I have thus based my social policy [*soziale Politik*] on a reworking of ethics, or rather, that policy is such a reworking (Fröbel 1850, p. IVf.).

Fröbel's text, as this passage, too, makes clear, stands in the tradition of Kant more so than of Hegel. He still lacks a separate theory of society, which is instead conceived as entirely dependent on the political. In a later tract written for the constitutional discussions in Frankfurt, Fröbel called for "the social republic, that is, a state in which happiness, freedom, and the dignity of every individual is recognized as the task of all, and the fullness of society's law and power arises from the understanding and agreement of all its members" (Fröbel 1848, p. 6). The change in terminology between the two editions of Fröbel's *Neue Politik* suggests that the pairing of "social" and "political" occurred in the years 1844/1846, that is, against the backdrop of the uprising of the weavers and the Prussian ordinance against it by Frederick William IV.

With a meaning similar to that of Fröbel's, the combination "*social-politisch*" is found in a polemical tract against liberal radicalism that appears to have been written in the spring of 1848:

> This party is the real leader of the revolutionary movement that is reaching out from Paris all across Europe. It is the socialist-political propaganda, the bearer and disseminator of the socio-political [*sozial-politischen*] ideas and doctrines, through which the world is to be moved and unsettled, through which absolutism is to be destroyed in order to make room for the socialist-democratic republic (E. Hofmann 1848, p. 9).

In this case, the compound "*sozial-politisch*" was intended to suggest a link between the democratic and socialist movements.

A crucial contribution to the spread of the pairing of "social" and "political" came from the Prussian district president and social scientist M. von Lavergne-Peguilhen. He maintained that "politics should emanate from the standpoint of the *societal cosmos*, and the politics derived from that is *German social policy* ["deutsche Sozialpolitik"]" (von Lavergne-Peguilhen 1863, p. IV). He posited this concept against the individualism and political centralism of French politics, and as a result emphasized the principle of the monarchy and the estates. He then explains his concept:

> The great manifestations of social life are subject to certain laws; by dint of political arithmetic, these manifestations must be predictable, and likewise the effects of the state reforms etc. Social policy draws the conclusions from these scientific axioms, it erects its doctrines on the basis of the same by seeking to test and confirm them through experience; alongside the rights and interests of the individual it simultaneously represents those of society and it seeks to establish the latter in its rights; it believes that it has no better way of serving the individual, no better way of preserving the interests of the nations, than through careful study of the laws on which the existence and development of society is based, through the state's treatment of society as dictated by these laws and with consideration for the Christian vocation of humankind. That is the position of this young science that is barely developed in its initial stages but promises to have future significance by virtue of that position (von Lavergne-Peguilhen 1863, p. 173).

This is the late articulation of ideas that go back a long way. As early as 1838, von Lavergne-Peguilhen had championed a "science of society" [*Gesellschaftswissenschaft*] (von Lavergne-Peguilhen 1838, 1841). In 1848 he appeared as the first signatory of a program of the *Verein für sozialpolitische Reform* [Association for Social-Political Reform], an organization that had emerged from the *Verein zum Schutze des Eigenthums und zur Förderung des Wohlstandes aller Volksklassen* [Association for the Protection of Property and the Promotion of the Prosperity of all Classes] and whose primary goal was to introduce the position of the owners of knightly estates into the constitutional discussion.[30] The program accordingly reflected the perspective of large agrarian landowners. At the same time, however, it did contain quite forward-looking elements, such as the demands for a progressive income tax, a reform of the banking system, freedom of association, the "creation of a suitable constitution for guilds and cooperatives," and, in order to "establish the welfare of the poorer classes," the demand for state doctors, salutary home construction, and a sanitary water supply; finally, the demand for a "vigorous cultivation of the science of the state and the social sciences."[31]

---

[30] Programm des Vereins für sozial-politische Reform. 20. September 1848 (Berlin 1848, p. 3).

[31] Ibid., pp. 35, 38f. – However, unlike the *Centralverein für das Wohl der arbeitenden Klassen*, the association does not seem to have left any historical traces. Incidentally, the Centralverein does not appear to have used the word pair "social-political," even though von Lavergne-Peguilhen was on its board; see Reulecke (1983, p. 172).

In line with the last-named demand, von Lavergne-Peguilhen brought the following proposal before the First Prussian Chamber in 1849:

> To establish a socio-political central institute, whose task it will be to studysocial conditions in continuous observation; to prepare or evaluate the relevant proposed laws or practical undertakings; to serve as the basis for the development of the science of society into an empirical science; to provide a center for all efforts aimed at understanding and reforming society, and to keep the state government in a constant reciprocal contact with the development of society (quoted by Geck 1950, p. 14).

Rarely has the complexity of social policy as a scientific task been formulated more succinctly.

The clashes of 1848/1849 already involved all political positions that have dominated the debates on social policy to this day: the liberal position, which expected the cure of the social ills to come from the self-healing powers of the market and from a strengthening of the capacities for self-help[32]; the revolutionary position, which predicted an overcoming of the capitalist system because of its inherent contradictions; the conservative position, which called for a return to the traditional ethos of the estate-based society in order to restore conditions of solidarity; and the reformist position, which was hoping to stabilize the political and social system permanently through institutional reforms. The word combinations of "*Sozialpolitik*" and "*Sozialreform*" [social reform] are found largely among conservatives and institutional reformers, sporadically also among liberals,[33] while the revolutionaries soon struck the world "*Sozialreform,*" which they had initially used, from their vocabulary. For the workers' movement, the alternatives "revolution or reform" subsequently became one of the fault lines of disagreements within the movement (Dipper 1992, p. 228ff.).[34]

2.2.3 Terminological Fixation

The failure of the political movement of 1848 subsequently caused questions of political reform to recede into the background, and the term "social reform" turned increasingly into a – politically – *conservative programmatic formula* for a reform that excluded the political rights of the subjects. The word "*Sozialpolitik*" was to some extent pulled into the same orbit.

---

[32] Representative: Von Mohl (1835); following Schulze (1970) also Karl Biedermann (1846).

[33] For example, in Robert von Mohl, who used the term "*sociale Politik*" for the first time in 1851 as a "doctrine of social utility . . . the doctrine of the means to achieve the purposes of individual social circles internally, compared to outside circles in relationship to the state," as the applied branch, in other words, of his "theory of society" (von Mohl 1835, p. 56). The term appeared again in von Mohl (1869, p. 473). On the spread of "social liberalism" see Scheer (1975, pp. 80–107).

[34] However, this pair of opposites is already found in the final sentence of Schuster (1835, p. 124): "You don't want to hear about *social reform*? Then submit to *social revolution*!" Quoted from Kowalski (1967, p. 78).

The first fixation of the concept occurred in W. H. Riehl, who conceived of his *Beiträge zur 'Wissenschaft vom Volk'* [Contributions to the Science of the People] as a "document which proves that a thorough examination of modern social conditions, undertaken with loving devotion to the peculiarities of the life of the people, must in the final analysis lead to the justification of a conservative *Social-Politik*" (Riehl 1851, p. 30).[35] He specified this program in more detail 3 years later:

> The point is to make the collected individual insights from the natural history of the people intellectually useful for the idea of the state, practically useful for the further development of our constitutional and administrative state, for rebuilding the shattered civil society; these facts of natural history must be used as a shield and sword against one-sidedly political (!) party doctrines that would like to cut and trim our political life according to a pre-drawn template. That is what I call *soziale Politik*. The point is to expand the science of the state on the basis of these natural historical facts, and to place an autonomous part of that science as the science of society alongside state law and the study of administration (Riehl 1854, p. 21).

In the spirit of this "natural historical" program, that is, one not oriented toward the voluntarism of the Enlightenment, he subsequently placed his ethnographic and socio-critical studies under the series title "*Naturgeschichte des Volkes als Grundlage einer deutschen Social-Politik*" (1845–1869) [Natural History of the People as the Foundation of a German Social Policy]. He imagined that the solution to the social question qua the workers' question would lie in the corporatist incorporation of the proletariat. Riehl was thus trying to solve what he most certainly perceived as new problems within the framework of the traditional ideas of order in an estate-based society.

By contrast, the work completed in June of 1848 by Karl Marlo, an economist who thought in "state-socialist" terms, was forward-looking. It already reveals a consistent distinction between the "social" and the "political" side of life:

> The word *social* comprises, in the broadest sense, all relationships that arise from the coexistence of human beings, but in the narrower sense only those that do not relate to the exercise of state power. Throughout, we will be using it only in the latter sense. By contrast, by *society* we understand the totality of all humans bound together into a state. In this sense, then, the life of society has a political and a social side . . . However, when it comes to this distinction, one must always bear in mind that the state . . . orders social life, and that the social situation of every nation thus also depends on its political conditions (Marlo 1859, p. 5f.).[36]

Here, the concept of society is the overarching concept, as in the notion of a national society common today, while the Hegelian and – following its lead – the Steinian distinction replaced the traditional unity with the *difference* between

[35] However, from what has been said before, it is evident that Riehl was not the first to use this word, as Lindenlaub (1967, p. 41) believed.

[36] Marlo (1850, p. 5f.). As Pribram (1992, vol. 1, p. 394) has said: "His three-volume work was intended to show that the manner in which the capitalist economy functioned led inevitably to a deterioration in the situation of the working classes and of small entrepreneurs. Like most German Socialist, he saw the organization of the socialist economy as a task of the government." On Marlo see also Scheer (1975, pp. 111–113).

"state" and "(civil) society." But the distinction between the political and the social is simultaneously maintained and a reciprocal interaction is already adumbrated.

A concise summary of the ideas of the first conceptual phase, which unfolded in the field of tension of the Hegelian distinction between state and civil society, is offered by the earliest essay which was devoted to the very concept of social policy:

> The embodiment of the conditions under which the benefits of birth, property, and understanding, as well as the social prestige based on these benefits, are distributed within a nation is called society. Until the beginning of this century, these conditions were never made the subject of scientific examination. Now that science has taken hold of this subject, it can never relinquish it again. We live as citizens of two worlds, of the state and of society. Defining the relationship of these two worlds to each other will be forever after a chief task of political research. In the future there can be no politics other than social politics [*Sozialpolitik*] (Meyer 1864, p. 319).

Meyer distinguished three stages of *social policy as a response to the relationship between state and society*: in the first stage, the distinction was denied and dissolved, either toward the side of "society" in the sense of the *societas civilis cum imperio* (restoration), or toward the side of the state (socialism). In the second stage, the relationship was posited as one free of contradictions and complementary, as in Hegel, Savigny, and in liberal economic thought (Bastiat). Only in the third stage "does social policy return in the concrete task of determining precisely the condition of society, as it has developed in the various nations, in order to erect on the diversity of the same the diversity of state forms." Here the "state form must ... adjust to the condition of society, but not in order to serve it, but in order to make it serviceable to itself." This "basic idea" is one that "social policy will have to work out in the future" (Meyer 1864, p. 327f.). *Social policy is here understood as a social science that establishes a society-shaping policy, one that derives its point of departure from the social conditions under the perspective of their solidified patterns of distribution.*

In contrast, Riehl saw the main task of the "science of society" in the precise description of human coexistence by means of "ethnography" [*Volkskunde*]. Only a government that knows the conditions of its "society" can engage in purposeful policies.

In summary, it should be noted that the social science or science of society that emerged against the backdrop of the political clashes between 1789 and 1848 had already come up with a sociologically grounded concept of social policy, though depending on the particular author, that concept proceeded from quite different social views. Especially L. von Stein already concretized social policy in the sense of state interventions through administrative action. In the process, a rather dialectical relationship of "state" and "society" became visible, one that can be described – following Hegel – as "mediation" [*Vermittlung*]. And yet, this socio-theoretical perspective did not shape the subsequent phases in the conceptual history of "social policy." *Under the impact of the national unification of Germany, ideas about functional differentiation that are crucial for a deeper theoretical conception of social policy receded in the background again.* A lasting contribution to this trend came from the Prussian historian Heinrich von Treitschke, who criticized the proposal of an autonomous "science of society" [*Gesellschaftswissenschaft*], but who now claimed the term "social political" [*sozialpolitisch*] for the "science of the state" [*Staatswissenschaft*] he put forth:

> The entire science of the state is socio-political; it must show how the idea of the unity of the people [*Volkseinheit*] is realized in the multifariousness of the particular endeavors of the people (von Treitschke 1859, p. 82f.).

This allowed Gustav Schmoller to remark, in a 1867 review of von Stein's *Verwaltungslehre*: "With this he creates, for the first time, a true system, but witnesses that the great majority of economists have so little understanding of his books, as though they were written in Chinese" (Schmoller 1867, p. 269). Until the end of the First World War, the concept of "social policy"developed so much under the premise of the national unification under *political* leadership that the autonomy of the social dimension disappeared from view.

3 The Workers' Question and Social Policy (1863–1918)

3.1 Latency of the Term Sozialpolitik

Compared to the lively phase of discussion during the pre-1848 period, the 1850s and 1860s brought few references to *Sozialpolitik*.[37] The claim by the long-time editor of a anthology of sources on the history of social policy – "And for all ideas and measures that were aimed at solving this very workers' question, the umbrella term '*Sozialpolitik*' was coined in the decade leading up to the founding of the Empire" (Born 1966, pp. 11–14) – is inaccurate, in two ways: first, it overlooks the emergence (described in the last chapter) of the concept as grounded in social theory; second, as will be shown below, it dates the institutional consolidation of the term nearly two decades too early. To the extent that a relevant conceptualization appears at all "in the decade leading up to the founding of the Empire," the phrase that dominated was "*sociale Reform.*"[38] These were years of continuous economic growth, a time when the rapid advance of industrialization raised hopes that the social question could be resolved by industrial progress. All the more so because the introduction of universal suffrage for men in the North German

[37] In addition to those already indicated, one should also list Joerg (1867); Joerg described as "social politician" [*Sozialpolitiker*] all those who were wrestling with the "social question" in the sense of the workers' question. On Joerg see Stegmann (1965). – The most comprehensive documentation on the literature regarding social policy up to the First World War, by Stammhammer (1896 and 1912), also mentions some tracts that used the pairing "*sozialpolitisch.*" To the extent that a specific trend is apparent, it seems to take its cues from Riehl.

[38] The *Realencyclopädie*, published by Brockhaus, already included an entry "*Socialreformer*" in the tenth edition (1851–1855), but it was dropped again in the next edition (1864–1868).

Confederation (1867), and the repeal of the prohibitions against associations, gave reason to expect that the political disadvantage of the workers would also be removed (Born 1959; Offermann 1979). The two decades before the founding of the Empire were also a heyday of economic liberalism in Germany, in terms of both political and entrepreneurial practice and in the social sciences. The field was dominated by the Manchester School around John Prince-Smith and Max Wirth, who joined in 1857 to form the "Congress of German Economists" [*Kongress deutscher Volkswirthe*] (Gehrig 1909; Herkner 1925).

What emerged ever more clearly during this phase was the distinction between the workers' question and the poverty question, which would lead to an "institutional division between a largely privatized care for the poor and a welfare-state regulated provisioning of essential services to workers" (Pankoke 1995b, col. 1227; Tennstedt 1981). And while the discussions around 1848 had reflected far more strongly the developments outside the country, the domestic conditions now moved into the center of the debates. Ferdinand Lassalle had founded the *Allgemeiner Deutscher Arbeiterverein* [General Association of German Workers] in 1863, thus giving the workers' movement – which had been suppressed since 1850 – clearly visible contours (Tennstedt 1983). Henceforth, the "*workers' question*" dominated the thinking about the "social question."[39] Contrary to what one might have expected, the liberal commercial code strengthened *both* sides, the entrepreneurs and the workers' movement, as a result of which the class conflict became more and more a historical reality. And the growing success of social democracy in the *Reichtag* elections – regarded by the bourgeoisie as a political threat – did its part to turn the workers' question into the most important domestic political problems of the new Empire.[40]

3.1.1 The Liberal Phase

A representative document from the 1860s is the work on the workers' question by the young Gustav Schmoller, which makes no reference to either "social reform" or "social policy" (Schmoller 1864/1865). The argument here is structured by the debate over "self-help," a position pleaded by Hermann Schultze-Delitzsch, or "state help," as proposed by Ferdinand Lassalle (Pankoke 1970, p. 174ff.). At that point, Schmoller believed there was "progress in overcoming the disastrous economic depressions" (Schmoller 1864, p. 411) and therefore saw the solution to the workers' question above all in private and public measures aimed at *strengthening the workers' ability to self-help*, that is, national education, promotion of savings,

[39] The much-cited, programmatic work by Lange (1979, first 1865) probably contributed to codifying the term, as did the fundamental manifesto of the Catholic-social movement by von Ketteler (1864).

[40] A good overview of "social reformers and social revolutionaries," especially of the most important protagonists of practical social policy, is provided by Lampert (1998, pp. 43–61).

and facilitation and support for various forms of cooperative self-help. Schmoller thus took a position that mediated between Schultze-Delitzsch and Lassalle:

> We are in complete agreement with the general tendency of our time to no longer tolerate the unjustified interference of the police-state [*Polizeistaat*], the arbitrary use of state power by a privileged aristocracy, as in the feudal state. Our entire modern age, and especially our modern industry, rests on the vigorous and not excessively constrained development of the individual; however, the correct development of the individual does not at all see law and the state, especially the constitutional state, which does not confront society as a foreign power with foreign interest, but grows out of the ethical connection with the entire nation, as a barrier and an impediment, but as the external guidelines for what is inherently good and right (Schmoller 1864, p. 535).

A remarkable blending of a liberal and conservative mindset becomes apparent here. One can describe education and the facilitation of wealth-formation as well as the self-organization of workers as a consistently liberal concept for a solution to the workers' question, whereby in keeping with the liberal position, the initiative to promote national education and savings was seen primarily as a task of the bourgeoisie.[41] For Schmoller, however, the intervention by the state remained a subsidiary but ethically necessary solution, and he accorded the state, as a "Christian state,"[42] greater insight into what constitutes the common good. Schmoller's harmonious image of society was based on faith in "the ethical tendency . . . that the healthy moral sense of the people will call forth tendencies and countercurrents against the kind of abuses and distortions that economic life creates or is in danger of creating."[43] This ethical consciousness, which repressed the conflictual consequences of von Stein's and Marx's diagnosis of society, became crucial not only for the founding of the "Verein für Sozialpolitik" (1872/1873), but also for Bismarck's social reforms: "That is why he should not help *anyone*? The state can."[44]

The founding phase of institutional social policy to which we will now turn took place against a new backdrop, however: the rise in labor conflicts and the co-occurrence of the founding of the *Reich* (1871) and a new economic crisis (1873ff.) caused the liberal hopes to vanish and made the state's power of shaping society appear more promising.

[41] The development in France from Napoleon III to the First World War corresponded roughly to this model.

[42] The phrase "Christian state" stems from Friedrich Julius Stahl, a jurist who was very influential at the time. On the influence of Christian motives and personalities on German social policy see Kaufmann (1988a) and Kaiser and Loth (1997).

[43] Schmoller (1864, p. 523); similarly Schmoller (1875). See also Harnisch (1994).

[44] Marginal note by Bismarck on the draft of a direct petition from the State Ministry to the Prussian king Wilhelm I dated February 21, 1865. Quoted in Tennstedt and Winter (1994, no. 41, p. 124). (In general, this source collection is hereafter cited only with reference to the source number, for longer documents also with the page number. Additional indications of the kind of sources are only given if relevant to the present context of a conceptual history).

3.1.2 The Political Use of Language in the Phase Preceding Bismarckian Social Legislation

The anthology of sources on the basic issues of social policy between 1863 and 1881 compiled by Florian Tennstedt and Heide Winter allows us to reference the political use of language even without painstaking research. Although the subject index lists 39 entries for *Sozialpolitik*, an analysis reveals that the noun *Sozialpolitik* does not appear even once in the source texts themselves, only in the commentaries. Where the references concern the texts themselves, we usually find there the adjective "*sozialpolitisch*," namely primarily in the combined phrases "*sozialpolitische Fragen*" [socio-political questions], "*sozialpolitisches Gebiet*" [sphere of social policy], and "*sozialpolitische Reform*" [socio-political reform]. The phrase "*sozialpolitische Fragen*" appeared only in 1872 in connection with an international conference.[45] The phrase "*sozialpolitisches Gebiet*" as well as occasional other combinations were used around 1878 by a single official in the State Ministry (Robert Bosse).[46] The phrase "*sozialpolitische Reform*" came to the fore only in the immediate run-up to the imperial message of 1881 (Tennstedt/Winter 1994, no. 153, p. 513; no. 189, p. 628; no. 191; no. 192, p. 633); before that, we hear mostly of "*Reform*" and a reference object, occasionally also of "*soziale Reform.*" The adjective "*sozialpolitisch*," too, was only sporadically used until 1879 and had not conceptually solidified. However, in the orbit of the accident insurance draft bill of 1879/1881, it came to be commonly used in the sense of a policy that promoted the integration of the workers into the *Reich* (Tennstedt and Winter 1993, e.g. nos. 133, 161, 226, 228).

A study of the language use within the framework of the Catholic-social movement yields the same finding: the word appeared for the first time on the occasion of the general meeting of Catholics in 1882, which issued the charge "to invite outstanding Catholic social politicians [*Sozialpolitiker*] to a conference about usury, wages, and basic relief;" out of this emerged in 1884 the "*Freie Vereinigung katholischer Sozialpolitiker*" [Free Association of Catholic Social Politicians],[47]

---

[45] Tennstedt and Winter (1994, nos. 88, 93, 110, 113). Also in the combination "*sozialpolitische und internationale Arbeiterfrage*" ["social-political and international workers' question"] in nos. 112 and 114; in no. 113, by contrast, we read "*soziale und internationale Arbeiterfrage*" ["social and international workers' question"]. All these sources refer to the "Preußisch-österreichische Konferenz über die soziale Frage" [Prussian-Austrian Conference on the Social Question], which was held in Berlin November 7–21, 1872. The word "*sozialpolitisch*" was used here to differentiate the domestic political from the international aspects of the workers' question (fight against the London International).

[46] Tennstedt and Winter (1994, nos. 154, 170, 204, p. 659). In addition, "*Social-politische Flugblätter* (Verlag Schindler, Berlin) are attested between 1874 and 1876.

[47] Hermans (1972, p. 479f.). An earlier use of this expression could not be found in this work. Ritter (1954) came up with the same finding. However, on p. 111 he mentions a letter by Ludwig Windthorst from 1873 in which he distanced himself from a "*sozialpolitischen Vorgehen*" ["a social-political approach"] in favor on the "protection of religion and the church;" this confirms once again that the term had not yet been codified.

which also published a Yearbook under its name between 1887 and 1889. The lexicographical finding suggests that the term "*Sozialpolitik*" was pushed especially by the Catholic side,[48] especially in the wake of Pope Leo XIII's 1891 encyclical on the workers' question, "*Rerum novarum*."[49] On the Protestant side, in spite of a remarkable charitable engagement of the "*Innere Mission*" [Internal Mission], a socio-political commitment comparable to the Catholic social movement cannot be discerned either conceptually or practically.[50]

The absence of the word "Sozialpolitik" in the political vocabulary of the 1870s becomes clearer still if we look at descriptions in which one could have expected to find the word "*Sozialpolitik*" in the linguistic usage after 1890. For example, Hermann Wagener, Bismarck's long-time advisor on social policy, said, on the occasion of the Prussian-Austrian Conference on the Social Question,

> that in order to deal fruitfully with the question, one cannot restrict oneself to the *workers' question*, but will have to look at the social question in the broader sense as the overall context of contemporary society, ... that one cannot assign and leave this task to society alone, but that the state and governments must also proceed to give political form to these things (Tennstedt and Winter 1994, p. 339).[51]

---

[48] The first lexicon article "*Socialpolitik*" appeared in 1879 in a Catholic encyclopedia and said the following: "S., the theoretical development and practical application of the principles of Socialism (see that entry). *Socialpolitiker* and *Socialreformer*, those who deal with a solution to the social question, the latter with the goal of a complete transformation of property and ownership relations. The former include the academic socialists [*Kathedersozialisten*], who seek reform by way of legislation." Herders Conversations-Lexikon, 2nd ed., vol. 4 (Freiburg im Breisgau, 1879, p. 474). Note the positive connotation of "*Sozialpolitik*" in contrast to (Socialist) "*Sozialreform*." In the next edition, "*Socialpolitik*" was highlighted through a special, four-column article (vol. 7, Freiburg im Breisgau, 1907, following column 1772). – The encyclopedias by Brockhaus (12th ed., 1875–1879) and Meyers (3rd ed., 1874–1878) around the same time do not use the word at all in the pertinent entries; however, the subsequent editions from the eighties (13th ed., 1882–1887 respectively 4th ed., 1885–1890) do have an entry under "*Sozialpolitik*." – The earliest handbook-like article appeared in the *Staatslexikon* first published in 1889–1897 by the Görres-Gesellschaft zur Pflege der Wissenschaft im katholischen Deutschland: Brüll (1897). By contrast the Handwörterbuch der Staatswissenschaften ignored the word in the 2nd ed (1898–1907), listed it in the 3rd ed. (1909–1911) only as a reference word, and included a separate article by the sociologist Leopold von Wiese only in the following edition of 1926.

[49] Following the encyclical "*Rerum novarum*," the claim to a "Catholic social policy" was put forth by Cathrein (1899), Alongside the already mentioned Bishop von Ketteler, Franz Hitze (1877, 1880) became especially influential.

[50] Shanahan (1962). In organized form one should mention only the short-lived "Christian-social Party" [Christlich-soziale Partei] of the Prussian court preacher and anti-Semite Adolph Stoecker (1878), and the "Protestant-Social Congress" [Evangelisch-Soziale Kongreß] founded in 1890. See Kretschmar (1972). – But at least some of the Prussian officials who were dealing with social-political questions considered their engagement a Christian task; see Tennstedt (1994).

[51] No. 118: "Protokoll(entwurf) der preußisch-österreichischen Konferenz über die soziale Frage."– Wagener also published his social-political ideas in book form, though without using the word itself. Instead, he speaks of "a social reform policy appropriate to the times." Anonymous (Hermann Wagener) (1878, p. 11).

Equally striking is the absence of the word "*Sozialpolitik*" within the framework of the discussions around 1878, which dealt with the question of how the Socialist Laws could be supplemented with measures useful to the working class. Here the preferred adjective was "*positiv*" (e.g. "positive policy") in situations where we today would expect to find "*sozial*" (Tennstedt and Winter 1994, nos. 151, 152, 187 [p. 615], 219 [p. 692]). Bismarck himself spoke occasionally of "social reform," but he also accepted the label "state socialist," which originally carried a negative connotation.[52] The only author of a source text who at least dared utter the phrase "*soziale Politik*" in a campaign speech in 1881 was the economist, public finance expert, and "state socialist" Adolph Wagner (Tennstedt and Winter 1994, no. 189, passim).

In summary it must be noted that the latency period of the term "Sozialpolitik" extended to the social legislation that is tied to Bismarck's name.[53] In this context, too, words and phrases like "*soziale Reform*" and "*Arbeiterpolitik*" were initially dominant, provided reference was not being directly made to concrete political postulates or measures.[54] A direct effect on political rhetoric from the founding of the "Verein für Socialpolitik" (discussed below) is not discernible.

3.2 *The Influence of the* Verein für Socialpolitik[55]

The turnaround in public opinion, from the liberal hope for a solution to the social question through economic progress and worker self-help to the need for political-social reforms, was initiated by a speech from the previously mentioned Adolph

[52] "The prince expressed himself more or less as follows: the mere persecution of the socialists is not enough. . . . He had come to believe that a moderate, sensible state socialism could exorcise the danger . . . Those people had to be stripped of their influence on the workers by showing the latter that the state is interested in them and looks after their welfare through practical measures, instead of deceiving them with false, impossible promises, as was being done by the Socialist leaders." Tennstedt and Winter (1994): No. 179: "Berichtsentwurf des bayerischen Gesandten in Berlin Hugo Graf von und zu Lerchenfeld-Koefering an den bayerischen Außenminister Krafft Freiherr von Crailsheim vom 18. Dezember 1880," p. 598. – On the conceptual history of "*Staatssocialismus*" see Thier (1930). Between 1877 and 1882, a journal with the title "Der Staatssocialist. Wochenschrift für Socialreform" was also published in Berlin; behind it stood segments of the Protestant-social movement.

[53] This impression is also confirmed by Stammhammer's *Bibliographie der Social-Politik*.

[54] In this era the Social Democrats also laid claim to the term "*Sozialreform*" for themselves: "The official social reform [*Sozialreform*] has nothing in common with our social reform except the name. The true social reform is the one promoted by Social Democracy." From "Aufruf der sozialdemokratischen Fraktion zur ersten Reichstagswahl unter dem Sozialistengesetz (27. Oktober 1881)," in *Die Sozialdemokratie im Deutschen Reichstag. Tätigkeitsberichte und Wahlaufrufe aus den Jahren 1871 bis 1893* (Berlin, 1909, p. 207, and passim). By contrast, the term "*Sozialpolitik*" was still rejected after the turn of the century, along with the "inadequate" policy connected to it.

[55] For this see in English also Grimmer-Solem (2003).

Wagner on the social question (October 1871), which resonated strongly in the journalistic media.[56] It earned those economists interested in social policy who joined together into an organization in its wake the nickname "*Kathedersozialisten*" [Lectern Socialists] by the Manchester camp [57] Subsequently, however, some also adopted this label to describe themselves.

3.2.1 Naming the Organization

While the founding history of the "*Verein für Socialpolitik*" has been documented in detail (Conrad 1906, p. 56ff; Boese 1939, p. 1ff.; Wittrock 1939), it provides no final clarity about the origins of the name. Wagner, in the speech mentioned previously, spoke of the "tasks of the state on the social question" and of "state policy on the social question," though he did use the adjective "*sozialpolitisch*" (Wagner 1872a, p. 11f.). At the Eisenach Conference of 1872, which set up a founding committee for the organization, Rudolf von Gneist, the elected chairman of the conference, gave this organization the "provisional title ... '*Social-Reform-Verein*,' to which, incidentally, an 'unnamed person' immediately objected" (Boese 1939, p. 12). According to Conrad (1906, p. 57), there had been talk of a "congress for social reform" already at a preliminary discussion on July 13, 1872 in Halle. The published record of the discussion speaks of the "Eisenach meeting to discuss the social question" (Boese 1939, p. 305). How and when the name was settled on cannot be precisely determined, as it would seem that not all meetings of the founding committee were recorded" (Boese 1939, p. 13). Apparently, however, Georg Friedrich Knapp used the phrase "*Verein für Socialpolitik*" in a letter to Gustav Schmoller in the runup to a meeting in November 1872 (Boese 1939, p. 13). The name also appeared in the draft of the by-laws that were presented to the participants at the Eisenach meeting on October 13, 1873. According to von Bruch (1985, p. 65), the name was accepted there without any discussion.

The carefully drafted "Call for the foundation of an Association for Social Policy [*Verein für Sozialpolitik*]" reveals implicitly how the authors understood the sphere and tasks of social policy at the intersection of "self-help" and "state help":

> Out of the totality of the more or less justified attempts at developing today's acquisitive society [*Erwerbsgesellschaft*], the clash between capital and labor is presently emerging as a threat. We believe that herein lie tasks of peaceful reform for the state and society.
>
> The first task will be to clarify the conditions of workers and their relationship to employers, to determine the needs of cooperative bodies, to support their successful development, and to promote any understanding between the contending parties.

---

[56] Wagner (1872a). On the context and impact of the speech see the vivid retrospective by Lujo Brentano on the occasion of the 25th anniversary of the organization (1875), reprinted in Brentano (1923, pp. 1–22).

[57] Oppenheim (1872). On this Wagner (1872b). For a good account of the controversies at the time see now Machtan (1988).

> In like manner, the other social and economic problems of our day, such as health care and education, transportation, stocks, and taxes, will be examined.
>
> We believe that the unfettered working of partly opposing individual interests of unequal strength does not guarantee the welfare of the totality, that instead the demands of the public spirit and humanity must assert themselves also in economic life, and that the well-considered intervention by the state to protect the justified interest of all those concerned must be aroused in good time.
>
> We do not see this state care as a makeshift or unavoidable evil, but as the fulfillment of one of the highest tasks of our time and our nation. With the earnest implementation of these tasks, the selfishness of the individual and the immediate interests of the classes will subordinate themselves to the lasting and higher destiny of the whole (quoted by Boese 1939, p. 248).

Schmoller's opening speech at the first Eisenach meeting on October 8, 1872, contained neither the term "*Sozialreform*" nor "*Sozialpolitik*." As in the above-mentioned speech by Adolph Wagner, Schmoller spoke of the "social question" and of "reforms," but the old terminology (see chap. 1) evidently played no role.

To be sure, the term "*soziale Reform*" was at this time common in scholarly writings, but not so the word "*Sozialpolitik*."[58] And that does not seem to have changed much during the 1870s. A survey of relevant works of that period yielded numerous instances of the term "*Sozialreform*," but only a few uses of "*Sozialpolitik*."[59] Even in the bibliographic survey by the editor of the conservative *Berliner Revue* (Meyer 1873), nearly complete and very informative for the period, contains only one entry with the title *Nationalökonomie und Socialpolitik in ihrer Beziehung und Wirkung auf die socialen Fragen der Gegenwart* (Sommer 1872).

---

[58] Dipper (1992, p. 333) suspects that the detailed review of Frédéric Le Play's La Réforme sociale en France (Paris 1865) by Albert Schäffle contributed to reactivating the term "*Sozialreform*."

[59] The following were exceptions: Von Scheel (1878) with an explicit definition, though one that harked back to the first conceptual phase: "*Socialpolitik* is the knowledge and art of arranging society, and since this arrangement can happen only through an uppermost, consolidating government, and since society is not conceivable without the state, the concept of the state is automatically included. *Socialpolitik* is thus a sum of efforts that are aimed at society, that is, at the historically evolved union of families and individuals . . . which is bound together by shared economic and personal connections and regulates the latter through morality and law in accordance with the same basic views; as a historically evolved union it is naturally also in the process of constant development" (p. 3); Contzen (1877), where the section on non-Socialist social reformers carries the title "Social-political movements in Germany since 1848," though without clarifying the term nor mentioning the Verein für Sozialpolitik; finally, Held (1878, pp. 123–140), where, "*Sozialpolitik*" was used merely in the sense of the intentions of the Verein für Sozialpolitik and as a way of drawing a distinction to those of the liberal "Volkswirtschaftlicher Congress". – Finally, the terms "*Sozialpolitik*" and "*sozialpolitisch*" appeared sporadically also in the controversy between Gustav Schmoller and Heinrich von Treitschke (1874/1875), though without undergoing a conceptual consolidation. For example, Schmoller (1874, p. 330): "The social movement that led to the Revolution of 1789 in France, did not occur in Germany. And that it did not occur here is due above all to the Prussian state and the *social policy* of its great kings . . . It was this *social policy* that protected the German peasants from abusive treatment and from being thrown off his land. . .This older German *social policy* largely concluded with the Stein-Hardenberg emancipation of the peasants and with the beginnings of the Prussian factory legislation". And von Treitschke (1875, p. 425): "In Sparta, Nabis and a depraved gang plundered the haves – a home-grown *social policy,* whose accomplishments you will surely not praise as 'thoroughly *kathedersozialistische* measures'."

This rarely cited work was dedicated to Chancellor Bismarck and was remarkably original: following Friedrich List, it took an approach that was explicitly focused on the theory of human capital and was in terms of social policy close to a Lassallian Socialism. The phrase it uses, "*Volkswirtschaft und Sozialpolitik* [national economy and social policy]," is broad and could be rightly called"societal policy":

> If we grasp the national economic systems and socio-political theories in their totality, ... we find the urgent necessity for a *Volkswirtschaft und Sozialpolitik*, which, with calm considerateness, on positive foundations, on humane, just, and legal paths, should set in motion a gradual change of the existing social conditions and antagonisms, the shortest road to reconciliation and at the same time to a higher, more fruitful culture, but also to make possible and prepare an organization of work and of the entire society that provides the entire population secure happiness, a decent life to all, without exception, in all strata of the people, that is, also and especially the laboring classes (Sommer 1872, p. 79).

The term "Sozialpolitik" solidified only in the 1880s, namely in direct connection with Bismarck's social legislation, and after that it appeared with great frequency in book titles as well as in the names of journals and the like.[60] Even though the "Verein für Socialpolitik" had been using that name since 1873, the term "*Socialpolitik*" was able to establish itself in scholarly terminology only after the word had also become commonplace in political language.

Perhaps the fact that the newly founded organization in 1873 chose the word *Sozialpolitik* to describe itself should be seen as the expression of a militant character and therefore rather be translated by "Social Politics." According to its original goal, the organization certainly did intend to involve itself in everyday politics with the help of resolutions that had a scientific basis and were adopted by the majority, in an effort to activate the government for the benefit of the disadvantaged classes.[61] The prevailing opinion was that the ethically-oriented economics of the historical school, for which most *Kathedersozialisten* felt an affinity, was also well suited to formulating well-supported recommendations on social policy.[62] It was only the unavoidable conflicts that arose along the way, and especially the engagement with the highly controversial Socialist Laws (1878) and the Protective

---

[60] For example: *Zeitschrift für Volkswirtschaft, Sozialpolitik und Verwaltung*. Organ der Gesellschaft Österreichischer Volkswirte (Prague, Vienna, Leipzig, 1892–1894); *Sozialpolitisches Centralblatt* (Berlin, 1892–1894), after 1894/1895 under the title: *Soziale Praxis – Centralblatt für Sozialpolitik* (this journal, was central to the social-political discussion until the end of the Weimar Republic; over the course of time the title was repeatedly modified). The *Archiv für soziale Gesetzgebung und Statistik*, first published in 1888, was issued after volume 19 (1904) – that is, after the editorship was taken over by Werner Sombart, Max Weber and Edgar Jaffé – as *Archiv für Sozialwissenschaft und Sozialpolitik*. The *Annalen für soziale Politik und Gesetzgebung* was published from 1911 to 1919, and the *Kölner sozialpolitische Vierteljahresschrift* between 1923 and 1932.

[61] On the political influence of the organization see Töpfer (1970); Plessen (1975); K.-H. Schmidt (1997).

[62] Gustav von Schmoller, especially, did much to come up with the methodological justification of this position. See Nau (1998).

Tariffs Bill (1879) that brought about the change "from the strike force of social reform to a discussion forum."[63]

The practical, directly political reformist intention – "Elevating the material and spiritual state of the wage workers" [64] – was subsequently revived by the "*Gesellschaft für sociale Reform*" [Society for Social Reform, fd. 1901], whose personnel overlapped noticeably with that of the Verein für Socialpolitik (von Bruch 1985, pp. 130–152; Ratz 1980). During the founding phase of the "*Verein fur Socialpolitik,*" the term "*soziale Reform*" thus referred more to the programmatic dimension, and the term "*Sozialpolitik*" more to the pragmatic dimension of the organization's activities. *Subsequently, "sociale Reform" retained its political connotation, while "Socialpolitik" became more of a specialized academic term.* Revealingly enough, "*Sozialpolitik*" sparked an extensive conceptual discussion that lasted until the end of the Weimar Republic. Similar discussions did not take place with respect to "*sociale Reform.*" Instead, "*Sozialreform*" turned into a term of political rhetoric that was open to a multitude of interpretations (Dipper 1992, pp. 336–343).

3.2.2 Confusions and Clarifications: The Historical Importance of the *Verein für Socialpolitik*

Established as a competitor to the liberal "*Kongreß deutscher Volkswirte*" [Congress of German Economists], the *Verein für Socialpolitik* soon turned into the dominant scientific organization in the field of political science, economics, and sociology. At the time the organization was founded, these fields of knowledge had not yet clearly separated from each other. Although the organization's membership was made up predominantly of economists, it also included some jurists as well as a large number of practitioners, most of them with academic training. Although statistically in the minority, the university professors always exerted a dominant influence.[65]

If one surveys the themes debated within the organization, often carefully researched through formal inquiries by its members, one is struck by the thematic breadth of the topics covered from the very beginning.[66] Those topics revolved by no means merely around the condition of industrial workers and measures for their improvement; rather, the focus was just as much on agrarian issues and with them

[63] Von Bruch (1985, p. 77). On this see also Schmoller's opening speech following his election as chairman of the organization at the Frankfurt meeting in 1890. In Boese (1939, p. 250ff.).

[64] As Freiherr von Berlepsch, for example, put it in the name of the Society for Social Reform (1903, p. 3).

[65] On the occupations composition of the *Verein für Socialpolitik* see Gorges (1980, pp. 70, 156, 216–218, 276f., 336f., 414–416).

[66] See the list of the organization's publications in Boese (1939, p. 305ff.), and the survey of the proceedings, Ibid., passim. Also, Gorges (1980, passim). The continuity with older administrative inquests is emphasized by Siemann (1989, pp. 293–311).

on rural workers, but also on small trade threatened by the expansion of industry – in other words, on all the social strata threatened by proletarization. Strongly represented were also themes dealing with economic policy, economic law, and finance. Great attention was paid to developments in other countries. Incidentally, even after 1879, the general meetings of the organizations remained a forum where entrepreneurs and union representatives had a chance to speak. If one considers as the topic of social policy everything that the organization dealt with, virtually the only way to circumscribe it would be by the disciplinary boundaries of economics and the social sciences.[67] However, boundary questions hardly played a role, at least in the first few decades of its activities. According to Pribram, the members of the first generation "even felt a conscious aversion to a clarification of the concept and of the theoretical foundations of social policy; as a result, discussions of a fundamental nature were initially deliberately excluded from the proceedings of the *Verein für Sozialpolitik*" (Pribram 1925b, p. 239). This may help to explain the discontinuation of the older current of discussion alongside the disciplinary differences, since the central power of definition had passed out of the hands of jurists and administrative scientists into those of economists.

The theoretical vagueness of the organization's program stood in stark contrast to the efforts by Lorenz von Stein or Robert von Mohl at conceptual clarification. While those men had a clear awareness of the *difference* between "state" and "society," historical-ethical economics, in reaction to the liberal "Free Trade School," emphasized precisely the *interconnectedness* of state, economy, and society. This ethically-mediated notion of interconnectedness can be regarded as a consistent trait of the German reaction to classic economics in England and France (Brandt 1993; Koslowski 1995a; Priddat 1995). But while von Stein was searching for the connection between what was analytically separated and saw in this separation both the possibility of progress and a structure that gave rise to the social question, the *Kathedersozialisten* lacked the corresponding structural insights.[68] As a result, "*Sozialreform*" and "*Sozialpolitik*" were to them no scientific categories, but collective names for a concrete, pragmatic engagement with existing problems, social goals, and political measures. In addition, the generally recognized ethical orientation offered little occasion to ponder the difference between objective assessments and value judgments in the wake of a scientific treatment of problems. *Within the setup of such an unproblematic interconnection of theory, applied science, and political judgment, "Sozialpolitik" too, appeared to be a self-evident concept.* The charge that economics had become a "science of sentiment"

---

[67] Lujo Brentano, in particular, repeatedly opposed this kind of expansion of the scientific program beyond the problems of social policy. See Neuloh (1961, pp. 30–35).

[68] Von Beckerath (1962, p. 76): "When Lorenz von Stein published the fifth edition of his work [i.e. *Lehrbuch der Finanzwissenschaft*], it had long since become foreign to most of his contemporaries ... As a result, a good deal of theoretical profundity and not a little historical-political insight, which could have also benefited later research, ... was thus lost in Germany."

[*Empfindungswissenschaft*] under the auspices of *Kathedersozialismus* (Wolf 1899, p. 17) touched on a conspicuous weakness.

The "directional struggles" and "methodological quarrels" between 1883 and 1914, which secure the activity of the organization and its prominent members a place in intellectual history beyond their impact at the time, should be seen as a reaction to the cognitive and normative problems that were associated with this position, whose most prominent advocate was Schmoller (Lindenlaub 1967; Nau 1996; Nau 1997). The main points of contention were the methodological problem in economic and social-scientific theorizing (general theory versus historism) and the question about the role of value judgments in scientific discourses.

Without going into substantive detail, it should be noted for our purposes *that the scientific status of "Sozialpolitik" became precarious in the wake of these disputes.* For one, and on this point there was substantial agreement, socio-political diagnoses and recommendations are always tied to concrete social conditions; but if social-scientific theory deals in principle with generally valid concepts and their relationships, there is no longer any room for a "theory of social policy."[69] For another, every judgment relevant to social policy presupposes normative criteria; those seem less and less secured by the unquestioned, culturally transmitted shared ethos of society, and increasingly as the almost irrational preconditions of human judgment and action. Max Weber's famous essay on the "objectivity" of social-scientific and socio-political knowledge not only had a significant effect on the outcome of the so-called "dispute over value judgments" within the *Verein für Socialpolitik*, it also represents a profound turning point in the history of the discipline:

> The connection of actuality with ideas of value which lend meaning to it, and the ordering and stressing of the parts of reality so colored, from the point of view of their cultural meaning, is a quite heterogeneous and discrete point of view as against the analysis of reality into laws and their arrangement into general concepts. The two kinds of rational ordering of reality have no sort of necessary logical relation to one another (Weber 1904).[70]

---

[69] Accordingly, the publishers of the *Archiv für Sozialwissenschaft und Sozialpolitik* saw "*Sozialpolitik*" merely as political practice, not a science: "We (describe) as the very own field of our journal the scientific study of the *general cultural meaning of the socio-economic structure of human communal life* and its historical organizations forms. – This and nothing else is what we mean by calling our journal 'Archiv für Sozialwissenschaft.' Here the word is supposed to encompass the historical and theoretical engagement with the same problems whose practical solution is the subject of 'social *policy*' in the broadest sense of the word." (Weber 1904, p. 165). Because of this extremely broad conception of the term "*Sozialpolitik*," this essays contributes virtually nothing to a closer understanding of the subject of social policy. – On Weber's material socio-political conceptions see "Ein Rundschreiben Max Webers zur Sozialpolitik. Herausgegeben und eingeleitet von Bernhard Schäfer," in *Soziale Welt* 18 (1967, pp. 261–271, esp. 265f.). A comprehensive theoretical determination of social policy following Max Weber was attempted by Rieger (1999).

[70] See also Weber (1968, p. 176).

As Lorenz von Stein before him, Weber insisted on the *autonomy of spheres of meaning* ["Sinnsphären"] between which no *systematic*, and at best only pragmatic, compromises were possible. Only today, within the horizon of a postmodern awareness of multiperspectivity are new paths of a controlled mediation between spheres of meaning being sought out (Welsch 1995). And the notion of laws of causality that can be identified by social science has yielded to more complex and "softer" strategies of inquiry.

It can be said, then, that the critical debates over methodology in the *Verein für Socialpolitik* created crucial preconditions for the discipline-specific differentiation of the political and the social sciences. Especially the emergence of economics and sociology as independent disciplines in Germany, and their institutional separation, can be traced back directly to these debates.[71]

3.3 First Conceptual Debates

With Wilhelm II's new course on the workers' question (von Berlepsch 1987), at the latest i.e. 1890, "*Sozialpolitik*" became a term of mass use, if not a public catchword.[72] Usage of the word became correspondingly vague, "for it would seem that the term *Sozialpolitik* still exerts a special attraction on the minds, which is why this term is used to designate the sphere or direction of politics that seems to the scholars or statesmen in question as the most important, the most significant one" (von Bortkiewicz 1899, p. 348). The publisher of the *Sozialpolitisches Centralblatt* identified the most important reason for this in his programmatic introduction:

> Of necessity, every economic manifestation and legislative measure confronted the question of the effect they would have on the condition of the various classes: these classes themselves stepped onto the stage of public life vigorously and energetically with their own demands on the economy and legislation. With all these manifestations connected by multifarious interactions we are dealing with social forces of extraordinary potency, which in incessant activity are reshaping our society. But everything here is in flux, instinctive feeling all too often outweighs purposeful intention (Braun 1892, p. 1f.).

It was precisely against this that the new journal sought to "emphasize the socio-political standpoint more completely and thoroughly than has been hitherto been the case. Since this is a principle that dominates the entire economy, the

---

[71] The *Deutsche Gesellschaft für Soziologie* was created in 1909 in explicit opposition to the "value-ladenness" of the *Verein für Socialpolitik*. Today, the *Verein für Socialpolitik – Gesellschaft für Wirtschafts- und Sozialwissenschaften* is the leading economic professional association in the German-speaking world.

[72] Wilhelm II, himself, in his speech from the throne on 22. November 1888, spoke of a continuation of the "social-political legislation begun" by his grandfather. In Vienna, a *Sozialpolitischer Verein* was founded in 1893 (with participation from Eugen v. Phillippovich), out of which developed the "*Sozialpolitische Partei*," which was active between 1896 and 1900 and combined liberal and social-democratic postulates. See Holleis (1978).

Sozialpolitisches Centralblatt will deal not only with what is understood by social policy in the narrower sense, but with *all* current economic questions from a social-political perspective" (Braun 1892, p. 2).

Here, the "socio-political" standpoint was oriented toward the social clashes, and it regarded the economic manifestations *and* legislative measures from the perspective of their effect on the condition of the various classes. This was a remarkably non-partisan point of view, one that would become crucial to the mainstream conceptualizations of social policy as a science.

In retrospect the confusion surrounding the term is not surprising, seeing that the social situations, and thus also the socio-political intentions and proposed measures, were defined in different ways, depending on the observer's political orientation. The *Verein für Socialpolitik*, too, was a gathering place for social reformers of various stripes (with Social Democrats largely absent), whose descriptions of the problems and "ideals" by no means overlapped (Sombart 1897). That is why the efforts at a substantive clarification of the term that now began mostly sought out generalizing categories that would make it possible to capture the broadest possible spectrum of political positions.

3.3.1 Preliminary Remarks on the Conceptual Question

Before we look at the protracted conceptual discussions that lasted until the end of the Weimar period, it is worthwhile to begin with a few clarifications *from a contemporary perspective* as a way of illustrating the difficulties that these discussions confronted.

In keeping with the two linguistic components of the word, the conceptual definitions diverged with regard to an understanding of both the "social" and the "political." For one, "social" was understood in the sense of a *normative* orientation toward a "shared humanity" [*Mitmenschlichkeit*], which was attributed, looking backward, to traditional ways of life. For another, "social" was understood in the *critical* sense with reference to modern, "capitalist" forms of social existence. What these two positions (grounded in either ethics or politics) shared was their critical opposition to an unrestrained individualism.[73] Finally, "social" was understood in the *neutral* sense of "referring to society," with the ideas about what constituted "society" differing in terms of what it encompassed (every form of human coexistence, national society, class society, and so on), and in terms of the sociological perspective one took.[74]

[73] Pribram (1924, reprint 1969, p. 96): "The unifying element that is strong enough to overcome these differences may be found in the opposition of all these world views to the atomizing tendencies of individualism, which fundamentally recognizes only individuals as the primary, purposeful entities within social life, and endows these individuals with full responsibility for their social behavior."

[74] A similar tri-partite division was made by Zacher (1980, p. 676).

When it came to the term "politics," the ideas were even more vague, which can be attributed not least to the complete absence at the time of a separate discipline of political science. In terms of our contemporary awareness, one should differentiate essentially four concepts of the German word "*Politik*," for which the English language has four different words:

Politik as *polity*: this refers to the community in its political constitution ("state") or the "political system" as a subsystem of society;
Politik as *politics:* this refers to the clashes among the political actors, that is, the struggle for power and for the content of specific decisions, especially laws;
Politik as *policies*: this refers to implemented political measures and their consequences;
Politik as *political science*: this refers to the scholarly study of politics in the three meanings distinguished above.

Of course, in historical reality, in our case with respect to the genesis of social policy, there are connections and interactions between what the four concepts of *Politik* try to distinguish. It is therefore not surprising that the contemporary debates about the term social policy often foregrounded aspects of selection that cut across these distinctions.

If one takes into account the multivalence of the two linguistic components of "social policy," it is no surprise that the attempts at definition trended in very different directions, with the result that there were soon complaints about the unmanageable number of different definitions of social policy.[75] It would therefore make little sense to document the whole range of conceptual discussions and proposed definitions.[76] Instead, I shall endeavor to use some influential examples to retrace important dimensions of the struggle for a concept of social policy.

3.3.2 Attempted Definitions Within the Horizon of Bismarckian Social Reform

To begin with, the definition in the *Staatslexikon* of the Görres-Gesellschaft (1897) shows that the broad socio-political perspective of the term that had taken shape in the fifties was still remembered:

> *Socialpolitik* or social theory in the narrower sense is the branch of the sciences of the state that deals with the relationship of public power to the various productive estates and to their mutual interests, especially in the economic sphere (Brüll 1897, col. 140).

---

[75] Günther (1922, p. 466ff.) distinguished 13 different conceptions of social policy. Neuloh (1961, p. 70) spoke of "more than 40 conceptual definitions of social policy around the year 1910"; that same author mentioned "about 60 different definition in the literature" in 1950 (Neuloh 1950/1951, p. 34). Of course, the classification of certain definitions as "different" is itself a question of definition.

[76] Overviews in Pribram (1925b), Hilberath (1930), Lütge (1932).

But the more scholars struggled for greater conceptual precision, the more specific and – with respect to the starting question – the more reductionist the definitions became.

A first occasion for a conceptual debate was provided by Bismarck's refusal to make measures for occupational safety the program of his social policy. That is why the "new course" of Wilhelm II constituted a first turning point in the history of German social policy. As the administrative practitioner Jastrow remarked in this regard:

> The linguistic usage in Germany has shifted since this message by Wilhelm II. The designation 'socio-political legislation' in the sense of worker insurance legislation has not entirely disappeared (one still finds it especially frequently in the daily papers). However, language usage now tends overwhelmingly to use 'socio-political legislation' as a combined expression for worker protection and worker insurance, together (Jastrow 1902, p. 8).

This is an example of an *inductive expansion of the term*, the kind that pushed to the fore time and again as socio-political measures were slowly broadened and increasingly extended beyond the circle of industrial workers. Here we can speak of an *institutional understanding* of social policy in the sense of *policies*. These concrete definitions that combined several complexes of measures under a single concept usually lacked a deeper theoretical foundation and not infrequently followed mere political opportunism, for example, later the creation of specific administration departments. I will pay little attention to them in the discussion that follows. However, this is not to say that the institutional developments had no effect on the scientific conceptualization, since they often provided the occasion for new attempts at systematization.[77]

One starting point for an *analytical examination of social policy* that had a sustained impact was the treatise by the prominent "state socialist" *Adolph Wagner*.[78] His intent was, from a position of explicit criticism of the historical school of economics, "to deal *in principle* with economic and socio-political questions." That intent gave rise to the following definition: "By social policy in general we mean the policies of the state that seek to combat *deplorable situations*

[77] The treatment of social-political questions in the textbooks at the time usually followed this institutional approach; frequently, however, the term "social policy" was not used at all.

[78] Wagner (1891). Wagner's concept of 'state socialism' reads as follows: "It must be recognized that the great mass of capital, especially also fixed capital, is in the hands of private owners, which are represented especially also through organizations such as stock companies and the like, where it accumulates to such a degree that it creates dangers for the autonomy of economic, social, and political life ... In consideration of this, state socialism demands ... that under certain circumstances, if it is technically and economically feasible, individual private enterprises are transferred to the state and the community." He mentions railroads, light companies, and transportation installations. He also called for restrictions on the free formation of prices "especially with important foodstuffs," and finally "a social and just financial and tax policy," that is, alongside progressive income taxes also a progressive wealth tax and "a strong inheritance tax." Wagner (1912, pp. 19–21). – On Wagner see Grüske et al. (1991).

in the area of the *distribution process* by means of legislation and administration" (Wagner 1891, p. 3f.). Wagner subsequently distinguished between, on the one hand, "fiscal social policy" as the use of "financial means, which refer in part to the *manner in which income is procured*, in part to the *uses of the expenditures*,"[79] and, on the other hand, "true social policy ... as a *correction* of the developments of the economy organized on a private basis, built on the institution of private property, and knowing only contractual regulations" (Wagner 1891, p. 8). He further distinguished the level of an "expansion of the historically handed down tasks of the state to those that lie primarily ... in the interest of the competitively weaker, non-propertied, lower, and working classes," from the level of their administrative instantiation (Wagner 1891, p. 10f.) – in modern parlance, between the development of a program and its implementation. No other writer at the time made proposals for the administrative development of political as well as communal measures in the interests of the disadvantaged strata with a comparably detailed knowledge. Characteristic for his scientific stance is the consistent examination of the economic and political conditions *from the perspective of the disadvantaged classes*. Accordingly, scientific social policy too finds its problem in the observable "deplorable conditions in the area of the distribution process." He paid very little attention to the criteria by which social conditions should be qualified as deplorable; instead, he postulated concrete circumstances as such by using plausibility criteria.[80]

Around the same time, the Center Party [*Zentrum*] politician Georg von Hertling, the social-political opponent of Bismarck and future Reich Chancellor, formulated the theoretical foundations of the *social policy* of the Center Party[81]: "The task of social policy in the first and most general meaning of the phrase ... is aimed at guiding, promoting, and harmonizing the various social circles through the state and in the interest of the state community" (von Hertling 1893, p. 4f.). In contrast to Wagner, he placed the greatest importance on the *criteria* under which socio-political demands on the state could be regarded as *justified*. He argued that social policy rested not only on "considerations of utility or even good will," but "on the unalterable principles of morality and the law" (von Hertling 1893, p. 7). In this context he invoked the Catholic doctrine of natural law (which had evolved over centuries) and rejected – on the basis of this doctrine – demands for the abolition of private property and for a general right to work. However, he did affirm a general "right to life," from which he drew far-reaching consequences for state intervention to combat unemployment and regulate the conditions of work and wages, and from which he derived the workers' right of association and other rights, for example,

[79] Wagner (1891, p. 4). On the history of the tax policy aspect, which is usually neglected in the discussion of social policy, see Mann (1978).

[80] Schmoller's reflections on distributive justice (1890, pp. 204–246) also remained attached to an intuitive criteria and thus lacked discursive plausibility.

[81] Von Hertling (1893; see also 1884). On von Hertling see Eickhoff (1932); Bauer (1974).

that of children to an upbringing and an education.[82] We find here the beginnings of the kind of *doctrine of social rights* that would become essential for the program of the welfare state after the Second World War (Kaufmann 2003).[83] With this von Hertling represented what was, compared to other proponents of the Catholic-social movement, a *liberal* position, because he fought against the state centralization of the Bismarckian reformist intention, which he called– in the sense of what is today referred to as the "subsidiarity principle" – "state socialism." Von Hertling was the most important champion of the principle of contribution-financed social security in the area of accident and old age insurance, in contrast to the "*Reichsanstalt*" preferred by Bismarck and financed mostly by public funds.

Widespread among the other Catholic social politicians was an organicistic way of thinking, which accorded the state the central role in organizing "society" in the sense of intermediary structures (estate, corporations) (Moenning 1927). On this point, they converged with Gustav von Schmoller and Adolph Wagner (Hermans 1972, pp. 472–476; Becher 1965). Among these politicians, *Franz Hitze*, the future secretary general of the *Volksverein für das katholische Deutschland* [People's Association for Catholics in Germany], held a prominent place. He was one of the first non-socialist writers to grapple with the thought of Karl Marx (Hitze 1880). Likewise invoking Catholic natural law and a *solidarism* derived from it, he rejected both economic liberalism and class struggle and advocated an organization of society around occupational groups, a form of organization in which the various occupational groups (workers, tradesmen, farmers, etc.) would participate in economic matters through public-law corporations.[84]

The *state-political dimension* of social policy was articulated by the jurist *Rudolph Sohm* in the formula that social policy was the embodiment of measures aimed at the interrelationships between the classes, to the extent that such measures promoted the *state's interests in power*.[85] This definition clearly took its cues from the intentions pursued by Bismarck, for whom social policy "was by its nature state politics, it did not have a specific social goal, it was a sub-field, but not a matter of a separate portfolio ... State and society should not be surrendered to particularist powers, parties here, stock corporations there, but should enter into an intensive reciprocal relationship: society shaped by the state, and the framework of the state filled by a well-structured social body" (Rothfels 1929, pp. 6f., 12f.). Arthur Salz

[82] See also Walter (1899). – An outsider's overview of the development of the Catholic position is given by Wermert (1885).

[83] Of course, the aspect of the *legal entitlement* (Bismarck's "Peculium" for the workers) was already of great importance to the social reform of the 1880s.

[84] On the often conflictual relationship between Hitze and von Hertling see Eickhoff (1932, pp. 86–90).

[85] "The mark of what is socio-politically just is that it makes the state *strong* ... What serves the *power* of the modern state? That alone is the political question inherent in the workers' question" – Sohm (1897, p. 593f.). For Sohm, the primary socio-political tasks of the state was the use of "smaller means" to slow the effects of the competitive pressure from the global economy on agriculture and the trades, but also to intervene in the development of modern industry "to link the free work contract of the present with the *freedom of the worker*" (ibid., p. 243).

later formulated the same more scientifically and combined the power-political and normative dimensions:

> From the concept of the state, then, nothing follows for the meaning of social policy. By contrast: the resolute *will* that a *people* [Volk] be and live, and that the worth inherent therein not waste away through the satiety of some and the indifference of others, pushes like an enchanting urge for action for and on behalf of the people and is always awake ... Only if we thus comprehend social policy, in what seems an abstract manner, as *product and guarantor of an existing collective consciousness* will we do justice to its nature in the midst of the institutions of our state and society (Salz 1914, pp. 27–29).

This "state-political" dimension of social policy played a considerable role especially in the discussions of the Weimar period.

The textbooks were dominated by a conception of social policy that was oriented toward the improvement of the social condition of disadvantaged groups, especially the working class. Van der Borght, for example, distinguished between "social policy in the general sense" as the "totality of measures whose intent is to promote the common welfare by influencing the conditions of the social classes that are part of the polity," and a "social policy in the narrower sense," whose intent was "to elevate the classes that must expend their labor in service to others in non-autonomous and dependent jobs ..., especially the industrial class of wageworkers."[86]

The first textbook on *social law*, identified as socio-political those laws

> that seek to eliminate certain harm in societal (social) relations – determined mostly by property and acquisition – between the citizens in the interest of the state as a whole, which is in danger of being threatened ... With respect to these persons (scil. the working class), there is a peculiar imbalance in our order of private law ... Our private law is dominated by the general principle of the equality of persons, among whom relationships, rights, and obligations are accordingly established by 'contract.' However, where the economic strength of the parties is not equal, this legal equality and reciprocal freedom remains merely a formal one (Rosin 1893, p. 139f.).[87]

This description likely captures the prevailing political opinion at the time precisely. With this, the public-law status of the workers, that is, the lack of suffrage in Prussia, and the constitutional question in general, was excluded. It was part of

[86] Van der Borght (1904/1923, p. 2f.). Notable is the explicit emphasis on the socio-political *intention* as a criterion of definition: "This determination of purpose is essential (otherwise) one would have to assign every conceivable branch of politics to it." However, the author does not reflect on *whose* intention we are dealing with. Given the dominance of the Reich government in German politics, that question may have been less urgent back then than it is in a democracy that lives by compromise.

[87] On Rosin see Hollerbach (1993, pp. 369–384). – Worth mentioning is also the textbook by Stier-Somlo (1906). With respect to the subsequent development, Zacher noted (1980: LX): "The law of social security, well cultivated even theoretically during the first decades of the century, had been continuously declining in jurisprudential quality during the Weimar period. The continual changes it was subjected to from the early thirties on had brought its jurisprudential culture to a halt – a deficiency that could be remedied only with Georg Wannagat's Lehrbuch des Sozialversicherungsrechts (vol. 1, 1965), at least with respect to its foundations."

the reason behind all Prussian social reform, namely to carry out social reform *instead of* political reform.

3.3.3 Werner Sombart: Social Policy as Policy for Economic Order

As early as 1897, these normative definitions of social policy were opposed by the economist Werner Sombart, whose ideas anticipated essential arguments of Weber's essay on the objectivity of knowledge in social science and social policy.[88] He criticized these definitions for allowing an exonymous determination of social policy by ideals external to economic life, and he called these ideals neither necessary nor useful. He was especially sarcastic in his remarks about "ethical" economics:

> By its nature it is always reactionary economically ... 'ethical' social policy is in its essence always obstruction politics ... 'Ethical' economic policy ... has the inherent tendency toward disjointedness, lack of planning, casuistry, politics of the moment, eclecticism ... Things are tinkered with on a 'case by case basis,' people are proud of that.[89]

Sombart's own approach to define social policy identified it largely with what we today would call *Wirtschaftsordnungspolitik* [a policy of political framing of economic life]. He began by introducing the important distinction between political measures aimed at the entire economic system, and measures that concerned "only the well being of individual economic subjects." Among the latter he included poor relief but also worker insurance and did *not* count them as part of social policy. He was able to do so because he established a close connection between various "economic systems" as forms of meeting basic needs and the class structure of contemporary societies: thus he assigned "*Junkerdom* and peasanty ... to a household economy, the petty bourgeoisie ... to the local barter economy, the bourgeoisie ... to the capitalist market economy," and the proletariat to a "socialist household economy at a higher step ladder" (Sombart 1897, p. 6f.). For Sombart, *social policy* thus encompassed "those measures of economic policy whose purpose or consequence is the preservation, promotion, or suppression of certain economic systems or their components" (Sombart 1897, p. 8). However, Sombart did not stop at this analytical perspective. Instead, he postulated an *immanent ideal* of the economic system, productivity, which thus became the criterion of social policy, and went on to conclude:

> A healthy social policy must make the best possible support for the social class that represents economic progress its task, because that is the only way its ideal – the greatest unfolding of the productive powers – can be realized, the realization of which, however, is regarded as necessary in the interest of cultural progress (Sombart 1897, p. 44).

---

[88] Sombart (1897, p. 10ff.). – Along with the ethical-social, Catholic-natural law, and national ideal advocated by the *Kathedersozialisten* and the Protestant social theorists, Sombart also discussed the racial-hygiene ideal that emerged during that time.

[89] Sombart (1897, pp. 33–35). For an anti-critique from the Catholic perspective see Walter (1899, passim).

This conclusion is diametrically opposed not only analytically, but also politically to what was understood by social policy until then. But it is quite compatible with more recent claims that the best social policy is a good economic policy. However, the lopsided partisanship for a "production policy" and against a "distribution policy" [90] is an analytically unnecessary choice and one that clashed with the postulate of value-neutrality; in fact, the concept of productivity would subsequently become a central example of the debate over value judgments (Weber 1924, pp. 416–423). However, given an increasing de-standardization of gainful work, the analytical approach of linking social policy with measures that promote or impede certain forms of meeting needs could become fruitful for future debates about the content of social policy.

3.3.4 Ladislaus von Bortkiewicz: Social Policy as Distribution-oriented Structural Policy

In this early phase it was especially the statistician Ladislaus von Bortkiewicz who dealt systematically with the question of definition. In the process, his thinking reflected the *dual meaning of the concept* as an institutional complex and a political intention, which made sense ever since Bismarck's worker insurance. He asserted that

> social policy is not a special area of legislation or administration, or, more precisely, social policy does not appear as a complex of legal norms and administrative measures that correspond to a specific area of the national economy or social life; instead, 'social policy' is more like *a direction* of state intervention in economic or social life (von Bortkiewicz 1899, p. 336).

Accordingly, he defined social policy as "the response of the state as manifested in legislation and administration to the social antagonisms."[91] It is a definition that goes beyond the worker question and the opposition of capital and labor (and also distances itself from ethical intentions), in that it also encompasses, for example, agrarian social antagonisms; moreover, taking sides for either party in this social conflict is not conceptually necessary. Von Bortkiewicz saw his own definition as an expansion upon the one by Adolph Wagner quoted earlier: "By social policy in general we mean the policies of the state that seek to combat *deplorable situations* in the area of the *distribution process* by means of legislation and administration."[92]

[90] This conceptual distinction was already made by Sombart, as well (1897, p. 4f.). – Amonn, whose essay of 1926 was one of the most thorough engagements with Sombart's essay, rightly objected that Sombart "understands social policy a priori as economic policy" (435).

[91] Von Bortkiewicz (1899, p. 334f.). This definition is in line with the intention of the *Socialpolitisches Centralblatt* cited earlier (note 66f.).

[92] Von Bortkiewicz quoted Wagner on p. 343 without indicating the source. Later, Adolph Wagner also offered a more neutral formulation (1912, p. 3): "Social policy is a conscious regulatory intervention in the large processes of economic life and in the area of the production and distribution of goods, in part also in the area of consumption."

His expansion was threefold: (1) we should speak of social policy not only with respect to "the participation of various social classes in national wealth and national income," but also "where power, reputation, and honor are at stake"; (2) the measures need not refer only to the liberal system of the private economy; (3) taking a judgmental position for any one side is not implicit: an intervention "for the benefit of the lower classes laboring with their hands" could be called a "positive social policy," though von Bortkiewicz did not recommend this usage.[93] Because of this, however, his conceptual definition remained vague, as later critics pointed out (Amonn 1924, pp. 159–199, esp. 163ff.).

This discussion articulated a problem that fully emerged only after the First World War and within the horizon of the *Werturteilstreit* (value judgment dispute): practical social policy is always a struggle for political changes in the name of certain normative ideas, and often in the name of a guiding model of politics and society. Moreover, champions of social policy acknowledge as *social policy* only the taking of sides on behalf of socially *disadvantaged* groups. In the face of this, how can the scientific engagement with social policy satisfy the scientific-ethical norm of impartiality without missing the very meaning of social policy?

3.4 The Influence of the First World War

The initiatives of Wilhelm II to introduce state worker protection and an independent industrial arbitration to settle industrial conflicts (1890/1891) remained the last substantial advances of a worker social policy until the First World War. A sustained public campaign against all forms of "Socialism" by large industry and personnel reshuffling at the ministerial level strongly constrained the socio-political impulse on the Reich level. The debates in the *Reichstag* over the so-called "*Umsturzvorlage*" (subversion bill) even culminated in the challenge issued by Freiherr von Stumm to Adolph Wagner to "settle the matter with the pistol" (Lindenlaub 1967, p. 53ff.).

Still, incremental improvements were made in the already established fields of worker insurance and worker protection, in Prussia also in the comparatively progressive mining law, and the principle of social insurance was extended to "private civil servants," what today are white-collar employees. Advances for the workers' movement occurred especially on the municipal level as well as through the incorporation of union representatives into the self-governing bodies of social insurance and the industrial arbitration courts.

While the scientific reflection did not go much beyond what had been achieved by the turn of the century (Pribram 1925b, p. 246f.), the first summarizing accounts did appear, many of which also included international developments.[94]

---

[93] All quotes in von Bortkiewicz (1899, p. 346f.). In this context, von Bortkiewicz invoked Lorenz von Stein, a peculiar reference for the time.

[94] Jastrow (1902); van der Borght (1904/1923); Herkner (1922); Wenk (1908); von Wiese (1910/1921); von Zwiedineck-Südenhorst (1911). On Herkner, von Wiese, and von Zwiedineck-Südenhorst

The development of social policy, however, also brought to the fore consequences that were unanticipated or at least had not been considered by its champions, and liberal opponents elevated these eloquently into a problem.[95] What is more, the corporatization of the socio-political actors began already before the First World War, with the emergence of national organizations – not only on the part of entrepreneurs and unions, but also in the area of medical insurance, for example – which acted increasingly as representatives of organized interests and participants in social policy (Born 1957).

By contrast, the main concerns of the workers' movement were left undone: a democratic constitution, full recognition of the right to organize, the statutory definition of a normal working day with restrictions on its length, and the recognition of unions as negotiating partners for the purpose of entering into collective labor contracts. Even though these concerns were supported not only by the Social Democrats, but also by the Center Party and other groups, they were unable to assert themselves against resistance from employers' organizations, the right-of-center bourgeois parties, and within the Reich government.

This hardened front was broken open only by the First World War. The national solidarity on the part of large sections of the workers' movement, something the bourgeois camp had not expected, the necessity of the forced recruitment of workers, and, in connection with this, above all passage of the National Labour Service Law (*Hilfsdienstgesetz*) in 1916 led to a growing political recognition of unions. Crucial to the "remarkably progressive" social policy was the War Ministry (advised during the initial phase of the war by members of the *Gesellschaft für soziale Reform*), which persuaded employers and unions to participate in the war, and mediation committees that were initially voluntary and whose composition was based on the principle of parity. These committees were then made obligatory in the National Labour Service Law (Feldman 1984, pp. 19f., 30f.). As Feldman noted: "Because of this law, membership numbers in the Socialist and Christian unions increased substantially, and the workers were extraordinarily successful in their demands for wage hikes" (1984, p. 108).

Once the end of the war was in sight, even leading industrialists felt compelled to enter into negotiations with the leaders of the free unions, and to accept, in the so-called Stinnes-Legien Agreement (November 1918), the essential demands of the workers' movement for recognition of the unions, collective bargaining agreements, parity in the area of labor mediation and conflict resolution, and the

(as well as other authors) see the collective review by Schmoller (1912). Also: Tönnies (1919); Gehrig (1914). Alongside von Philippovich (1908), the study by Gehrig is the most useful for a history of social-political thinking.

[95] See especially Bernhard (1912). This essay went through three printings in 3 months. Moreover, Marr (1923, pp. esp. 547–551) has shown that the socio-political impulse was waning already before the outbreak of the First World War even among the earlier champions.

introduction of the 8-h day (Feldman 1984, pp. 118, 122). Social democrats attained leading positions within the Reich government. A Reich Labour Office and a Reich Ministry of Labour were created, the latter a demand that had been put forth as far back as 1848 (Valentin 1998, vol. 1, pp. 421, 472, 479). The idea of an "organization of the economy" on the basis of committees of equal representation, and the guarantee of socio-political services made their way into the Weimar Constitution, which, thanks to its democratic structure, also held out the prospect of equality in the future. It thus seemed that the social-policy movement, to the extent that it was oriented toward the workers' question, had essentially achieved its goal: not through a revolution of property relationships, but through a progressive reform of the relationships of production in capitalism and through the state guarantee of social protection. A decade later, Eduard Heimann articulated the logic of this movement very concisely:

> The social idea springs from the economic-social ground of capitalism, it takes form in the social movement, and asserts itself with economic-social means within capitalism and against capitalism ... Social policy secures the capitalist basis of production against the dangers threatening from the social movement by yielding to the social demand; it dismantles capitalism piece by piece and in so doing preserves what is left; it achieves success when, and only when, the fulfillment of a piece of the social demand becomes a necessity for production. This is its dual conservative-revolutionary nature (Heimann 1929/1980, p. 171f.).

4 The Crisis of Social Policy (1920–1945)

It may seem too imbalanced to affix to the entire period from the end of the First to the end of the Second World War a label that characterizes its beginning. This epoch saw no small number of institutional innovations – for example, in the area of social welfare and housing, the introduction of unemployment insurance, progress in occupational safety, indeed, the first steps toward a youth and family policy.[96] However, if one looks at the programmatic ideas that had been associated since the *Vormärz* and down to the turn of the century with the notion of social reform and increasingly also with that of social policy, we can observe for both the Weimar Republic and the Nazi "Third Reich" a dismantling of the previous leading ideas for social policy from a variety of different motivations.[97] Since this dismantling went hand in hand with a recoding of the notion of social policy, it is especially significant to our concerns here.

---

[96] For a good overview see Tennstedt (1988, pp. 77–96); also Hentschel (1983, pp. 55–144), Frerich and Frey (1996, vol. 1, pp. 171–244); Stolleis (2013, German Social Policy, vol. 2).

[97] It should be noted that the "crisis of social policy" was merely one aspect of a much broader crisis in orientation in the German Reich (and in Austria).

As far as the Weimar Constitution is concerned, it can be described as the first social or welfare state constitution in the world, even if a relevant conceptualization of what that meant did not exist yet.[98] It contained an entire section on the economic and social order, which was introduced by the following general clause: "The organization of economic life must accord with the principles of justice, with the goal of guaranteeing everyone a life of dignity."[99] In this way a close connection between economic and social policy was postulated, though in practice it revealed itself more as a poorly conceptualized juxtaposition.[100]

4.1 *The Crisis Discussion and its Context*

The change in the frontlines of the discussion over social policy first became apparent in 1922, on the occasion of a meeting to celebrate the fiftieth anniversary of the "*Verein für Sozialpolitik*" [Association for Social Policy]. The then-chairman of the Association, Heinrich Herkner, delivered the introductory talk on the first topic of the day, "The future of social policy." After a look back at the previous activity of the Association, he diagnosed the changed situation as follows:

> The founders of the Association believed that Germany should be governed in the main by a scientifically highly educated class of civil servants who stood above class interest and parties ... How very different it is today! ... no one will believe any more that a class of civil servants who stand above the parties will ever again be able to gain control of the government. Least of all the state bureaucracy, regardless of how numerous it has become. Much greater power is possessed by the bureaucracy of the large economic organizations,

[98] The word "*Wohlfahrtsstaat*" (welfare state) is first found in Adolph Wagner within the context of his doctrine of the purposes of the state (1876, Part 1, p. §168, 257): "And the state of advancing nations, and thus especially the modern state, ceases increasingly to be a one-sided *Rechtsstaat* (state under the rule of law), in the sense of the most autonomous possible realization of the purpose of law and power, and is becoming more and more a *culture and welfare state*, in the sense that its efforts in the area of cultural and welfare purposes are continuously expanding and taking on a richer and more varied content." A quite modern-sounding interpretation was given by Tönnies (1914/1915). The term also appears in the 1922 *Richtlinien der deutschen Zentrumspartei* (Ritter 1954, p. 417). However, Abelshauser (1957, p. 10) notes: "Contemporaries of the twenties preferred to speak of the 'social people's state' [*sozialer Volksstaat*], 'social state' [*Sozialstaat*], or 'social *Rechtsstaat*' if they wished to characterize the social charge of the new polity in the transition from the 'bourgeois' *Rechtsstaat* to the interventionist state that provided for and secured people's existence." Though, this "transition" itself is a theoretical construct that does not accord with the German pattern of development. – On the conceptual-historical background see Rassem (1992); Stolleis (1998).

[99] Art. 151 of the Weimar Constitution.

[100] Still the best survey is Preller (1949); see also Hartwich (1967); Bogs (1981).

> the workers, white-collar employees, civil servants, employers and entrepreneurs, by the bureaucracy of the parties and of the press controlled by the parties and organizations ... What happened is that the power of the state in relationship to the natural laws of economic life was overestimated, and those laws are revenging themselves bitterly ... One must get away from the prevailing mercantilist thinking and relearn to think in terms of free trade (Herkner 1923a, pp. 93–95).[101]

This thrust was also underscored by the next lecture. Ludwig Stein demanded that one "recognize, alongside and prior to distribution, the production problem in all its force and power, its brutal ruthlessness in creating profits."[102] Both speeches were met with "thunderous applause," which shows just how far the economic *zeitgeist* had moved away from the positions of the *Kathedersozialisten*. The background to this change was not so much criticism of the accomplishment of the workers' movement as such, but rather the dismal economic situation of the post-war years and the period of inflation along with the concrete policies pursued by the unions, which seemed to many economists an impediment to Germany's economic recovery. Moreover, state authority had largely exhausted itself during the world war and its aftermath and no longer inspired any hopes. The "inability of industry and the workers to arrive at effective compromises in the economic and social sphere" found its starkest expression in the controversy over the 8-h day that was carried on between 1922 and 1924 (Feldman and Steinisch 1978, p. 353).

Herkner, who enjoyed great esteem within the social movement thanks to his standard work on the workers' question, drew the consequences for social policy a short while later in the publication of the German Employers' Associations (Herkner 1923b), and it was probably as much the place where he published his essay as its content that triggered a vigorous debate and put the notion of a "crisis of social policy" into the public space.[103] Herkner's former assistant Charlotte Leubuscher was first to impart some structure to this vague but highly plausible idea. She distinguished

- A "crisis for social policy," brought on by the question "whether, given the current economic situation, we can still afford a social policy of the conventional kind";
- A "crisis within social policy," "to the extent that the methods of social policy applied today are controversial"; in the process it was especially the focus on measures by the centralized state that were questioned;

[101] The liberal, anti-bureaucratic thrust of Herkner's socio-reformist thinking appears early on in his work, so that the "turnaround," as he himself always emphasized, as well, was by no means as radical as the subsequent discussion assumed. See Herkner (1895, pp. 575–596).

[102] According to Boese (1939, p. 173), Ludwig Stein's talk was entitled "Die wirtschaftlichen Grundlagen der Sozialpolitik" [The Economic Foundations of Social Policy]. The conference volume does not list a title. Quote from *Die Zukunft der Sozialpolitik*, p. 103.

[103] Important contributions in volume 32 (1923) of *Soziale Praxis*. Ibid. (1923ff.) an ongoing chronicle of the discussion as it was carried on in other publications.

- A crisis "of social science with regard to its position on socio-political problems" (Leubuscher 1923, p. 341).

This differentiation could also be helpful in today's "crisis discussions." For the present purposes we are interested only in the third dimension of the crisis, though its problems were derived from its first two dimensions.

As far as the contested practical measures were concerned, Herkner himself, in an essay that concluded the debates, offered a clarifying overview. He emphasized that "the primary causes of the misery we confront today have nothing whatsoever to do with social policy" (Herkner 1924, p. 202), but resulted from the consequences of war and inflation, from which, he noted, the middle classes suffered greater losses than the workers. The problem of social policy resulted merely from the circumstance that in spite of the economic disaster, people were clinging to rights and demands that were merely suited to making it worse. Herkner described as especially problematic "the introduction of the *8-h day* that was carried out in a hasty manner and therefore without the indispensable preparations," and the development of the local *aid to the unemployed*, which in many places was undermining the incentive to seek work (Herkner 1924, p. 204f.). As he saw it:

> Not only the entirety of social policy of the prewar period (worker protection, worker insurance, unions and cooperatives) therefore lies outside the area of contention, but so does an essential part of what was added to this social policy only during the war and after, such as the equal codetermination of employees in regulating working conditions, the recognition of freedom of association by the employers' associations and the unions as the appointed representatives of the interest of the workers, the collective bargaining contract, the parity-based mediation system, the works' councils, the public work performance record, and the aid to the seriously disabled" (Herkner 1924, p. 202f.).

He regarded as controversial only those elements of social policy that seemed to *directly* impair the economic recovery. On this point he received support from von Zwiedineck-Südenhorst, who argued "that social policy has trampled all over the principles of a sound economy," and he also held it responsible for the inflationary developments of the post-war period. Moreover: "Changes in distributions through shifts in the nominal wage incomes are . . . no solution to the problem of balancing out a production deficit for the broad mass of the population" (von Zwiedineck-Südenhorst 1923, pp. 121, 135). The result of this situation was that the socio-political discussion in the Weimar Period focused heavily on distribution and its impact upon the economy. This was combined strikingly with a substantially *weaker empirical orientation* of the social sciences, and especially of the *Verein für Sozialpolitik*, than had been the case in the period before the First World War.

Götz Briefs, whose analysis of the crisis discussion was one of the most illuminating contributions at the time, also emphasized that "social policy as such . . . appears less in dispute than some of its methods and institutions" (Briefs 1923, p. 9). The crucial questions were, first, the relationships between economic and social policy, and, second, the shortcomings of the methodology:

> This social policy through the public authorities worked necessarily through institutionalization, oversight, and regulation, it was individualized only in the roughest way, in short, it was bureaucratic . . .. It had no contact . . . with the soul of the common man; it worked from

> the outside and 'top-down': harsh, cold, generalizing, objective; and found from no side the warmth of recognition that it would have deserved based on its objective performance – it was and remained to the feelings of the common man just another branch of the state administration, in which, as in so many others, he was an object. It did not achieve its meaningful purpose: social peace (Briefs 1923, p. 11).

The "haggling weighing and balancing of the dose of work that must be performed for a wage" corresponded to the "commercialization of living work, ... [to] the legitimate product from the individualistic-liberal doctrine that the economic society is purely a market bond" (Briefs 1923, p. 15). The generalizing of practical individualism was not the "principle of a possible society," and Briefs argued, with a critical glance at Bentham: "To be sure, an 'enlightened,' 'well understood,' 'rational' self-interest absorbed into itself the interests of others, but the attachment of interest that followed from this and *only* from this is too weak and random to be able to constitute society and a societal economy."[104] The crisis of social policy, Briefs concluded, "is truly not the crisis of a few elderly gentlemen among the social politicians ... Its roots reach into the structure of our modern economy, into the animating principle of this economy, into the German form of the relations between state and the economy and between state and society, into the historical situation of the relationship between capital and labor" (Briefs 1923, p. 16). The previous juxtaposition of an individualistic economic policy and state social policy was untenable; instead, the "socio-political minima" had to be built into the economy itself. We can only suspect that Briefs was urging greater formative power for the system of collective labor agreements compared to social policy pursued by means of state laws.

4.2 *Social-Democratic Perspectives: Between Socialization and the Social* Rechtsstaat *(rule of law)*

Even if the word "*Sozialpolitik*" played only a marginal role within the context of the socialist program, we must briefly look at the influence that the representatives of this potent social movement exerted on the socio-political thinking of the Weimar period and after. However, if we limit ourselves – as we are doing here – to the conceptual side, the result is meager. Within the sphere of tension created by the developments in the Soviet Union, the movement's own tradition, and the precipitous changes in the country, the German socialist workers' movement remained not only fragmented,[105] but also largely without any clear, long-term

[104] Briefs (1923, p. 14). The problems of collective action that were already raised here were analyzed in a more differentiated way by Olson (1968).

[105] On the diversity and inevitability of the fault lines see the retrospective by Winkler (1987, pp. 951–954).

political outlook. That is especially true of the social-democratic movement that asserted itself within the horizon of the Weimar constitutional process. Although it was among the pillars of the democratic order, it was unable to formulate a clear model for social policy. The relationship between social democracy and the intellectuals and scientists that were near to it remained ambivalent and strained.[106]

With the split of political Socialism into a social-democratic and a communist wing, the programmatic term "Socialism" had lost the clear Marxist identity it had achieved since the Erfurt Program (1891) already in the "revisionism debate" [*Revisionismusstreit*], and all the more so since the end of the war and the revolutionary movements in its wake. On the surface, the debate was only over competing methods in pursuing the goal of a socialist society: through civil war and revolution or through the parliamentary path? Eduard Bernstein (1890) had already challenged important arguments of revolutionary Marxism. The goal of abolishing the private ownership of the means of production remained alive during the Weimar period not only among radicals, but also within the social-democratic base. But the leading minds of social democracy moved away from the idea of socialization once they attained political influence (Winkler 1984, pp. 191–198). But what alternative blueprint should take its place, since an affirmation of the capitalist economic system was of course out of the question? After all, it was generally believed that the creation of political democracy did not offer a sufficient guarantee that the alienating work conditions of the capitalist process of production would be abolished.

The Social Democrats' dominant programmatic concepts of the immediate post-war period were, alongside "socialization/nationalization," the demand for "workers' councils" and a "collectivized economy" [*Gemeinwirtschaft*]. All three concepts were incorporated into the Weimar Constitution, although Article 156 (nationalization, collectivized economy) constituted non-binding directives, and Article 165 (workers' councils, economic councils) embodied abstract, formulaic compromises, which could be approved by conservative proponents of representation based on occupational estates as well as by the champions of "workers' councils" (Ritter 1994). Especially the free trade unions were skeptical of the idea of councils, since they feared their competition. But the notion of a guidance of the economy in social partnership, as foreshadowed in the founding of the "Central Association" of employer's groups and unions in the wake of the Agreement of 1918 by the Leaders Hugo Stinnes (Employers) and Ludwig Legien (unions), already faltered in October 1919 and ended in the struggle over the 8-h day.

Although one can describe the practical policy of Social Democracy during the Weimar period as "reformist," clear reformist concepts are found only among a few writers who were close to the social democratic movement, men like Hugo Sinzheimer, Fritz Naphtali, and Hermann Heller. All three were of Jewish background and had to leave Germany after the Nazis came to power. While the

[106] Winkler (1985, pp. 709–716). A survey of the substantive positions can be found in Heimann and Meyer (1982), and in Blau (1980).

practical influence of their concepts remained modest in the Weimar years, they became important for the later development of social policy in West Germany.

4.2.1 Hugo Sinzheimer: Social Self-Determination in the Law

The most lasting influence on the social-democratic position was exerted by the jurist *Hugo Sinzheimer*, who perhaps more so than any of his contemporaries combined theoretical clear-sightedness and practical political engagement.[107] Sinzheimer can be regarded as the founder of labor law in Germany, which has become a model also for other countries in continental Europe (Sinzheimer 1907/1908; 1916, 1927). In a clear departure from the Roman-legal concept of *Dienstmiete* [contract for lease of services], and drawing on Karl Marx and Otto von Gierke, he conceived of the labor contract as a "legal relationship of subordination" [*rechtliches Gewaltverhältnis*] between an employer and the employee dependent on him, and he tried to bring out the roots in German law of *collective-contractual* regulations of such relationships (Sinzheimer 1916, pp. 40–45).

Sinzheimer's basic social-reformist idea referred to a separation of the legal spheres of the state and of the economy. More clearly than other contemporary social thinkers he clung, on the one hand, to the shaping power of the state, and, on the other hand, to the need for an autonomous economic system – with this he was moving conceptually within the sphere of what can today be regarded as the characteristic quality of the European form of the welfare state (Kaufmann 2001)

Sinzheimer's concept of "labor law" – a term that took its place only gradually alongside the older and more comprehensive notion of social law (Scherner 1996) – goes beyond the regulation of the labor contract and encompasses the totality of the legal norms that deal with the state of being an employee: "It includes the relationships that emerge out of the right of association, aid for the unemployed, the work performance record, worker insurance, the law of enterprise councils, the collective bargaining agreement, work groups, and so on" (Sinzheimer 1927, p. 6). In keeping with his social-reformist ideas, these legal spheres were to be "social law," that is, they should emerge out of the formative power of the freely organized forces of social life, and not out of processes of law-making by the state.[108]

At the center of his conception of social law stood, in addition to labor contract law, the law of *labor constitutions* [*Arbeitsverfassung*]. Because the labor contract was not seen primarily as a relationship of exchange, but a relationship of subordination or authority, it was necessary to legally regulate this relationship (which encompassed the labor contract), namely on the basis of the *equal participation of the employee*. The work relationship and the work constitution therefore of necessity contained elements of public law: at issue was the state's guarantee of "social

[107] See Ritter (1994, pp. 91–97). On Sinzheimer's importance see Kahn-Freund (1976).

[108] A good summary of Sinzheimer's position is provided by Fraenkel (1972, pp. 105–112). For a reinterpretation see Blanke (2005).

self-determination in the law."[109] Either the labor constitution itself, as the framework of economic guidance, must become the object of democratic legislation, or relevant collective bargaining agreements between employers and employees must be given a basis in state law that makes them compellable. The first approach concerns the notions of a state economic constitution [*Wirtschaftsverfassung*], of the kind that was put in place in the Weimar Constitution and has been preserved to this day in the laws on codetermination; the second approach concerns state *legal foundations of autonomy in negotiating pay agreements*, as were laid down in West Germany with the Collective Bargaining Agreement Law in 1949 and 1953.[110] Sinzheimer can therefore be called the first theorist of corporatism.

The analytical achievement that led Sinzheimer to his positions, which seem nearly self-evident to us today, becomes clear only against the background of the Prussian understanding of law and the state, on the one hand, and the exclusively individualistic-private law conception of the work relationship that was grounded in Roman law, on the other. It is for this analytical achievement that Sinzheimer deserves attention in the present context. His pioneering ideas can be concisely summarized as follows:

1. In opposition to all syndicalist attempts at a "*Rätedemokratie*" (democracy of local councils), but also to all unitary notions of German national statehood, he emphasized the *difference between the political and the economic constitution*, analogous to Hegel's distinction between "state" and "civil society."

   > The purely political democracy can act upon the social conditions only through laws and the state administration. However, both are inadequate to serve the social development in a way that we Social Democrats must desire . . . It follows from this that political democracy necessarily requires supplementation. Social, and especially economic, interests need special forms in which they can operate directly and autonomously. Political democracy must create these forms. They are created when alongside the political constitution in the state, a separate economic constitution is established that accomplishes the economic-organizational tasks through the economic forces themselves on the ground of basic norms by the state (Sinzheimer 1919).[111]

2. In opposition to the juristic positivism of his day, he emphasized the calling of jurisprudence to be a "legislative jurisprudence" [*legislative Rechtswissenschaft*], through which Sinzheimer became the promoter of a theory of legislation [*Gesetzgebungslehre*] (Sinzheimer 1976b). He distinguished

[109] See the subtitle of Sinzheimer (1916).

[110] As Fraenkel (1973, p. 136) has said: "Current German collective bargaining agreement legislation, indeed the collective bargaining agreement law of countries that are built on legal principles different from the German ones, is largely based on ideas that were first legally grasped and articulated by Hugo Sinzheimer."

[111] This is probably what Ritter (1994, p. 91) mentions as "Sinzheimer's speech at the party conference of the SPD on 'The system of local councils and the Reich Constitution' on 6.14.1919." – A differentiated balancing of the relationship between state legislation and social processes of normativization is also found in Sinzheimer's discussion of Georges Gurvitch's theory of social law (Sinzheimer 1976a, vol. 2, pp. 164–187).

legislative jurisprudence from the mere application of the law as well as from legal sociology or legal philosophy. It was not supposed to "examine the justification of social aspirations and derive forms from principles," nor stop at the investigation of the facts of the law. It

> takes the social aspirations as a given ... The jurisprudential task vis-à-vis the existing social aspirations lies in bringing these aspirations in harmony with themselves in their legal conditions. What legal forms must be present to allow certain social goals to be realized without contradiction and impediment? (Sinzheimer 1916, p. 7).

Legislative jurisprudence thus stands between science and political praxis. However, it can impart an appropriate legal form only to the currents pushing for change that arise on their own through the social conditions and the aspirations of will working in them. That, precisely, is what Sinzheimer was able to accomplish in exemplary form with his doctrine of the collective bargaining agreement.

3. In the wake of Max Weber's sociology of law, Sinzheimer also integrated the knowledge of the relevant social facts into the scientized legislative discourse. The jurist who makes himself available to the legislative processes in the manner described needs not only legal, but also sociological knowledge:

> Critical sociology of law does not ask what the norm wants, but what it means and accomplishes socially. Critical sociology of law seeks to grasp what norm makes of reality and what reality makes of the norm, and how the norm then works in reality. It directs its attention not at the content of the norm, but at its social power, manifestation, and function (Sinzheimer 1916, p. 7).

The power of this approach becomes clear once we understand the interrelationship of the three aspects he talks about: because Sinzheimer recognizes that the sphere of the state and that of society differ, he arrives at the postulate of a legislative jurisprudence that merges juristic and social knowledge. Although the word itself does not appear in his writings, Sinzheimer thus articulated the function of *social policy* as *mediating* between "society" and the "state" more clearly than any of his contemporaries. Characteristically enough, labor law and social law are understood to this day as spheres of law that link public and private law. In this context Sinzheimer also referred back to Lorenz von Stein, in whose "science of the state" [*Staatswissenschaft*] he saw a comparable intention (Sinzheimer 1976a, vol. 2, p. 156).

4.2.2 Fritz Naphtali: Economic Democracy

The concept of works' councils was a legacy of the attempted revolution at the end of the First World War and made its way into the Weimar Constitution chiefly with a view toward restoring and pacifying the prostrate economy. Substantial segments of the business class also believed that a social partnership relationship to the workers – as had already established itself in the "Central Association of German Industrial and Commercial Employers and Employees" – would bring about a more rapid recovery of the economy. Moreover, this movement stood within the tradition of association-forming and thinking in terms of occupational estates and groups (Ritter 1994, p. 75f.; Fraenkel 1972, pp. 78–105). However, the relevant constitutional provisions were put into practice only in the hotly contested Enterprise Council Law of 1920 and in the creation of a "Preliminary Reich Economic Council," though the latter lacked any institutional foundation and thus led to nothing (Winkler 1984, pp. 236–238). The social democratic model of an economic order that was not nationalized but collectivized and "carried by vital bodies of economic self-governance" got bogged down already in its early stages. The councils did *not* become "organs of a future socialist economy growing within the capitalist state" (Sinzheimer 1976a, vol. 1, p. 334f.).

In search for a guiding concept for social policy, the General Federation of German Trade Unions (*Allgemeiner Deutscher Gewerkschaftsbund*) chose the programmatic term "economic democracy" [*Wirtschaftsdemokratie*] at its Breslau Congress (1925) and charged a commission (which included, among others, Hugo Sinzheimer, Rudolf Hilferding, and Fritz Naphtali) with fleshing out the concept. The result was a document written mostly by Naphtali, who also spoke about it at the trade union congress in Hamburg in 1928.[112]

The backdrop to the program of economic democracy was Rudolf Hilferding's diagnosis of a necessary transition from free to *organized capitalism*. The increasing concentration and trend toward the formation of monopolies in the capitalist economy led to a growing collectivization of the functions of entrepreneurs and to the necessity of planning processes (Hilferding 1910/1973; Winkler 1974). It was precisely this, according to Napthali, that formed the prerequisite for the possibilities of "economic democracy," that is, the *institutionalized participation of workers in economic decision-making processes*. Picking up on various forms of an already existing "collectivized economy," he identified an already present trend toward democratization in the economy, which led him to this conceptual description:

> The democratization of the economy, intimately linked with the growing influence of the democratic state on the economy, demands that the direct participation of workers organized as producers (i.e. the unions) in all organs of economic policy continuously expand . . . The critical point is that economic activity is no longer pursed in the private but the public interest, not on behalf of private persons, but on behalf of an entity that stands above the individuals, and to whom the profit redounds. The picture of economic democracy is the reflection of political democracy, only in a different form (Napthali 1928, pp. 137, 152).

Surprising in retrospect is the matter-of-fact way in which the unions, as the trustees of the interest of the workers, are simultaneously set up as the trustees of the public interest. In accordance with the notion of councils underlying the Weimar Constitution, the chief accent was grounded in *codetermination above*

---

[112] Naphtali (1928). On the creation of the document see Louis (1969, pp. 35–45). On its content and reception see Weinzen (1982, pp. 28–160).

the level of individual enterprises within the framework of sector-specific or regional "economic councils." However, even Naphtali's essay was unable to develop any workable proposal how the project of a "collectivized economy" could do justice to the clashing demands of a balancing of competing interests, the increase in productivity, and the focus on the customer. Moreover, the claim that the implementation of democratic-economic maxims represented an evolutionary road to Socialism remained controversial within the workers' movement because of its implicit negation of class struggle, while at the same time rendering the concept suspect in the bourgeois camp because of its socialist goal.[113] However, the bourgeois camp itself could offer no convincing concepts on how to deal with the undesirable consequences of a growing cartelization and monopolization of the economy.

The significance of the concept of economic democracy largely adopted by the free unions of the time after the Second World War tended to be only a tool of criticism. The continuing demand for a democratization of the economy focused on other alternatives. That was true of the union demands for codetermination, which were now directed largely at individual enterprises and thus remained compatible with the bourgeois concept of the "social free market economy" [*Soziale Marktwirtschaft*].[114] But it was also true of the Social Democratic Left, who, with an eye toward large enterprises and monopolies, pursued nationalization plans that were more far-reaching than what seemed compatible with the concept of economic democracy. The weakness of the idea of the collectivized economy remained the fact that while it had some plausibility as a concept, it was unable to develop any generalizeable structural principles for an economic system.

4.2.3 Hermann Heller: The Social Constitutional State

Although he was no less engaged in the workers' movement than Sinzheimer and Naphtali, the influence of Hermann Heller – who died in exile in Spain in 1933 at the age of only 42 – remained small during the Weimar period; however, his conception of the state became groundbreaking for West German social democracy.[115]

Generally speaking, Weimar democracy lacked a concept of the state that was capable of attracting a social and political consensus. Jurisprudential positivism, as articulated with respect to state theory in Hans Kelsen's Pure Theory of the Law, the political science decisionism of the likes of Carl Schmitt, or the idealistic

---

[113] On the contemporary criticism see Weinzen (1982, pp. 121–160). Gerhardt (1930) did a differentiated examination of the concept of economic democracy from the bourgeois point of view.

[114] However, the codetermination legislation by no means exhausted the idea of economic democracy on the enterprise level; see on this von Nell-Breuning (1968a).

[115] On Heller see especially Müller and Staff (1984).

conception of the state of Rudolf Smend could all draw upon the intellectual traditions of the Empire. But the democratic state that bound itself through its own constitution could arrive at a consistent self-understanding only by overcoming conventional theories of the state. This was the project to which Hermann Heller dedicated himself, and he did so against the background of his social democratic convictions.[116]

Heller's theory of the state is interdisciplinary and grounded in cultural studies. He understood the modern constitutional state as a political form that owed its emergence to the development of western culture and society. To him, the state was therefore not simply a mere power state or a mere outgrowth of the legal system, but *the evolved product of historical forces* of the most varied kind and one that changed with them. "The state remains always merely a partial content of the complex reality of life, from which the theory of the state isolates it. However, the insights of this theory have value only when this act of isolation continuously refers back to the totality of reality, in which alone it has life and truth" (Heller 1934, vol. 3, p. 123). The state was understood as "an organized decision-making and action-taking entity" (Heller 1934, vol. 3, p. 339). What legitimized it was legal security: "The institution of the state is thus justified by the fact that once the division of labor and social intercourse have reached a certain level, the certainty that the law has meaning and will be enforced makes the state necessary" (Heller 1934, vol. 3, p. 333). However, since this says little about the concrete shape of the state, a theory of the state, as its theoretical justification, must do justice to the institutional demands of the legal system, as well as to its cultural preconditions and the effective social forces.[117] Such a theory therefore emphasizes the *constitution*, which is suited to endowing the state simultaneously with stability and openness toward the social forces:

> The novel content of modern constitutional documents lies in the tendency to carry out the objective legal restraint on the power of the state and secure it through the citizen's subjective rights of liberty and participation vis-à-vis the power of the state, so that the basic rights of the individual are protected by way of the basic organizational structure of the state. That the separation of power and the basic rights have recently been regarded as two mutually independent institutions is a fundamental and dangerous misunderstanding of the constitutional state under the rule of law. In actuality, the tendency toward the planned, constitutional [*rechtsstaatliche*] organization of state power and the tendency directed at guaranteeing liberty are mutually interdependent (Heller 1934, vol. 3, p. 388).

The normative justification of the state is thus not transcendental, but results from the *ideas* that are at work in the foundation and development of the state, and which, in the democratic state, find their form in the constitution.

---

[116] See Heller (1926, vol. 2, pp. 3–30). The most important work is his *Staatslehre* (1934), now in Heller (1971, vol. 3, pp. 79–406).

[117] On Heller's theory of the state see Schluchter (1968); Blau (1980, pp. 62–214); Penski (1982); Albrecht (1983); Hebeisen (1995).

The connection that is today commonly made between Heller's position and the concept of the *social state under the rule of law* [*sozialer Rechtsstaat*] is primarily the result of the prominence of this concept in West German discourse (see Articles 20 I and 28 I of the Basic Law) and finds only modest attestation in his own writings.[118] What remained crucial to his notion of the state was the postulate of the *material quality of being a "Rechtsstaat,"* which, in contrast to Kelsen, sought to bind the law to the normative ideas of the social forces at work within a society.[119] In this context, the "social idea" advocated by social democracy

> appears as the logical continuation of political democracy toward economic democracy. The former eliminated the estates, the latter opposes the political classes . . . It thus wants to transform the pure *Rechtsstaat* into a democratic-social welfare state by seeking to replace the 'anarchy of production' with a just ordering of economic life and to that end limits private property as much as possible (Heller 1930b, vol. 2, p. 291).

However, Heller sees this "*rechtsstaatliche Vergesetzlichung der Wirtschaft*" – the "juridification of the economy by the constitutional state" (Heller 1930a, vol. 2, p. 461) – as a very precarious process in which the class struggle comes to the fore again:

> The economically weaker party seeks, by means of legislation, to bind the economically stronger party, to force him to greater social benefits or even displace him from his property. Thus capitalism has taken the democratic principle to the point where the rule of its own creator, the bourgeoisies, is threatened" (Heller 1930a, vol. 2, p. 448). "This divergence of political and social-economic power is not a condition that can last. Either the state must be given the possibility – by having a separate economic foundation to its power – to make itself politically independent vis-à-vis private economic influences, or the struggle among the leaders of the economy must have at least the temporary result that they eliminate the democratic laws to their advantage (Heller 1971, vol. 3, p. 236).[120]

Unlike Sinzheimer, Heller thus did not perceive the possibility of a welfare state-compromise, a pacified though permanent tension between capital and labor. With respect to the economic and social constitution, Heller remained much more vague than Hugo Sinzheimer, with whom he shared many basic premises of his reflections. In particular, he lacked the sense for the inescapable autonomy of the economic sphere, which formed the starting point of Sinzheimer's design of a "social law." As Stephan Albrecht has said (1983, p. 197): "With respect to all these problematic areas, Heller's strength lay more in analysis than guidance, more in critiquing than

[118] To the best of my knowledge, the phrase "*sozialer Rechtsstaat*" does not appear at all in Heller's *Staatslehre*; it is found sporadically in his political writings, on rare occasions also as "*sozialistischer Rechtsstaat*" or "*Wohlfahrtsstaat*" ["socialist *Rechtsstaat*" or "welfare state"]; more often we read "*soziale Demokratie*" ["social democracy"]. See also Robbers (1983, pp. 68–71).

[119] Ch. Müller (1984) has shown that Kelsen recognized more clearly than Heller that this gives rise to problems.

[120] Thus, Heller interpreted the rise of National Socialism also as the response by the bourgeoisie to the growing power of the workers' movement in the Weimar Republic.

showing feasible alternatives. This, however, was in turn intimately related to the condition of the social democratic movement as a whole."

4.3 "Christian Social Reform" and the Failure of Corporatist Solutions to the Conflicts

A strategy of corporatizing social conflicts was also envisioned by the proponents of Catholic social doctrine. During the Weimar period they knew better than most others how to chart a middle course between social democratic endeavors at socialization, on the one hand, and the demands, motivated by economic policy, to limit the "socio-political achievements," on the other. This strategy was also favored by the long-time Reich Minister of Labour, the Catholic priest Heinrich Brauns (Mockenhaupt 1977). Catholic social doctrine essentially accepted free enterprise and the profit principle, though it subordinated them to the highest purpose of the economy, which was to meet human needs. A "corporatist organization of the economy" constituted the further development of the idea of vocational estates, which characterized the *solidarist conception of society* that Catholics held in opposition to the socialist idea of class struggle and to the liberal idea of competition, and the general tendency toward the formation of organizations and associations during the Weimar period seemed to favor this approach.[121] The relationship between state and society, and thus social policy, as well, should be shaped by the *principle of subsidiarity*. Theodor Brauer, for example, argued

> that the confusion in all our conditions arises from the troubled relationships between the state and society. The modern sovereign state knows only itself. The social entities, however, have largely accommodated themselves to this state egotism by largely dispensing with their autonomy and laying down at the feet of the state. The primary reason for this is that all modern groupings are above all interest groups . . . Today, the state engages in social policy as part of its state policy, not to support society and its structure, but at least in part to weaken it . . . The state that is best off is the one that allows the family and the community, the professional groups and the church, to live and develop as freely as possible. In so doing it lets loose forces that must unfold and develop, and which, if suppressed out of egotism, will in the long run invariably turn against it, even if only by clinging to the state with their needs and concerns – for in the end they will develop into so many blood suckers who will sap its vitality (Brauer 1931, p. 82f.).

This "Mönchengladbach School" of social Catholicism[122] that was dominant in Germany faced a romanticizing "Vienna School." In Austria, in the wake of Adam Müller and Carl von Vogelsang, a conception of society had endured that was oriented toward pre-democratic, estate representation. According to this scheme, the building

[121] For a concise account see Messner (1930, p. 44ff., quote: 48). A corporatization of industrial relations was also advocated by Mitscherlich (1927).

[122] Summary accounts of social Catholicism in its relationship to social policy are given by Briefs (1925); Bauer (1931); Kaufmann (1988a); Lindgens (1987).

of post-feudal society had to be carried on the basis of socio-economic, especially professional similarities, in analogy to the older estates, in order to do justice to the principles of Christianity, and to find a third way between liberal individualism and socialist collectivism. This camp was also suspicious of contemporary social policy. It countered the notion of social policy with that of "Christian social reform":

> The much more far-reaching miscarriages of a *social policy without a solidly established social order* are becoming fully apparent today: it is becoming one of the factors in the collectivization of people and society. Social insurance carriers, because of the enormous mass of the insured and the interests connected to them, have become one of the *social powers*, whose importance is enhanced especially by the fact that unions and parties with socialist goals see in them an instrument to expand their position as social powers. And social policy itself becomes for them a means of bringing about the socialist-planned economic system (Messner 1956, p. 144f.).

"Christian social reform," by contrast, lay "in efforts to solve the social question according to Christian social principles" (Messner 1956, p. 293). Those principles included the rejection of capitalist interest and the affirmation of production cooperatives in which the workers were equal owners of their enterprise.

The Mönchengladbach School, which stood close to the People's Association of German Catholics [*Volksverein für das katholische Deutschland*], in contrast, accepted the given form of industrialization and democratization and therefore saw in social policy fundamentally a useful means for combating deficiencies in the capitalist system (Höffner 1962b). However, because it did not regard a perspective that was oriented toward individual interests as adequate, it also demanded a "Christian social reform" that paid greater attention to concerns affecting society as a whole.[123] It was Heinrich Pesch, in particular, who sought to provide a scientific foundation for a "solidarist" economic and social order:

> The reciprocal dependence on the welfare of others in society is therefore not a *mere factual* relationship. Because the mutuality and commonality of interests seems grounded in rational human nature as a demand of the latter itself, solidarity simultaneously represents a *moral* relationship of people to one another. Even if the destruction of one's fellow human beings were to provide advantages, one must not will it, let alone bring it about ... Therefore, even if the individual looks to his own interests, he must at all times be simultaneously considerate of the legitimate interests of others, who as humans have a claim to happiness, well-being, to the fruits of social life (Pesch 1924, p. 33).

These ideas of industrial partnership found their embodiment – though in a conceptually altered form – in the codetermination legislation after the Second World War.

The basic idea of the corporatist right to free collective bargaining was not able to prevail in the Weimar Republic. A state-administered system of mediation seemed like the only way out, given the intensity of the clashes between the negotiating sides (Richter 1932; Hartwich 1967, pp. 23–44). Eventually, however, the entrepreneurs

[123] Dipper (1992, pp. 346–348) sees these impulses from Catholic social doctrine as the innovative element in the social reform discussion after the First World War.

waged their battle also against this system of mediation, and this led to the brutal labor conflict of the *Ruhreisenstreit* in 1928 (Feldman and Steinisch 1980, pp. 57–117). The global economic crisis that began soon after rattled especially the already fragile German economy and eventually led (in an act of capitulation in the face of problems financing unemployment insurance) to the end of the ability of a democratic regime to govern and to the transition to presidential government (Timm 1952; Maurer 1973).

Less attention was paid to a second circumstance that challenged the previous concept of social policy oriented toward the workers' question. The end of the First World War and the subsequent inflation and currency reform had given rise to *new social problems*. These concerned no longer only the working population, but also a middle class impoverished by the devaluation of its assets. Added to this were the victims of war and many other widespread problems, also and especially among young people. Initially these new social problems were overwhelmingly addressed at the local level; in fact, during the interwar period there developed, particularly in the areas of health-care, housing, and welfare, something like a *communal social policy*, though it was not subsumed under this label (Rudloff 1998; Sachße and Tennstedt 1988, vol. 2, pp. 184–202). Slowly these new challenges also became the object of national regulations. Moreover, to the extent that the social question was framed not in state-political but socio-ethical terms, it was no longer possible after the First World War to say that there was a *special* discrimination against workers. Yet in spite of these factual and normative shifts in the existing problems, most theorists of social policy in the Weimar period were not able to break with the focus on the workers' question.[124]

Lastly, and especially disquieting, was the "anxious question of whether that concept of social policy, which operates with an ethic directed at the common interest, can still be sustained at all, now that the very factor that previously embodied this common interest and asserted it powerfully against the forces active in economic life, namely the state, seems to have fallen completely under the spell of the interest organizations that have become excessively powerful" (Pribram 1925b, p. 252). This question touched on the very substance of the conventional, and especially the Protestant-bourgeois, legitimizations of socio-political interventions.

4.4 Reactions from Scientific Social Policy

The indicated shift in the perception of the problems social policy had to deal with, but also the growing institutionalization of social policy as a separate specialty within the framework of the economic and social sciences that were differentiating into their own disciplines (von Mayr 1921), led in the 1920s to a burst of intellectual

[124] One exception was Spann (1912) who had already demanded before the First World War "that a social policy focused on education and the family must be placed as an autonomous, equal-value system of measures alongside every other group of socio-political institutions of support".

activity that manifested itself above all as a debate over the *concept of social policy*. However, this would not be able to remedy what Marr had perceptively diagnosed as early as 1923 as "the *divergence that has been growing for nearly 30 years between social insight and socio-political action*" (Marr 1923, p. 571). Leaving aside what was probably the primary cause of this, namely the continuing structural differentiation between politics and science, reducing this divergence would have required two things from the social sciences: first, on the policy level the articulation of technical doctrines [*Kunstlehren*], that is, concrete problem analyses from the perspective of ends and means[125]; second, with a view toward the "great" socio-political questions (politics), social analyses against the backdrop of a yet-to-be developed theory of the relationship of social science thinking and political action. The first steps in this direction are found in the literature to be discussed, but they rarely led to analyses of contemporary situations.[126]

4.4.1 Conceptual Discussions

It was obvious that "the *common conception* of the term social policy, as the embodiment of those domestic political measures that have been taken since the beginning of the proletarian movement to appease or at least calm the pressing class

[125] The word *Kunstlehre* goes back to the distinction between "*scientia*" and "*ars*" and was used since the nineteenth century. In Max Weber (1904, p. 186), *Kunstlehre* has the meaning of a scientifically grounded medical "technology." However, Weber believed that this expression of a "*glaubensfrohe Stimmung des naturalistischen Monismus*" ["sanguine attitude of naturalistic monism"] was impossible in the social sciences because of the clash of values that underpinned all social policy. – Von Zwiedineck-Südenhorst, by contrast, understood the term programmatically: "As a field for the exercise of human study, social policy is not a science in the strict sense of that word, but a *Kunstlehre*. But it can – and if it wants to be rational, it must – pursue scientific paths, it must take advantage of the achievements of the sciences that fall within its sphere of action." Following Weber, he then went on to formulate two scientific tasks : "1. Testing the suitability of the means that serve the achievement of the desired ends, and in connection with this the determination of all possible consequence that *could* occur, not only the intended ones . . . 2. In the end even the *critique of the socio-political ideals* will also become a scientific task. Those ideals can and must be tested, as M. Weber has said, against the postulate that what is intended should be free of inherent contradictions." (Von Zwiedineck-Südenhorst 1911, pp. 62, 66) – The term *Kunstlehre* was repeatedly picked up in the conceptual discussions of the 1920ies, on this see Kleinhenz (1970, pp. 44f., 52f.). It played a certain role even after the Second World War; see, for example, Weddigen (1951/1952, pp. 156–163, here 161): "The science of 'social policy' is a *practical*, that is to say, an applied, discipline, a so-called *Kunstlehre*. While the systematizing, theoretical sciences seek to establish a system of the most generally valid laws and rules regarding the object of their knowledge, social policy, as a science, . . . makes it its task to show socio-political practice the path to its goals." See also von Wiese (1956).

[126] Needless to say, there were a great many scientific responses to individual socio-political problems, but they cannot be considered here. Noteworthy was especially the development of a separate discipline of labor law by Sinzheimer and others; see Kaskel (1920); Sinzheimer (1927). – Likewise, I can only mention the important public finance treatises by Goldscheid, Schumpeter, and Sultan: Goldscheid and Schumpeter see Hickel (1976), Sultan (1932).

of wage laborers" (Sombart 1897, p. 3), had become obsolete. But even the scientific definitions of the prewar period came in for sustained criticism in the conceptual discussion that now began. That discussion,[127] which ended largely without any consequences, was too extensive to examine in detail here.[128] However, it is worth noting that a comparatively intensive scientific discussion about "social policy" developed in the 1920s, a discussion that evidently also involved the attempt to *consolidate social policy as an independent scientific discipline.*

While Lorenz von Stein had still dealt with "social policy" as part of administrative science, socio-political questions were subsequently discussed within the framework of textbooks on "economic policy" or "practical economics." Until the First World War, social policy was thus largely a domain of economists, who, if they were sympathetic to "ethical economics," did not make a systematic distinction between economic and social policy, in any case. When German economics turned to the questions of the British classics and neo-classicism, and with the partial renaissance of liberal thinking, social policy was marginalized in the field of economics (Kurz 1989). This change, however, was quite gradual, and in the Weimar period, too, the influence of historical stances in the border region of economics and sociology (often called "social economics") remained considerable. The guiding idea of a "unity of the social sciences" persisted in Germany until after the Second World War and dissolved only under the influence of Anglo-American economics and sociology.[129] Even if clear affinities emerged in the Weimar period between scientific social policy and sociology,[130] that is not reason to interpret this as an abandonment of the economic sciences. The processes of self-understanding among the academic social politicians remained largely beholden to *the notion of a unified social science.*

What seemed sustainable in this context was the old idea, already hinted at by Lorenz von Stein and developed by Sombart and von Bortkiewicz in various ways, *that social policy dealt with the conduct of the state with respect to social class conflicts.*[131] With this, the measures to relieve economic and social misery, which

[127] See especially Adler (1927), Albrecht (1928), Ammon (1924, 1926), von Balás (1926), Bauer-Mengelberg (1925), Bloch (1932), Brauer (1931), Geck (1931), A. Günther (1922), A. Günther and Heyde (1924/1969), E. Günther (1930), Heimann (1924), Heimann and Weber (1931), Heyde (1966, fist 1920), Hilberath (1930), Klotz (1927), Lütge (1932), Nelson (1924), Pieper (1947, first 1933), Pribram (1925a, b, c, 1926, 1932), Spann (1931), Spindler (1922), Voss (1925), A. Weber (1931b), Weddigen (1930, 1933), von Westphalen (1931), von Wiese (1926), Wilbrandts (1926), Wunderlich (1924), Wyott (1927), von Zwiedineck-Südenhorst (1923).

[128] A systematic overview is offered by Kleinhenz (1970, pp. 28–57).

[129] See Häuser (1994), as well as other essays in the same volume. For continuities in the area of the relationship between finance and the free market economy see Schulz (1987, pp. 149–188).

[130] Sociologists who published repeatedly on socio-political topics included, alongside Leopold von Wiese and Götz Briefs, especially Alfred Weber and Ferdinand Tönnies; see also Oppenheimer (1912).

[131] As early as 1880, Franz Hitze had defined the solution to the social question as a "question of socialization [*Vergesellschaftung*]," "the question of how the existing social system, the system

were particularly numerous in the post-war period, were excluded from the term social policy and instead associated with "poor relief" or "welfare."

Already before the First World War, *von Zwiedineck-Südenhorst* had taken a stab at a social theory that was open to new problem groups. Similar to what Herkner (1922) had already done he differentiated between means and goals, that is, between the "bare account of everything that appears as social policy, and . . . a debate about what ought to be in social issues, in other words, ideas about the politeia with the right social structure and about what needs to be done to bring it about.[132] Von Zwiedineck-Südhorst was the first who sought to place this issue on a *sociological* foundation. He did this by erecting his definition of social policy on a "theory of socialization" that proceeded, on the hand, from a growing division of labor and professional specialization, and, on the other hand, from the formation of the political community. In the broader sense, social policy seemed to him "*the politics aimed at securing the ongoing achievement of society's purposes.*" (Von Zwiedineck-Südenhorst 1911, p. 38). And following Albert Schäffle, he believed that the "purpose of society" seemed to lie in the "most extensive possible participation of the totality in the goods and services that promote civilization by drawing on all available forces."[133] To him, the greatest threat to the "purpose of society" was thus the class *struggle*, that is, the fight against another class that went beyond the inevitable clash of interests and sought to *weaken it.* Avoiding these conflicts that damaged the common interest was for him the central task of any social policy, as the bearer of which he recognized not only state actors, but also social actors. Social policy in the narrower sense he then linked to the specific conflict between capital and labor.

This *simultaneously class-theoretical and integration-theoretical approach* can be seen as the dominant paradigm most readily in those positions in the debate over social policy that ranged from socialist (e.g. Adler) to organicistic (e.g. Spann, von Westphalen). It was picked up especially by Amonn, von Wiese, and the influential Heyde; Weddingen maintained this position also after the Second World War.[134] Its particular rationality is illuminated by the following quote from a jurist:

---

of capital and labor must be reshaped, reorganized in order to set the increasing fragmentation of society the goal of bringing the contrary forces back into balance and harmony" (Hitze 1880, p. III).

[132] Von Zwiedineck-Südenhorst (1911, p. III). On von Zwiedineck-Südenhorst see Neuloh (1961).

[133] Von Zwiedineck-Südenhorst (1911, p. 7). Similarly, though less progress-oriented, von Balás (1926, p. 1): "Society's greatest interest lies in the greatest possible welfare of humanity within the state, the nation, society. This welfare is characterized by the feeling of contentment that prevails among an ever growing number of members of society, a feeling that emerges in the course of development through the conjuncture of the requisite satisfaction of their physiological and intellectual needs."

[134] Weddigen (1957, p. 1): "The concept of social policy as an activity encompasses the measures which, in an effort to preserve common purposes, are aimed at influencing the relationship of social groups – especially of estates, classes, or castes – to one another and to society as a whole."

> The [state-theoretical] meaning of social policy lies in the fact that it seeks to counter the tension and division that develop within every social entity from the divergent conditions and the . . . striving of the groups that are present in it and form it, and threaten to destroy it. This indicates at the same time that social policy cannot limit itself to the level of the economy, and that its treatment is not just a matter for the discipline of economics. *For the society threatened by tensions there arises the inner necessity to engage in social policy.* Especially the state that wants to preserve its existence must act socio-politically, and its socio-political action takes direct hold of its innermost nature; it is in the highest sense political action. To that extent mediation is also a political function. With it, too, the state serves to maintain its existence (Richter 1932, p. 20f.).

Toward the end of the Weimar period the aspect of class receded, and the problem of integration was combined even more strongly with the call for a "strong state" and for a solution to the social question within the framework of *social policy at the level of economic enterprises* (Geck 1931; Albrecht 1930). In addition, arguments about heredity and racial hygiene, which had been discussed since the beginning of the century, gained in importance (Sachße and Tennstedt 1988, p. 136ss). All this had also created plausibility structures that led fairly smoothly to the Nazis' understanding of social policy.[135]

From our perspective today, von Zwiedineck-Südenhorst's discussion, which already drew on Simmel's theory of differentiation (Simmel 1989) still seems undifferentiated, but it already contained the *guiding notion of inclusion*, which has shaped welfare theory in recent times. It is possible to bring the same objection against the notion of "societal purposes" as against Sombart's idea of productivity: are we dealing with anything more than the scientifically dressed up perspective of a single discipline, in this case sociology? The attempt – inherent in a discipline – to establish a general societal consensus on a rational foundation remains as much dependent on general societal acceptance as all other proposals for a "basic consensus." "The notion of society is far too indeterminate to be usable at all for a clear conceptual determination."[136] The move to invoke the (national)societal integration problem as a problem addressed by scientific social policy becomes understandable if one takes into account the "collectivism" that dominated social scientific thought also in the interwar period, and which contrasted noticeably with the individualistic social theories of the Anglo-American world (Acham 1994; Backhaus 1994).

However, social science thinking in the Weimar period did not move substantially beyond the illusion of an Archimedean vantage point of scientific independence. Many attempts at defining social policy got bogged down already in the snares of semantic differentiations.[137] Where attempts were made to draw definitional boundaries, these often amounted to juxtapositions that strike the observer today as merely different perspectives or the expression of different political

---

[135] For a summary account see Krohn (1985); Sachße and Tennstedt (1992, pp. 18–97).

[136] Pribram (1932, p. 23); similarly von Wiese (1926, p. 616).

[137] An early example of this kind of effort is provided by von Wiese (1921, first 1910, p. 7ff.). Here also already the tendency toward a boundless conceptual broadening, which is likewise found in Heyde and, most pronounced, in A. Günther.

orientations. For example: social policy as a set of political measures or as a political intention? Social policy as economic or social policy?[138] State-focused or society-focused social policy? Social policy to shape or to supplement economic life? Worker social policy or consumer social policy? Present-focused or future-oriented social policy? *The number of conceptually relevant aspects always remained much larger than any possible theoretical perspective.* And so the relationship between sociology and social policy was aptly described as a "permutational task the results of which are too vast to fully grasp" (Bauer-Mengelberg 1925, p. 701). However, the search was in most cases for *a single*, central perspective, for it was believed that this was the only way one could establish social policy as an autonomous discipline.[139]

Towards the end of the Weimar period there are signs of a more carefully thought-through view. For example, von Zwiedineck-Südenhorst specified that the tasks of a scientific social policy were a theory of ends and means: "It is the fate of science that as such it essentially can never say much more – and therefore is not permitted to say more – than this: *Tell me which goal you are pursuing, and I will tell you whether the means you are employing to that end are suitable for getting you there*" (von Zwiedineck-Südenhorst 1961, p. 181). A dynamic view of social policy was postulated by Gerhard Albrecht (1928). Hilberath was harshly critical of all definitions that elevated a specific goal or intention to a defining characteristic: "Nearly all authors who have published a textbook on 'social policy' define the concept of 'social policy' in a very diverse way in a *theoretical* part. In the *practical* part of the textbooks, however, they strangely limit themselves to 'worker protection,' without paying the least attention to the definition they posited" (Hilberath 1930, p. 284). What becomes clear also is that writers were turning away from the class-specific definition of social policy and turning increasingly toward more comprehensive notions of welfare.[140] Still of interest today is the discussion instigated by the *Gesellschaft für soziale Reform* [Society for Social Reform] about the *economic value of social policy*, which picked up older ideas from Rudolf Goldscheid (1908, 1911) and anticipated the discussion after the Second World War dealing with the theory of human capital.[141] However, this broadening of the

[138] Pribram (1925b, p. 243): "No serious attempt was ever made ... to include in the systematic elaboration of that discipline those areas of politics that lay outside economic life, and to which, in the consensus opinion of most authors, social policy also extended – legal policy in the broadest sense, educational policy, and the like."

[139] Of course, there were also accounts of social policy that dispenses with a uniform perspective and either took an inductive-descriptive approach or emphasized precisely the plurality of motives and carriers: e.g. Rauecker (1926).

[140] For example, A. Weber (1931a, p. 25): "Social policy is the embodiment of measures and institutions which, in the interest of society, are supposed to promote togetherness, freedom, and the dignity of working people, in conjunction with a sustained improvement in their relationship to the world of goods." See also Balás (1926), with the beginnings of a line of argumentation focused on the theory of institutions and order.

[141] See Briefs (1930a; 1931). On the revival of the topic see Vobruba (1989).

inquiry also led to the loss of the connection to state policy, which was most suited to endowing the prevailing intentional definitions with a certain coherence. The state-focus of the German concept of social policy also became a problematic issue against the backdrop of the rising importance of international social policy (Weddigen 1932).

4.4.2 Eduard Heimann's Historical Theory of Social Policy

Among the discussions over the concept and theory of social policy during the Weimar period, discussions that were on the whole rather divorced from reality, the work of Eduard Heimann stands out.[142] It is among the small number of first-rate social democratic contributions to the discussion at the time about the relationship between capitalism and social policy.[143] His main work saw itself as a "theory of social policy" (1929) and simultaneously triggered a broader discussion.[144] How that discussion dealt with his work reveals the weaknesses of the contemporary reflections about social policy, and with a view toward the history of Heimann's output, it transitions us to the discussion after the Second World War. Heimann placed social policy into a context of intellectual and social history, and against the backdrop of the theory of capitalism and socialism. He did not see social policy as a timeless intention or definition, but as a phenomenon closely linked to the development of modern capitalism. Accordingly, there were

> no specific theoretical foundations of social policy; rather, sociological theory shows the historical direction in which social policy is moving forward, and economic theory indicates the means for analyzing the given economic situation, for balancing the socio-political success and the sacrifices they may have demanded (. . .), in other words, to show the concrete possibilities, necessities, and limitations (Heimann 1931a, p. 82).

Social policy was for Heimann "the institutional manifestation of the social idea in capitalism" (1929, p. 167). By "social idea" he meant the historically effective set of normative images for a life of freedom and dignity, images that – starting

---

142 This judgment is shared by Krohn (1985, p. 322f.); Krohn points further (p. 321) to the "so-called Kiel School with Adolf Löwe, Gerhard Colm, Hans Neisser, and Fritz Burchard, and in addition Emil Lederer in Heidelberg with his students," most of whom subsequently taught with Heimann at the New School of Social Research in New York. For a summary overview of Heimann see Rathmann (1988); Ortlieb (1975).

143 The authors introduced in Sect. 4.2 pursued more focused and specific view of the problem.

144 The discussion was set in motion by an extensive review by Götz Briefs in *Sociale Praxis* 38 (1929), and continued in the subsequent volume 39 (1930) with contributions from Carl Landauer (pp. 177–182), Karl Pribram (pp. 225–230, 249–252), Otto von Zwiedineck-Südenhorst (pp. 273–278, 297–301), a reply by Heimann (pp. 585–588, 609–613), a response by Landauer (pp. 929–933), as well as a contribution from Gerhard Albrecht (pp. 886–889). See also Tönnies (1930).

from the Christian tradition and the liberal social model of the Enlightenment – had taken shape in the wake of the development of capitalism. The most important carrier of the "social idea" was for him the workers' movement, though what it invoked were not primarily its own ideals but those of the liberal bourgeoisie as it demanded the freedom and dignity of the individual also in the working life. Accordingly, for him the crucial elements of social policy were the measures of occupational safety and the emergence of a collective labor law (including codetermination), *not social insurance*. On this point he agreed with Sinzheimer, whom he quotes repeatedly.

Heimann referred to Marx to illustrate the unsocial consequences of capitalism, though he parted ways with him on economic theory. Apparently unfamiliar with Lorenz von Stein, he argued similarly that social policy was *necessary* to stabilize capitalism. This necessity arises, first, from the demands of production policy, to the extent that the advances of capitalism also required more productive workers, and, second, from the striving for freedom and human dignity on the part of the workers themselves, who, in the wake of the development of capitalism, recognize every more clearly the tension between their exploitation and the expanding spheres of action available to them and demand changes within the framework of collective organizations. Social policy therefore has no fixed program; instead, "capitalism begins historically and conceptually explicitly without social policy, gives rise to it ineluctably, and undergoes profound changes through it" (Heimann 1931a, p. 257).

This is not the place to examine the substantive argumentation in greater detail. Suffice it here to indicate the major advances and weaknesses of Heimann's theory:

1. His theory of social policy is not speculative and static, but historical and dynamic.
2. It distinguishes *and* integrates the economic into the sociological perspective and relates social policy to the development of the economic system and its necessities in terms of production policy.
3. It is the first approach that is able to integrate the normative content of social policy in the form of descriptive theory in the Weberian sense.[145]
4. It insists on an antagonistic relationship between the social classes and uses it to explain the dynamic character of social policy.
5. It should be noted critically that the overemphasis on the state in the concepts of social policy prevailing at the time had its counterpart here in a striking neglect.[146]

[145] This does not rule out that Heimann identified personally with this social idea and the perspective of a "socialist" order, something critics also accused him of. However, he certainly knew how to keep his wishes and his diagnoses separate: "Whether social policy is indeed a path to socialization, as the social democrats and the bourgeois opponents of social policy believe, or whether it integrates the working class into the bourgeois world, as bourgeois social politicians believe and the communists fear, depends on the growth and change of the forces of history." (Heimann 1931b, p. 654)

[146] In his response to a critique by Briefs about this, Heimann specified the role of the state in the direction of the notion that only its binding prescriptions could overcome the dilemma between a ruinous competition, on the one hand, and advances in production policy, on the other. However,

While the critics pointed out that the argumentation had other gaps and had been given an idealized gloss, that does not alter our appreciation for the fact that Heimann was the first to present an *explanatory* theory of the genesis and dynamism of social policy that is in line with our current macro sociological thinking.

Like many others who were actively engaged in social policy, Heimann had to emigrate as a German of Jewish background, though he returned to the field of the German social sciences after the war. If we compare his later writings with his earlier ones, we can note continuities and ruptures. What continued, in particular, was an interest in social theory, which placed the development of capitalism into a larger context. Heimann retained his emphasis – now even more charged with respect to religious factors – on the ideational and moral elements for the success of social integration.[147] Largely gone, however, was his reference to social policy as a socially integrative, *institutional* development. Evidently his hopes for an advance of social policy in the direction of a "socialist" system had evaporated; instead, he now described "social reform as a synthesis" of capitalist and socialist, individualistic and collectivist elements:

> It is very misleading to describe the system of economic and social reform as a mixture of contrary elements; for that description blurs precisely the crucial element, namely that a higher and new principle has guided the reform. One can compare this more readily to an immunization, through which a living but endangered body is immunized with its opposite, a poison, against the effects of that poison; ... Our account reveals that the principle of dialectic reform is mental, and that it finds its manifestation in institutions ... Marxism, which has set out to turn western life upside down, was absorbed into western life as a healing force. That is the blessing of the dialectic (Heimann 1961, pp. 339–341).

Thus he believed that the role of social policy in the continuation of the capitalist development had been fulfilled. He maintained that the new problems of modern societies no longer had to do with class struggle, but with the emergence of an affluent society and the inner dynamic of the economy this entailed. That is why he pointed to new risk potentials, especially the consequences of colonial imperialism, to the new possibilities of a structural weakness in demand, to the individuality-destroying, anonymizing effects of the technological-economic rationalism, and – already at the beginning of the 1960s! – to environmental threats (Heimann 1964). According to his analysis, the main issue remained the limitation on economic demands: "The perversion of mere means, the elevation of the technological and financial degree of efficiency to the highest purpose, and the corresponding shaping of the human type are the historical result of late-capitalist society" (Heimann 1954, p. 236). His hope for renewal was once again directed at

Heimann restricted the socio-political role of the state to the beginning phase of social policy; the stronger the workers' movement became, the more it became the real carrier of social policy. See Heimann (1930). – The fact that this argument had no corporatist underpinning (as in Sinzheimer) or grounding in democratic theory reveals a clear weakness in Heimann's *political* theory.

[147] See especially Heimann (1954). Heyder (1977, pp. 113–201; 1982, pp. 75–94) has worked out Heimann's largely implicit social theory.

intellectual forces, though he does not suggest who the historical carriers of these new ideas might be.

4.5 *Social Policy Under National Socialism*[148]

Already toward the end of the Weimar period, the term "social policy," which previously had described either the context of political clashes or of academic reflection, established itself also as a comprehensive term in institutional practice.[149] It subsequently came to prominence also under the National Socialists, though the latter replaced all of the personnel of the relevant publications and forced especially Jewish social scientists into emigration.

One example were the changes in the name and the editorial staff of the publication that was the leading channel of communication between the science and the practice of social policy and the welfare system, which is consistently cited here as *Soziale Praxis*: from 1909 to 1927, the journal formerly published as *Soziale Praxis – Centralblatt für Sozialpolitik* appeared under the title *Soziale Praxis und Archiv für Volkswohlfahrt*. In 1928, the name was changed to *Soziale Praxis – Zentralblatt für Sozialpolitik und Wohlfahrtspflege*.[150] Beginning in May 1933, publishing passed into the anonymous hands of the "Office for Social Policy" already set up by Francke, with Dr. Werner Bohnstedt as managing editor.[151] With the 1935 issue, the venue of publication changed from the long-time publisher Gustav Fischer in Jena to the Weidmannsche Buchhandlung in Berlin. In the middle of 1936, the editorship passed from Bohnstedt to Dr. Fr. Sitzler; the Office of Social Policy was no longer mentioned as the publisher. Beginning with volume 1937, the journal appeared in the Verlag Franz Vahlen in Berlin. Beginning with volume 47

---

[148] See the standard work by Sachße and Tennstedt (1992), and Stolleis (2013, German Social Policy, vol. 2).

[149] As symptomatic let me mention the publication of a semi-official *Jahrbuch für Sozialpolitik* by the state secretary of the Reich Labour Ministry, Dr. Geib (Berlin, 1930/1931), along with the *Internationales Jahrbuch der Sozialpolitik* of the International Labour Office in Geneva (from 1931 on).

[150] The name change came with the following editorial note: "'Soziale Praxis' had been founded by Dr. Heinrich Braun and Dr. N. Brückner, had been continued by Prof. Dr. J. Jastrow and (1898–1921) by Prof. Dr. Ernst Francke." From 1921 to 1931, Prof. Dr. Ludwig Heyde served as the publisher (in conjunction with Prof. Dr. Wilhelm Polligkeit and Dr. Frieda Wunderlich); Polligkeit and Wunderlich continued as editors until the *Gleichschaltung* in April 1933.

[151] The prominence of the term "social policy" finds expression also in the name *Monatshefte für NS-Sozialpolitik*, which were published between 1934 and 1943. The year 1937 also saw the return (for a single year only) of the *Jahrbuch für Sozialpolitik* (already published in 1930/1931), now issued by the press adviser of the Reich and Prussian Labour Ministry.

(and with the addition "Neue Folge") it came out as *Soziale Praxis. Zeitschrift für Aktienwesen, Gesellschaftsrecht und Sozialpolitik*. It was now published by Dr. Schlegelberger, state secretary in the Reich Justice Ministry, and Dr. Fr(iedrich) Syrup, president of the Reich Office for Job Placement and Unemployment Insurance (later state secretary in the Reich Labour Ministry); Sitzler remained the editor. Volume 52 (1943), under the title *Soziale Praxis – Zeitschrift für Sozialpolitik und Gesellschaftsrecht*, lacks any information on the publisher and editor. The 1944 issue and a few issues in 1945 appeared once again under a new title, "for reasons related to the war economy": *Die deutsche Sozialpolitik. Gemeinschaftsarbeit der Zeitschriften 'Soziale Praxis' und 'Monatshefte für NS-Sozialpolitik,' zugleich Kriegsausgabe der Zeitschrift 'Soziale Zukunft,'* co-published by Kohlhammer and Vahlen.

Of note is not only the turnover of the journal's editorial staff that accelerated during the Nazi period, but also the reorientation in terms of content to *Akienwesen, Gesellschaftsrecht und Sozialpolitik* [Stock Market, Corporate Law, and Social Law] after 1938. This is a perfect reflection of the decreed absence of conflict in industrial relations within the framework of the German Labour Front.

The example of *Soziale Praxis* can be used to show what was generally true for social policy at that time: it became an ideological instrument of leadership for the state and the party, and that included the authorized publications on the topic. Thus the editorial of 1934 already illustrated the new course:

> The new yardstick for this system has been found: in the future, the value of the individual within society and to it will not be measured by property but by work . . . work that finds its meaning in what it achieves for the nation as a whole . . . The place of the pure worker and white-collar social policy, which always ran the risk of ignoring or harming the concerns of other groups of the nation, is taken by the *societal policy* [*Gesellschaftspolitik*] that stands under a uniform idea. It is its task to ensure the most effective forms for the possible collaboration of the various groups and the factors of economic processes (Bohnstedt 1934, p. 3f.).

An academic publication interpreted the difference to the "social policy in the old Reich" much the same way:

> The new Reich has brought for social policy, as well, an orientation to its true goal: an orientation toward the German *Volk* as a whole. Social policy can no longer serve merely to preserve and strengthen the power of the state, for the state, too, is only an organ of the entire nation. The new German social policy has been given the goal of *realizing German socialism*: . . . No longer shall social policy merely created 'outlets' for manifestations of social tensions, it shall not be inserted after the fact as a corrective into an economic constitution that reveals social mistakes in its construction; instead, it shall from the outset avoid such tensions by building certain institutions into the national economy. And that is why social policy no longer takes its place 'next to' or 'after' economic policy, but constitutes its necessary component (Gerhardt 1939, p. 2).

Social policy was now given a decionistic-voluntaristic twist: the party and the Führer supposedly knew what the German people needed. Accordingly, in the systematic accounts the productive factor work and its economic meaning were now accorded significance in creating the basic framework; moreover, the labor constitution and the order of national work moved into the center of the examination.[152] The formula of the economic value of social policy that was developed at the end of the Weimar period was now given an offensive, strictly "human-economic" character. *Only the economically usable and sociobiologically acceptable life capable of creating community was still seen as worthy of support.*

This *völkisch* dimension also had precursors in the Weimar period:

> German social policy of today, and even more so that of the future, is a *policy concerning the structure of the nation.* Its goals are: the healthy structuring of the nation, its social unity, and thus the best possible development of the people's productive and social forces. Consequently, the workers are no longer the sole object of social policy; instead, without regard as to the tradition of social policy, the object is *every stratum of the people whose existence, and thus also its communal value to the whole, is in danger* (Winschuh 1929, p. 10).

From this collectivist perspective it was but one more step to

> the national socialist concept of the formation and shaping of the 'national body' in accordance with racist principles of hereditary biology and population policy ... The reference point for care-providing services and measures was now no longer the needy individual, but the 'national community.' The production of the 'healthy people of the future' became the goal of welfare provision, not the integration of disadvantaged individuals (Sachße and Tennstedt 1992, p. 11f.).

In the realm of work and social insurance, the disastrous effect of this new doctrine showed itself in a weakening of legal entitlements, most clearly with racially or politically undesirables (Bonz 1991). However, it manifested itself most directly in the welfare system: the establishment of a party-run welfare organization, the National Socialist People's Welfare [*Nationalsozialistische Volkswohlfahrt*], created the mass basis for the social control of "individuals unfit for communal life" and rigorously enforced the principle of selection.[153] Social policy, even if the "People's Welfare" was not conceptually assigned to it, thus developed not only into an ideological, but also a practical instrument for shaping the nation, one that was also deployed deliberately for purposes of "race hygiene" and race policy.

This amounted to a fundamental rupture with the guiding humanistic ideas that had always legitimized social policy, all national and power-political motives notwithstanding. Even under Stalinism, the de facto neglect of the non-productive segments of the population was not elevated into a program. In addition, the recognition of individuals as bearers of social *rights* largely vanished. Social entitlements could be revoked at any time for political reasons, and any form of self-organization or collective assertion of entitlements was prohibited.

Still, the Third Reich did not simply abolish – "in the name of the people's community" – all forms of self-governance in the institutions of social policy and outlaw the unions; especially in the early years, it also introduced significant

[152] Gerhardt (1939, Chaps. 1, 3, and 4). On the actual development see Mason (1977). For more recent research building on his work see the survey by Frese (1993).

[153] See Sachße and Tennstedt (1992, pp. 110–150); Hammerschmidt (1999). Also, as a self-description Althaus (1939).

improvements in wages and social services.[154] Moreover, the inner structure of the social insurance programs remained largely untouched.[155] However, during the war social policy shifted essentially into the areas of the labor economy and wage policy (Recker 1985). At any rate, one cannot speak of a dismantling of the social sector. It is therefore difficult to question whether the Nazi polity was a welfare state.[156] The differentiation between "welfare state" as the political guarantee of social rights, and of "welfare sector" as the totality of all socio-political institutions (Kaufmann 2013, pp. 35–39) may allow us to draw a specific distinction, in that the guarantee of social rights presupposes a state under the rule of law, which usually (but as the German Empire before 1918 shows, not invariably) goes hand in hand with democracy.

For our purposes in terms of a conceptual history and reflections about social policy, the time of the Third Reich yields little directly. However, the experiences with totalitarianism, with the "political tilt of social policy" (H. Achinger), and also with the defensive battle against the attempts to create a universal, uniform insurance, have had a lasting influence on the socio-political orientations of the post-war period in Western Germany.

5 Social Policy Since the Second World War

An account of this, the most recent phase in the thinking about "social policy" poses much greater problems of exposition than before. For one, the sphere of problems and measures subsumed under the concept of social policy has continually expanded. At the same time, however, the concept has lost structuring force and has turned from a label for a political program into a largely descriptive term for an expanding field primarily of domestic politics, but in part also of interstate and transnational politics (European Union). Finally, one must bear in mind that in connection with the Second World War and under the key labels of "social security" and "welfare state," a broad movement of institutional reform began also in other countries, which corresponds essentially to what is called *Sozialpolitik* in Germany. More recently, the term "social policy" has also established itself internationally.[157]

It should be added further that we have no overall accounts of the history of terminological usage and intellectual reflection for this period. What follows is therefore a first attempt to structure and pin down a theme that is fraying on various

[154] For a summary assessment see Lampert (1985).

[155] For an account by a representative of the regime see Seldte (1939). On social security see Teppe (1977). For a remarkably objective contemporary survey see Guillebaud (1941); for a newer survey see Frerich and Frey (1996, vol. 1, pp. 245–329).

[156] Thus Sachße and Tennstedt as well as Hockerts (1998a, p. 17) explicitly affirm that it was.

[157] On the explicit terminological reception of the German word see Cahnman and Schmitt (1979).

sides. In the process, I must dispense even more so than before with a complete account in order to prevent the topic from becoming unmanageable.[158]

5.1 Normative Orientations

5.1.1 Social State and Social Market Economy as Conceptual Frameworks

After it had proved impossible to arrive at a stable economic and social order during the Weimar period, and after National Socialism had discredited also the older national tradition and with it the "collectivist" faith in the state, now dismissed as "authoritarian," a comprehensive reorientation of society was indispensable. The question on what foundations the polity should be rebuilt in Germany was caught up in the tension between the emerging East-West confrontation and eventually gave rise to two German states. This account is limited to the development in West Germany.[159]

In the three western zones, the debates over the political and social reorientation crystallized initially around the creation of constitutions. In the process, the state constitutions continued the tradition of the Weimar constitution of casting social entitlements and guiding ideas into constitutional norms (Hartwich 1970, pp. 27–33). The creators of the Basic Law [*Grundgesetz*, GG], by contrast, shied

[158] Some initial surveys of the development of practical social policy since the Second World War are given by von Bethusy-Huc (1965), Kleinhenz and Lampert (1971), Tennstedt (1988), Hockerts (1980), Frerich and Frey (1996, vol. 3), Zacher (1980, pp. LVI-CI), Lampert (1998, pp. 86–115). – For a comprehensive account of social policy in the two German states see Bundesministerium für Arbeit und Soziales and Bundesarchiv (2001–2008).

[159] While it was originally asserted in the GDR that "social policy was superfluous in a socialist state that is 'by its nature' social," the term *Sozialpolitik* played a certain role within the political semantics of East Germany. "In the relevant writings of the GDR, great importance is placed on the demarcation between 'socialist' and 'capitalist' social policy. 'Genuine' social policy supposedly existed only in socialist states, for only socialist social policy was oriented toward the interests of the workers. By contrast, capitalist social policy, as an instrument in the hands of the ruling class, supposedly sought to secure the continuation of the system of exploitation" (Lampert and Schubert 1977, p. 130). – Even though the social-scientific institute in the East German Academy of Sciences bore the name "Institute for Sociology and Social Policy," as far as we can tell, the term had no structuring *scientific* importance. The representative "publication, serving scientific and propagandistic purposes, on the development of the first Workers' and Peasants' State from 1945 to 1985" saw social policy as an "integrated part of the uniform policy of the working class and its allies. It is policy to shape social relationships and conditions between the classes, strata, and social and socio-demographic groups." As the goal it indicates social security and promoting the development of the classes and strata: (G. Winkler 1989, p. 9f.). – On the history of social policy in the GDR see Frerich and Frey (1996, vol. 2), Hockerts (1998b); and M. G. Schmidt (2013, German Social Policy, vol. 4).

away from social-state promises that could not always be realized, and they restricted themselves to affirming a commitment to the "democratic and social federal state" (Article 20 I GG) and the "democratic and social *Rechtsstaat*" (Article 28 I GG).[160] As the standard work put it:

> The affirmation of the social state is a general clause and dilatory compromise formula in one: a general clause as a reflection of the shared normative will of the constitution-shaping political forces, a dilatory compromise formula as a non-decision about the diverse, open disagreements of opinion with respect to the shape the social state should take. Sphinx-like, silently, ambiguously, and laden with interpretation ... the concept of the social state became the equally overlooked and overestimated constitutional law foundation of the constitutional reality of the social state (Zacher 1980, p. 675).[161]

At the least, Article 74 GG laid down far-reaching social policy jurisdictions for the federal legislature, though these were essentially oriented toward the existing laws and did not open up any substantive perspectives for the future.

The creators of the constitution had deliberately left open the decision about the economic order to be created in the coming Federal Republic of Germany. In principle, initially both a nationalization[162] in line with the concept of "democratic socialism" and a predominantly free-market system were possible. The decision was made, at the latest, with the election of the first Bundestag and the appointment of Ludwig Erhard as Minister of the Economy. He pushed for a *social market economy* ["*soziale Marktwirtschaft*"], and this term coined by Alfred Müller-Armack became the signature and interpretive framework not only for the economic order but also for the so-called "social order" of the Federal Republic to the end of the first era of "bourgeois" government in 1966.[163]

The term "social state" was given a jurisprudential interpretation only after the fact and referred only in a material-legal sense to the social policy laws created already in the German Reich, which – with a few exceptions, such as the Nazi child allowance legislation – remained in place also in the Federal Republic, which regarded itself as the successor state. As a guiding concept for social policy, the term "social state" gained influence only from the 1970s on (see Sect. 5.3).[164]

The continuity in the sphere of the legal system was far greater than in the realm of the economic system. The discontinuity of the latter was the result, not least, of the advances in economics, especially in the 1930s, which were reflected in a changed, "more systemic" view of economic activity and exerted lasting influence on the understanding of social policy. The most influential writers were John

---

[160] On the development of the idea of the social state see Grewe (1951), Ritter (1991, pp. 10–13).

[161] There also an overview of the interpretive discussion up to 1960. Also, Zacher (1968a); on the academic discussion see also Forsthoff (1968).

[162] See the relevant discussion within the Verein für Sozialpolitik: Weddigen (1950).

[163] On the emergence of the guiding concept "social market economy" see Helmstädter (1989, pp. 247–249).

[164] For a remarkably early interpretation of the social state clause in the sense of a welfare state program of intervention see Dürig (1953).

Maynard Keynes in England (Keynes 1935), Gunnar Myrdal in Scandinavia (Myrdal 1939, 1958; Myrdal and Myrdal 1935), and Walter Eucken in Germany.[165] In various ways, they engaged critically with the conventional equilibrium economics of the Marshall-Walras variety and with the unenlightened state interventionism of the interwar period. They also developed new concepts of a *more differentiated* link between the economy as a whole and the state.[166] Initially, Eucken's "order-political" concept became influential for the rebuilding of West Germany. Although Keynesian ideas were already evident in the "Mackenroth Rule," according to which "all social expenditure must be paid for always out of the national income from the current period,"[167] they became decisive only in the Stability and Growth Act of the Grand Coalition (1966–1969).

Eucken's great achievement lay in a fundamental reformulation of the issue of economic policy, which he encapsulated in two postulates:

> First postulate: the policy of the state should be aimed at dissolving economic power groups or limiting their functions. Every consolidation of the power groups reinforces the neo-feudal diminution of the authority of the state ... Second postulate: the economic activity of the state should be aimed at shaping the structural forms of the economy, not at guiding the economic process (Eucken 1952, pp. 234, 236).

Characteristic for Eucken's thinking and the *ordo-liberalism* built upon his ideas was the ideal-typical distinction between the exchange economy (*Verkehrswirtschaft*) directed by the markets and the central administrative economy guided by central planning. With this, the ordo-liberals were equally opposed to a nationalization of the economy and to unregulated capitalism, which, as the Weimar period had shown, tended toward the formation of cartels and other concentrations of power. The task of the state in economic policy thus lay in the continued promotion of competition against the oligopolistic and monopolistic tendencies that were at work also in exchange economies ("order policy"). The "order" metaphor soon entered into scientific and political rhetoric, which henceforth spoke no longer about capitalism and socialism, but of the problem of the economic and social order.[168] In the process, conceptions of society based on class theory disappeared and were replaced by ideas of a "leveled middle-class society."[169]

[165] Especially Eucken (1950, first 1940;1952). The emergence of order-political thinking already during the Third Reich was noted by Abelshauser (1991).

[166] Similarly intellectual groundwork was done in jurisprudence by Hugo Sinzheimer; see Sect. 4.2.1.

[167] Mackenroth (1957, first 1952, p. 45). This programmatic text was probably the most influential one for the discussions about social policy in the 1950s.

[168] See, for example, the dominance of the order metaphor in Lagler and Messner (1952); also, the standard work by Lampert (1997a). – Incidentally, since 1957, the Ministry of Labour has been called Federal Ministry for Labour and Social Order [*Bundesministerium für Arbeit und Sozialordnung*].

[169] The widely adopted formula of the "leveled middle-class society" [*nivellierte Mittelstandsgesellschaft*] first in Schelsky (1965, first 1953; printed in 1965, pp. 311–336). For a diagnosis of the times in the post-war period see now the summary by Nolte (1998).

The guiding social image of ordo-liberalism had a middle-class imprint and to that extent resembled its old-liberal counterpart. In the face of the "trends toward massification" at the time, a broad diffusion of property and the state's prevention of the formation of economic power were to protect the realm of private autonomy and "personal responsibility."[170] Ordo-liberalism believed that the conventional social policy was also partly responsible for the tendencies toward massification:

> The illusion that central guidance is 'social' is still widespread . . . Let us go into households and factories. There we see what the social question is at our historical moment. There it becomes clear how the concentration of property and of economic guidance in the state and in other public-law entities, on which private power groups also exert a sustained influence, make the supply with goods worse, promote massification, create coercion and dependency, lessen personal responsibility, and endanger the forces that strive for realization in each individual (Eucken 1949, p. 131).[171]

Without the need for a minimum of collective protection being denied, social security was thus expected chiefly from the formation of private property and private insurance (Eucken 1952, pp. 43–48, 185–193, 312–324). Property for all those gainfully employed was to come about, almost automatically, as a result of the release of economic initiative in the competitive system and the rapid economic growth this made possible within the framework of a currency policy that stabilized the penchant for savings. Eucken understood "social policy primarily as a policy of the economic order" (Lampert 2001). In contrast to Anglo-American liberalism, the Ordoliberals thus emphasized the leading role of the state with respect to the economic system: against the backdrop of a Protestant-Lutheran political and economic ethics, "the competitive system is seen by the Ordoliberals as an instrument of disciplining . . . The market, supervised by the state, is the disciplining instrument of coordination that gives rise to the asceticism of professionalism and work that has always been individually presupposed in the New England sects" (Manow 2001, p. 192).

Ludwig Erhard invoked the basic principles of Ordoliberalism when he advocated the social market economy and described a good economic policy as the best social policy. On this he differed from his state secretary Müller-Armack, who noted critically:

[170] See especially Röpke (1949). A comprehensive account of ordo-liberal ideas is given by Blum (1969, pp. 47–89). For a derivation of these ideas from the history of theory see Brandt (1993, pp. 397–415).

[171] Similarly critical toward the dominant socio-political views was Müller-Armack (1947, p. 106f.): "All those who, as politicians or scientists, see themselves chiefly as social politicians considers themselves in all currents and parties obligated to denounce any responsiveness toward free market necessities as outdated liberalism and thus avoid an intellectual confrontation that is nevertheless still unavoidable today. That the social political results of such a collectivism were rather meager in all countries that embraced it did not detract from the pious approval."

> Neither the social starting data that enters into the market process, nor the income structure that emerges from it need coincide with our social criteria ... We know today that the market economy does not adequately satisfy certain demands for social equalization and social protection, and we must take care to build in appropriate stabilizers (Müller-Armack 1952, p. 30f.).[172]

Subsequently, free market principles were able to prevail only in the area of manufacturing and trade. The "social order," which was essentially equated with the institutional side of social policy, was characterized by substantial continuity with the Weimar period.[173] But there was good reason to question to what extent this was an "order" at all:

> In the nearly 80 years of its existence, German social policy has grown wildly ... This corpus of social laws and ordinances has proliferated into a confused tangle in which nobody can get his bearings any longer, least of all the pitiable creatures for whose benefit the whole matter was undertaken. This is an intolerable condition, one that was no intended and must be done away with. That is to say, the demand for a social plan, for a social policy that is erected according to plan must be fulfilled and carried out once and for all (Rüstow 1959, p. 20).[174]

The connotations of the term "social market economy" remained as diverse as "social policy" and are contested to this day. In practice, the liberal market aspect of Ordoliberalism has prevailed and marginalized the emphatically socio-reformist components in Wilhelm Röpke, Alexander Rüstow, and others (Becker 1965). In recent years, some commentators have asserted a contradiction between social market economy and social policy, at least with reference to the actual development in Germany.[175] There is a renewed demand for "thinking in terms of orders" also in social policy, in order "to clarify the question of how indispensable social state interventions should be carried out if they are supposed to actually reach the economically weakest" (Volkert 1991, p. 110f.). However, the systemic character of social policy is not nearly as evident as that of the market economy. What "the social" means in distinction to the economic and the political, or in other words: which social phenomena and problems are relevant as the effective sphere of

---

[172] Differences in the interpretations by Erhard and his state secretary Alfred Müller-Armack is analyzed by Blum (1969, pp. 90–128); Part II of his book offers an account of the reception history of this concept. On the relationship between the views of Eucken, Röpke, and Müller-Armack; see Starbatty (1982).

[173] That also holds for the principle of the *Gemeinwirtschaft* [collective economy], which continued to be advocated with socio-political arguments. See Thiemeyer (1975, 1979). On Thiemeyer, who developed a consistent – but little noted – position between "social market economy" and "socialism," see Schulz-Nieswandt (1992).

[174] The programmatic term "social plan" [*Sozialplan*] first in Mackenroth (1957, first 1952). On Rüstow see Lenel (1986).

[175] See, for example, Gutowski and Merklein (1985), and the anti-critique by Lampert and Bossert (1987). On the discussion see also Grosser et al. (1988), Schwarz (1990), Klein (1994), Kleinhenz (1995).

social policy and why – to this day no clarity has emerged on this question.[176] As a result, for the recent period, as well, we can do no more than sketch the change in views.

The concept of the social market economy was not without consequences for the socio-political development and its conceptualization. Still during the occupation period, the principle of *free collective bargaining* was carried through, and it strongly curtailed the weight of the state with respect to labor relations compared to the Weimar period. After the founding of the Federal Republic, the primary emphasis of the long-term legislation lay initially in the area of *industrial order* and later in the sphere of *income security policy*. Both areas of intervention were compatible with the free market functioning of the economy and were therefore frequently described as "the social" of the German market economy. For it became clear early on that even the most successful market economy could not by itself regulate the distribution problems arising from the maintenance of those not gainfully employed, that this was thus a case of "market failure." Moreover, the topicality of a wealth building policy for the dependent workers in the period up to 1966 can be attributed to the suggestion of the guiding principle of the social market economy.

Beyond the institutional aspect of social protection, "social security" became a programmatic term that stood alongside "social justice" (Kaufmann 1973, pp. 91–139) and benefited from a widespread "striving for security" (Braun 1978). Initially, however, the programmatic term "social reform" became more important to the socio-political debates in the Federal Republic. After Chancellor Adenauer had announced a "comprehensive social reform" and a "comprehensive social program" in his inaugural speech at the opening of the second legislative period,[177] *social reform* became a guiding principle of a reform of the social protection that was fought over from the second to the fourth legislative periods, but which led to far-reaching results only in the pension reform of 1957.[178] Thus, from the middle of the fifties, the problems of income security and thus of income distribution moved into the center of the socio-political debates, while labor law and the expansion of social services moved to the margin of political interest. This has earned the Federal Republic the reputation of a "social insurance state" [*Sozialversicherungsstaat*] compared to other welfare states around the world.

---

[176] See, for example, the periphrases of "*Sozialordnung*" in Lampert (1989); in this context the state of the sociological discussion and research on social order is even not mentioned.

[177] On the prehistory and course of the discussion over "social reform" see Hockerts (1980, pp. 216–319).

[178] See the documentation edited by Richter (1955ff.). On the conceptual and interpretive context see Kaufmann (1973, pp. 111–115).

5.1.2 Christian Social Doctrines

Initially the disillusionment following the defeat in the war gave a new impetus to *normative reflections*. We have already encountered them in connection with the concept of the social market economy, which was inspired above all by Protestant influences (Manow 2001; Honecker 1971). More immediately influential for social policy was Catholic social doctrine,[179] whose most prominent proponents were the later cardinal of Cologne, Josef Höffner, and Oswald von Nell-Breuning, S.J., who had drafted the Papal encyclical "Quadragesimo anno" (1931).[180]

Höffner's handbook article on social policy is notable in the present context for its systematization of socio-political tasks according to (1) social protection, (2) socialsecurity, (3) social promotion, and (4) structural policy tasks such as a broad diffusion of wealth and settlement policy (Höffner 1962a, col. 349). Moreover, Höffner made a lasting contribution by elaborating basic concepts of Christian social doctrine: personhood, subsidiarity, solidarity, and the common good.[181] A certain affinity between the original concept of the social market economy and Höffner's position is unmistakable, especially with respect to the demand for a policy of widely dispersed wealth and a limiting of the state's policy of protection to providing basic security.[182]

Von Nell-Breuning contributed to a Christian articulation of social policy immediately after the war, and he advocated above all for the codetermination of workers[183]; however, his decades-long engagement was reflected less in systematic works and more in establishing a bridge between Christian social doctrine and the trade unions and social democracy.[184] Worthy of note is especially his development of the dialectical connection between solidarity and subsidiarity as basic principles of the social order (von Nell-Breuning 1957, 1968b).

The effects of the Christian social doctrines on the socio-political development in the Federal Republic tend to be indirect. After the war, the churches were accorded considerable moral authority. The clear alliance between Catholicism and the CDU and simultaneous affinity of a substantial segment of Protestantism for the SPD were also reflected in the positions on social policy. However, both

---

[179] Langner (1980). On the relationship between Catholic and Protestant social teachings see Karrenberg (1965).

[180] Worth mentioning is also Utz (1961), but being located in Switzerland he was not so influential.

[181] See his often reprinted textbook *Christliche Gesellschaftslehre* (Höffner 1962c). Höffner was also a co-author of the so-called "Rothenfels Memorandum" (Achinger et al. 1955), and became influential through his active publishing activity; see his anthology *Gesellschaftspolitik aus christlicher Verantwortung* (1966). On Höffner see Große Kracht (2006).

[182] Kaufmann 2006; see esp. Höffner (1953, 1960).

[183] Von Nell-Breuning and Sacher (1949); in the appendix an impressive international survey of the Christian-social movement at the time. Von Nell-Breuning (1968a). On von Nell-Breuning see Schultz (1978), Schwaderlapp (1980).

[184] Von Nell-Breuning's publications have been collected into several volumes (1956–1960; 1970a; 1979).

churches shared a commitment to a middle course between capitalism and socialism, and this – in conjunction with a strong continuity of socio-political institutions – stabilized the path of German social policy also in a post-war situation that was open to new developments. Contrary to the prevailing interpretations of the "German way" in the international literature, a "third path" was laid out not only by Catholic social doctrine, but found its justification (in different terms, though) in the economic and social ethics of *both* large confessions.[185]

5.2 Social Policy as Social Science Between Tradition and new Orientations (1946–1966)

The preceding sketch has already illustrated that a multitude of competing concepts for "social policy" are available for a generalizing view of socio-political measures. Nevertheless, the term has asserted itself especially in the *theoretical* discussion of economics and sociology, in which, needless to say, real political changes have also been reflected.

The misery immediately after the war left little room for general considerations of social policy. But theoretical reflections on social policy regained their importance already before the establishment of the Federal Republic. The influential publications at this early state included an essay by Ludwig Preller, later the first chairman of the *Gesellschaft für sozialen Fortschritt.*[186] That organization arose in 1949 as the successor to the *Gesellschaft für soziale Reform*, which also had a successor publication to "Soziale Praxis," which became an important organ of socio-political discussion, at least in the initial years.[187] The *Verein für Socialpolitik* was also reestablished as early as 1948, with its archaicizing spelling and with the addition *Gesellschaft für Wirtschafts– und Sozialwissenschaften* (Albrecht and Arndt 1948). In the wake of the differentiation between economics, jurisprudence, and the social sciences in the narrower sense (sociology, political science, demography, ethnology), and between these disciplines and social philosophy and social ethics, that is, in the *process of the dissolution of the communicative interconnection or "unity" of the social sciences that was characteristic of the German-speaking tradition,*[188] the *Verein für Socialpolitik* turned into a specialized

[185] The same has been argued by Manow (2001, p. 195).

[186] Preller (1947). Among the leading contributions one should mention also Jostock (1946), a programmatic tract that picked up on the tradition of Catholic social doctrine, and the earliest textbook by Tormin (1949).

[187] *Sozialer Fortschritt. Unabhängige Zeitschrift für Sozialpolitik*, has been published monthly since January 1952. However, this publication was never able to become as important as the weekly *Soziale Praxis* had been before 1933.

[188] See von Mayr (1921), Kaufmann (1989).

society for economics. Since that time, the relationship between economic policy and social policy has also become increasingly polarized.[189] Since the Second World War, we have not seen again the kind of dense communicative context about social policy that existed between 1871 and 1930. To be sure, in the era of "social reform," scientific expertise was repeatedly drawn upon for inspiration and to legitimize practical social policy (Krüger 1975; Kaufmann 2007a), but these scientific actors were individuals without the backing of a scientific community.

5.2.1 Conceptual Diversification

Initially the term "social policy" became once again a structuring theme of the impending reorientation, although complaints about its vagueness did not cease in the wake of attempts at reformulating it.[190] All I can lay out here are currents and differentiations that would subsequently give rise to theoretical reorientations.

The resumption of the *conceptual discussions* did not prove very fruitful in this context (Hoffmann 1948; Weber 1953; Lepsius 1955; Pütz 1967; Müller-Heine 1977). For in the intent at arriving at an unambiguous term, the scientific conceptual constructs must take their guidance from a societal preconception, which has a primarily political or institutional imprint, as well as from certain normative ideas. If at the same time a certain intention or "goal of social policy" is implied, theorists rarely succeed in freeing themselves from the normative ideas of specific socio-political actors and in developing an independent *scientific* perspective. Since the experiential subject of social policy proves to be heterogeneous with respect to the relevant institutions or measures and the possible intentions or goals of the actors involved, and turns out to be feebly structured in epistemological intent, the task of ordering and selective decision-making necessary falls to the researchers. In the process they confront the dilemma of simplicity: the more clearly they construe the object of cognition, the less they do justice to the heterogeneous nature of the experiential object. Conversely: the more complex the theory, the less suitable it will seem for providing guidance for practical decisions.[191] One possible way out, in order to reconcile the theoretical and practical perspectives, is the scientific

---

[189] A conciliatory attempt at clarification was undertaken by Schulz-Nieswandt (1991).

[190] Gerhard Weisser (1969, p. 1048), one of the most intellectually consistent theorists of social policy at the time, offered this assessment: "Thus the doctrine that is traditionally called social policy in the German-language realm offers a picture that becomes blurred in the fog of a good deal of vagueness. No consensus exists on either the subject of the doctrine or the ways in which to justify its theses. There is not even clarity. But there is an urgent need on the part of society-shaping practice and theoretical possibilities to give the doctrine fixed contours and a clear internal structure."

[191] Similary, Winterstein (1969, pp. 10–13). For an attempt at a theoretical grounding see Kleinhenz (1970), and building on this work, Leenen (1978).

reconstruction of social and socio-political problems in their interconnection.[192] But since these are multifarious, they cannot be reduced to *one* "socio-political" problem.

Already toward the end of the Weimar Republic there were signs of a diversification of the concept, when the conventional understanding of social policy focused on the workers' question was joined by broader reflections, with the suggestions being made soon to refer to these as "*Gesellschaftspolitik*" [societal policy].[193] One can see in this a return to an intention already defined by Lorenz von Stein, and in a different way by Wilhelm Heinrich Riehl (see Sect. 2.2):

> Just as a 100 years ago social policy, in the sense of a societal policy, was thus already based on the notion of an orderly society, the preservation or restoration of which appeared as the task of social policy, modern scientific social policy qua societal policy also seeks to influence society, that is, the co-existence of human beings, on the basis of insights into social life, namely in the way that social science brings them forth (Geck 1950, p. 15f.).

The term *Gesellschaftspolitik* was widely adopted in the post-war period, though without ever acquiring an unambiguous connotation (e.g. Achinger 1979, first 1958; Höffner 1962a; Kraus 1964; von Nell-Breuning 1970a; Weisser 1978). In all likelihood this shortcoming can be explained by the fact that this subject matter was not permeated by social science and remained initially largely within the horizon of issues in economics. Still lacking at that time was a clear theoretical concept of society. Few were as clear-sighted as Müller-Armack, who articulated the problem of the post-war period as follows: "Crucial aspects for the preservation of our economic culture will depend on whether we will succeed in preserving the free market form on account of its high efficiency, while at the same time placing it within a consciously designed overall system" (Müller-Armack 1947, p. 94). Here already we can see a clear difference but also relationship between "economy" and "society."

In addition, an approach developed that was oriented toward shaping workplace conditions and which laid claim to the term "*betriebliche Sozialpolitik*" alongside "*soziale Betriebspolitik*" (Briefs 1930b; Geck 1931; von Nell-Breuning 1970b, pp. 27–34; Reichwein 1965). This issue became politically relevant also in the discussion over co-determination and was pursued further by the field of "*Betriebssoziologie*" ("industrial sociology") (Pirker et al. 1955; Dahrendorf 1965). However, it was of only marginal importance to the subsequent course of the discussion over social policy.

The term "*kommunale Sozialpolitik*" ("municipal social policy"), which can likewise be traced back to the Weimar period, played hardly any role at all in the

---

[192] As was already done by Mönch (1949, p. 156): "A true theory must, in abstracting, proceed not only from pure concepts, but chiefly also from current problems and systematically develop their nature and significance." – On this more systematically Kaufmann (1977b), now in Kaufmann (2009).

[193] See, for example, Klotz (1927); Geck (1931) – The word was already used by von Philippovich in 1914; see Geck (1950, p. 11).

post-war era. Social policy was now clearly understood as a federal issue.[194] The term assumed new relevance only with the expansion of the concept of social policy beyond income maintenance into the area of social services and social infrastructure in the 1970s.[195]

The international development also exerted an influence on the social policy discussion in Germany, but its reception was largely ambivalent. Institutional solidifications in Germany had created historical heavyweights and a web of interests that opposed the direct adoption of new models (especially in the so-called Beveridge Plan[196]) of a social protection system that encompassed the entire population and was uniformly administered.[197] While the central Anglo-American term "social security" was adopted, it did not acquire a weight comparable to "*Sozialreform*." The term "*Wohlfahrtsstaat*" (welfare state) was adopted largely in the sense of a negative concept of the "*Versorgungsstaat*" (provisioning state) that set itself apart especially from the Swedish model.[198]

While the established term *Sozialpolitik* therefore remained dominant, it was no longer able to assume a function of structuring the discussions. Its primary characteristic now lay in denoting a field of politics that initially comprised the institutional areas connected to the "workers' question," namely occupational safety, collective bargaining policy, the collective right to work, codetermination, and the various areas of social security, but to which additional political fields, such as housing policy, the regulation of the war burdens, wealth policy, and relief or welfare policy were gradually assigned. The field of politics defined as "socio-political" was subsequently expanded chiefly by focusing on specific groups: the middle class, families, young people, the disabled, women, foreigners, and – finally – seniors were discovered as the target groups of social policy.[199] Most recently, even the right to pensions of civil servants is being increasingly integrated into the perception of social policy (e.g. Frerich 1996). The expansion of the field of social policy can also be read from the organization of the federal ministries: for

---

[194] On the issues connected with this see Münch (1997).

[195] See Becher (1982) as well as other essays in the same volume; Mundt (1983), Krüger and Pankoke (1985).

[196] Lord Beveridge presented his plan to Parliament in November 1942. Beveridge's concept of social policy encompassed not only a reform of the social security system, but also an active full-employment policy. See the early reception by Liefmann-Keil (1949). On the political significance of Beveridge's proposals see Bremme (1961, pp. 39–80).

[197] For one attempt at a reception see Auerbach (1955, 1968). The SPD's "*Sozialplan für Deutschland*" (Hannover 1957), co-developed by Auerbach, also reveals clear influences from the Beveridge Plan. Even the "Rothenfels Memorandum" requested by Chancellor Adenauer in competition to his labour minister called "for *one* situation essentially *one* service through *one* provider." Achinger et al. (1955, p. 135).

[198] Kaufmann (1973, pp. 108–115). A polemic use of "*Wohlfahrtsstaat*" is already found in the government declaration by Reich Chancellor von Papen (1932); Stolleis (1998, col. 1487).

[199] Hippel (1982) even takes the orientation toward target groups as the overarching systems criterion for his account of social policy.

example, the Federal Ministry of Labour that existed from 1949 to 2002 (after 1957: Ministry of Labour and Social Order) was joined in 1953 by a Federal Ministry for the Family, which today, after several changes in name, is called the Federal Ministry for Family, Seniors, Women, and Youth; in addition (1961–1969 and again from 1991 on a Federal Ministry of Health was created as a third department of social policy, which combined sections from the two other ministries.[200] However, this brief overview, which illustrates institutionally the still-to-be examined fraying of the German understanding of social policy, is a chronological leap forward.[201]

5.2.2 Diversification of Perspectives

Like conceptual discussions, claims of disciplinary exclusivity do not seem to lead anywhere.[202] Social policy as a contested (politics) or institutional practice (policies) invariably has historical, legal, financial, organizational, social problem-oriented, and often also social-psychological aspects. If one examines the utilization of scientific knowledge for such a practice, this kind of analysis of problems and measures results ineluctably in the combining of the stock of knowledge from different disciplines.[203] However, when it comes to such necessarily particular "techniques" (*Kunstlehren*) or "systems of recommendations and warnings" (G. Weisser) – e.g., questions of pension insurance, occupational safety, and the like – it makes sense to use "social policy" only as an umbrella term, since it has always referred to a perspective that *overarches* certain institutional complexes and is oriented toward a higher degree of generality. But even if we understand by "social policy" a realm of experience demarcated only by political or other conventions, there is no reason why only *one*

---

[200] In a broader sense, the Federal Ministry of Housing that was set up in 1949 (1969–2002: Federal Ministry of Urban Planning and Housing) should be counted among the departments of social policy. An overview of the development of the social policy departments and their subordinate agencies is given by Kahlenberg and Hoffmann (2001).

[201] As far as the "semi-official view" is concerned, the expansion of the measures subsumed under the label "social policy" can be traced especially well in the informational brochure published by the Federal Ministry of Labour, *Übersicht über die soziale Sicherung* ("Overview of Social Security"; Bundesministerium für Arbeit und Sozialordnung 1962–1977), since 1994: *Übersicht über das Sozialrecht* ("Overview of Social Law") and, in addition, *Übersicht über das Arbeitsrecht* ("Overview of Labor Law"; Bundesministerium für Arbeit und Sozialordnung 1994ff.). On this see also the expanding systematics of the relevant textbooks and comprehensive accounts: Tormin (1949), Heyde (1966, first 1920), Schieckel (1955), Albrecht (1955), Erdmann (1957), Weddigen (1957), Burghardt (1979, first 1966), Preller (1970), Sanmann (1972, pp. 188–205), Christmann et al. (1974), Brück (1981), Lampert (1998, first 1980), Molitor (1987/1988), Bäcker et al. (2000), Blüm and Zacher (1989), Frerich (1996), Kath (1995).

[202] For example, see the debate between Weddigen (1951/1952) and Geck (1952/1953), and the reply by Weddigen (1955).

[203] See, for example, the schematic account of the multi-disciplinary contexts of scientific systems that pronounce on social policy in Engelhardt (1991, p. 48).

specific discipline should be in charge of its analysis. Rather, the character of the practice in question seems to demand that it be examined from the perspective of *different* disciplines (Lampert 1992; Zerche 1993).

This poses the problem, however, of how the research results of different disciplines can be brought to bear on the questions raised by practical, society-shaping social policy. Ingeborg Nahnsen has tried to derive from this very problem the necessity and possibility of a separate discipline of 'social policy," "by means of the integration of findings from other disciplines under the umbrella of a supraordinated approach that brings them together" (Nahnsen 1961, p. 129). But this unifying approach is anything but self-evident *as a supraordinated one*. By contrast, Gerhard Weisser, who probably provided the strongest impulses for a scientific reflection on social policy in the post-war period, argued that one could certainly do without the establishment of a separate discipline of "social policy."[204] Of far greater importance to him was to place the process of scientific consultation under intersubjectively controllable criteria by explicitly posing the question about the normative premises of scientific recommendations and warnings and relating it to a "normative social science."[205] This impulse led to a resumption of the values debate in a new context[206] and to further debates on how recommendations in economic and social policy could be justified.[207]

As a result, in recent years we have seen within some disciplines a differentiation of certain subdisciplines or at least research communities concerned with questions of social policy, whose participants establish contact with each other and collaborate in the analysis of problems.[208] The scientific study of social policy is necessarily

---

[204] A discussion of the problem that was refreshingly free of disciplinary interests was also offered by Schreiber (1963).

[205] See the scattered statements by Weisser collected in Stelzig (1977); also the contributions by Werner Wilhelm Engelhardt, Friedrich Fürstenberg, Siegfried Katterle and Bernhard Schäfers see Henkel et al. (1998).

[206] In addition to Weisser, and going beyond him, it was especially Weippert (1939) who argued the possibility of normative recommendations grounded in social science. Hofmann (1961) emphasized that the normative effects of the social sciences were inevitable. For critical and differentiating counterpositions see the anthology edited by Topitsch (1965). In a direct engagement with Weisser, Hans Albert, in particular, articulated a position which then exerted an effect in the "positivism debate" in German sociology, which was also referred to as the "second value-judgment debate." See Adorno et al. (1972). This debate once again failed to have a clear result. It became clear, however, that value references were inevitably contained within social science arguments, and that the point was not to eliminate them, but merely to control and contain their effects. On this see Beck (1974).

[207] See especially von Beckerath and Giersch (1963).

[208] For example, today we find the *Sozialrechtsverband* (established in 1965 under the title *Sozialgerichtsverband*), a committee on social policy within the *Verein für Sozialpolitik*, a section *Sozialpolitik* in the *Deutsche Gesellschaft für Soziologie*, and a section *Politk und Ökonomie* (focused on issues related to labor market policy) in the *Deutsche Vereinigung für politische Wissenschaft*. Research centers include the *Max-Planck Institut für ausländisches und internationales Sozialrecht* [Max Planck Institute for Foreign and International Social Law,

multifocal (i.e. focused on a variety of problems) and *multidisciplinary* (i.e. involving various disciplines). Which discipline should take the lead in providing the theoretical framework in any concrete case remains a question of heuristic expediency, that is to say, it depends on the particular characteristics of the issue in question. Depending on the research setting, such a problem will be taken directly from the context of practical political concerns, or freely chosen by the researcher. In the latter case, the researcher's disciplinary orientation will often prove decisive for both the selection of the problem and the way it is theoretically structured. There is nothing fundamentally objectionable about this, since imbalances and biases can be corrected by scientific critique. Today, progress in the social sciences can be expected to come, not from methodological restrictions, but from a process of analyses, critique, and synthesis that is based on a division of labor and is invariably redundant. And the translation of social-scientific knowledge into political practice takes place through varied but mostly indirect paths (Kaufmann 1977b).

5.2.3 New Conceptual Orientations

If we look at the advances in socio-political thinking after the war in relationship to the dominant paradigm of the Weimar period, three aspects, in particular, were challenged from a substantive point of view: (1) the state-centered conception, (2) the reference to the workers' question or the relationships between social groups or classes, and (3) the dominance of socially integrative issues. The first two aspects are the topic of this section, the third will be examined in the next section.

First to be questioned was the *state-centric* nature of the concept of social policy. Experiences with the state's mediation system in the Weimar period and even more so the experiences with the totalitarian state of the Nazis argued in favor of an emphasis on the socio-political autonomy of *social* actors, of the kind that was practically implemented in the principle of free collective bargaining, the restoration of forms of co-determination in the area of industrial relations, as well as in the self-governance in the four branches of social insurance (influential Böckenförde 1976b). In the process, a limitation on the reach of state interventions was in line with both the *principle of subsidiarity* as propagated by Catholic social doctrine and, above all, with the new *ordo-political thinking* in the sphere of industrial policy (see Sect. 5.1). Accordingly, the *question of providers* now received systematic attention in the accounts of social policy.[209] According to Weisser, three types of *providers* of

since 1980; since 2011: "… for Social Law and Social Policy"] and the *Zentrum für Sozialpolitik* [Centre for Social Policy Research, Bremen University, since 1988]. Moreover, thematic anthologies are increasingly bringing together contributions from other disciplines, and bibliographies contain a growing number of references to works outside the discipline. However, the state of interdisciplinary collaboration is by no means satisfactory, though all sides acknowledge its necessity.

[209] See the independent discussion of this topic by Weddigen (1956). Sections on various carriers of social politic can also be found in many textbooks.

socio-political benefits can be distinguished: public institutions (i.e. those set up by the state), associations (e.g. partners in a collective wage agreement, welfare associations), and private businesses. With the recognition of this diversity of providers, scientific social policy is confronted with the question about the criteria for a practical demarcation of competencies. (Weisser 1956a).

Especially contested initially was the question of the *object* of socio-political thinking. Following Amonn (1927, pp. 21, 32), a first distinction can be made between the object of experience and the object of cognition.[210] As an *object of experience* one must define social policy with an eye toward the concrete clashes and realizations that constitute the history or current social policy of a given experiential realm (e.g. Germany, England, Europe, international agreements) or certain actors (state, local communities, partners to collective wage agreements, political and social movements). A considerable heterogeneity is unavoidable here. Social policy constitutes itself as an *object of cognition* in the process of the scientific formation of concepts and theories. The goal here is the development of a basic conceptualization that makes possible *consistent* choices and descriptions. The growing heterogeneity of the experiential object "social policy," that is, what is generally understood by the term, does not fundamentally impede the theoretical observer from imparting sharper contours to this only loosely describable object and to analyze it *from a specific perspective*. In that endeavor, *divergent* perspectives are, of course, fundamentally legitimate: for example, approaches based on class theory, distribution theory, integration theory, or welfare theory. In like manner, the same object of experience – e.g. collective labor law or statutory sickness insurance – can be examined from the perspective of different disciplines (economics, law, sociology, political science).

The post-war discussion as well as the conceptual discussions of the Weimar period were, however, not yet familiar with these distinctions. Rather, for most observers there was a *congruence between the experiential and the cognitive object*, that is, they posited a scientific framing of the problem that was dictated by the practical issues. In the process, they became invariably entangled in the problem of a circular strategy of definition: instead of selecting *different* analytical perspectives from the standpoint of their heuristic usefulness for specific problems, they posited the existence of *one* central problem that was to be the central problem of both practical politics and science simultaneously.

Until then, observers had usually defined this fundamental problem as the "workers' question," and then preferred to treat it from the perspective of class theory.[211]

[210] This was also suggested by von Wiese (1956), probably the most incisive contribution to the theoretical discussion at that time.

[211] Subsequently, the class-theoretical perspective in social policy receded strongly into the background, with the exception of a few neo-Marxist attempts to revive it in the 1970s. However, a revival that developed this approach further is found in Lepsius (1979), who introduced the expression *Versorgungsklassen* for those social categories who depend on social benefits to live their lives.

Depending on one's political viewpoint, the workers as a homogenous class appeared either as a threat to the existing order, as a social group in need of the state's special protection, or, finally, as a power factor that impeded economic or even social progress via the influences from unions.[212] Once the conflicts over the extent of the co-determination of employees had been settled (Schneider 1993), *labor law* receded increasingly into the background as the object of social policy.[213] Henceforth, all major conflicts were no longer resolved in parliament, but within the framework of labor law jurisdiction or, in rare cases, by the Federal Constitutional Court; initiatives for a comprehensive codification of labor law made no headway. Instead, *social law* moved into the center of the clashes over social policy, and in 1953/1954 a separate *Sozialgerichtsbarkeit* ["social jurisdiction"] was created for it (Zacher 1980, pp. LVIII–LXV). And into the center of social law moved social insurance law, or – as the new linguistic usage put it – the *law of social security* ["*soziale Sicherheit*"] (Bogs 1955).

This also had repercussions for the scientific approach. The term "social security" became central to the theory of social policy (Weisser 1956b; Külp and Schreiber 1971). In economics, the perspective of distribution theory now moved fully into the foreground.[214] In part, one can even detect a tendency to exclude social policy in the productive sector (occupational safety, labor law, co-determination) entirely from the systematics of social policy.[215] At the same time, though, the problem of social security was now seen more comprehensively and the separation between worker policy and poverty policy was overcome[216]; in social-political practice this corresponded to the connection between the pension reform of 1957 and the *Bundessozialhilfegesetz* [Federal Social Assistance Act] of 1961. Sporadic efforts were made, following the approach of Beveridge, to place all of social policy under the goal of social security, a move that placed special emphasis on the connection between economic policy (full employment policy) and social policy (e.g. Schachtschabel 1952, Pütz 1954). At that time, however, this perspective did not yet play a dominant role. The primary emphasis lay on the demand that the social benefits – which varied in terms of the reason triggering the benefit (*principle of causality*) – be standardized from the viewpoint of their role in providing social

---

[212] The last-named threat is one that Briefs (1952), in particular, warned about.

[213] For a summary account see, for example, Zöllner (1977); Nipperdey and Seifert (1990). An up-to-date survey is provided by the period publication issued by the Federal Ministry of Labour and Social Order: *Übersicht über das Arbeitsrecht* (Bundesministerium für Arbeit und Sozialordnung 1994/2000).

[214] See already Schumpeter (1916/1917; after Adolph Wagner, cf. Sect. 3.3.2); also the pioneering work of Liefmann-Keil (1961). Problem-oriented analyses: Pfaff (1978a, 1983). On the state of the theoretical discussion see Bartmann (1981). For the application to social policy see Zerche and Gründger (1996).

[215] For example, this area is entirely absent from the textbooks of Brück (1981) and Frerich (1996). Since state labor law is less developed in the Anglo-American and Scandinavian world, the international discussion tends to overlook this area or to construe the topics of the "welfare state" or "social policy" differently. On this see Kaufmann (2013, German Social Policy, vol. 5).

[216] The pathbreaking work in this regard was Achinger (1939).

protection (*principle of finality*), and that the social benefits be coordinated through a "social plan."[217] It was also within this context that there emerged for the first time the problem of the intergenerational link, and thus within the scientific discussion the need for a family support as correlate to economic protection in old-age – in other words, the problem of the "three-generations contract."[218]

5.2.4 New Theoretical Perspectives

Finally, compared to the paradigms of social policy of the Weimar era, the *theoretical perspectives of the fundamental problem of social policy* changed. If the class conflict and the problem of integrating marginalized groups through state policy were in the foreground back then,[219] the perspective now shifted, for one, onto the area of *individual welfare*, and, for another, onto the *problems of providing services*.

The shift in the focus of welfare theory from the condition of classes to the *comparison of individual life situations* is closely connected to the change in the guiding images of social order (see Sect. 5.1). Under the program of creating a "middle class society" [*Mittelstandsgesellschaft*], the question about the *equalization of opportunities* had to move into the center. Moreover, ideas about *social weakness* changed: "The modern development has turned other social groups into typically weak strata . . . One can say that the social problematic has today become a total social one, and that it cuts straight across the 'old' class layers of the independent and the dependent, of employers and employees."[220] It was this very idea that prompted the programmatic title of Hans Achinger's book *Sozialpolitik als Gesellschaftspolitik – Von der Arbeiterfrage zum Wohlfahrtsstaat* [Social Policy as Societal Policy: From the Workers' Question to the Welfare State, 1958]. This reorientation, however, was by no means without controversy:

> The approach that lies at the basis of the cognitive object of social policy as a science (in the traditional sense) is aimed at the significance of the economic-social differentiation and group formation for the prospering and functionality of the whole of society in the interest of the nation and the state . . . If the focus there rests on the social organism that depends for the exercise of its function on the relationship of its group-organized members, here it is on the living conditions and forms, on the social living standard of the elementary cells of

---

[217] See the volume by Boettcher (1957), which is especially representative of the discussion in the 1950s. A good survey over the state of the discussion at the time is offered by Molitor (1957).

[218] Alongside Mackenroth (1957, first 1952), this was constantly pointed out especially by Ferdinand Oeter and Oswald von Nell-Breuning. See already Oeter (1952a, 1952b). A summary of von Nell-Breuning's position can be found in von Nell-Breuning (1979). On the more recent state of this issue see Borchert (1994) and Kaufmann (2007b).

[219] As Weddingen put it as late as 1957 (p. 2): "Social policy is the policy aimed at the integration of social groups into a social whole."

[220] Pütz (1954, p. 9). The unpublished dissertation of Lepsius (1955) already pointed in the direction of the new orientation traced in the account that follows.

> the societal cosmos, on the individual members of society that belong together in families and households (Albrecht 1959, p. 362f.).[221]

A theoretical-normative basis for this individual-centric view was developed by Ludwig Preller, who sought to ground social policy from an anthropological perspective:

> *Economic policy* seeks to satisfy human needs by producing and distributing goods; *social policy* deals with the human being who produces and works for these goods, with the people to whom they are distributed. Economic policy and social policy relate to each other as economic good and human being (Preller 1962, p. 85).

In line with this thinking, he offered the following descriptive-normative definition; "*Social policy produces impact from the aspect of the working life to the structure of human society in the sense of people as a value in their own right*" (Preller 1962, p. 291). Notable here is the linkage of the "personal-functional" and the "systems-functional" aspects of social policy, which Christian von Ferber illustrates as follows:

> Seen from a consistent materialistic cognitive position, the 'reference problem' of social policy arises not with collective subjects, but with individuals, who, embedded within the metabolism of nature and fixed to an irreversible temporal horizon, receive substantial life opportunities from societal production as social goods. This material cognitive position, as it was formulated in the anthropology of Helmut Plessner, ... has the ineluctable consequence for the sociological theory of social policy that it must incorporate the individual in sociologically structured statements. Without a categorical processing of the physical/temporal dimension of the human being, no discipline is able to work on problems of social policy (von Ferber 1977a, p. 31).

The term "*Lebenslage*" [life circumstances] coined by Gerhard Weisser became the basic theoretical concept of this new social-science perspective: "*Lebenslage* is the latitude that the external circumstances offer the individual for the fulfilment of basic concerns, which he regards as the meaning of his life upon unimpeded and deep self-reflection."[222] What is remarkable about this definition is its broad tailoring beyond the realm of economics. This is not about the mere "satisfying of needs," as the yardstick of which one could regard the level of income (Thiemeyer 1963; Schulz-Nieswandt 1991). Rather, it was about the *latitude* to pursue "basic concerns" [*Grundanliegen*], whereby Weisser posited "that people have not only interests that are physical in nature, but are also capable of intellectual interests and attachments, which, where they occur, determine action out of their inherent dynamic" (Weisser 1959, p. 638). Moreover, he assumed that "upon unimpeded and deep self-reflection," that is, especially after eliminating attempts to exert propagandistic or commercial influence, it would be possible to ascertain a set of "basic concerns" on which virtual consensus was possible thanks to given

---

[221] In the same sense also Weddigen (1967).

[222] Weisser (1959, p. 635). Weisser offered various versions of the definition; on this see Möller (1978). On the more recent discussion see Clemens (1994).

cultural values; as a result, it was possible to determine *Lebenslagen* and their differences independent from mere subjective preferences.[223]

> What is distributed are not income and possible wealth; rather, what is distributed are – far more comprehensively – *Lebenslagen* . . . Distributed are opportunities for self-realization, distributed are the places of people in the social or productive process (Thiemeyer 1988).

The advantage of the concept of *Lebenslage* thus lies in the fact that it makes it possible to examine – from *various* vantage points – the differences in welfare or the "social inequality" among individuals as dependent on existing institutional and contextual structures. As such it constitutes a concept that acts as a bridge between legal, economic, and sociological analyses.[224] A new, standardizing reference point of social-political thinking becomes evident in the concept of *Lebenslage*.

While the notion of *Lebenslage* allows for a conceptualization of the *field of action of social policy*, it does not conceptualize social policy itself as an *interventionist process*. In this regard, Weisser was still strongly shaped by the voluntaristic conception of the older doctrine of social policy, which proceeded from an idealized, uniform actor "the state," and in which the task of scientific social policy was to offer this actor rational suggestions on how to achieve the goals it has set for itself. In his concept, Weisser, too, presupposed a *shared horizon of advisory social science and political decision makers*, and he problematized neither the process by which the social policy will was created, nor the implementation of social-political decisions.

Under the influence of advances in sociology and political sciences, this conception became increasingly problematic. Good political intentions, guiding images, or "target systems" [*Zielsysteme*] (Sanmann 1973) are no guarantee that they will achieve the intended economic or social effects. Rather, institutions of social policy, once created, develop an *internal dynamic* and often unforeseen side effects. Where the older thinking about social policy had proceeded from *intentions* or the "direction of state intervention" (von Bortkiewicz), the *effects of state interventions* now moved to the fore of scientific interest. The *contingency of the relationship between science, politics, and administration* slowly became

---

[223] The social indicator scholarship can be seen as the operationalization of this approach. See Engelhardt (1991, pp. 38–46).

[224] The perspective indicated by the concept *Lebenslage* has been widely adopted by now. Although the leading textbook by Lampert avoids the word, its definition is very similar in meaning: "In this sense, practical social policy can be defined as the political action that is aimed, first, at improving the economic and social status of groups of persons that are economically and/or socially weak in absolute or relative terms, through the use of suitable-seeming means in the spirit of the basic societal and social goals pursued in a society (free development of personhood, social security, social justice, equal treatment), and, second, to prevent the occurrence of economic and/or social weakness in connection with the appearance of existence-threatening risks" (Lampert 1980, 5th ed. 1998, p. 4). – Related to the *Lebenslage* concept is also the term *"Lebenschancen"* ("life chances") introduced into sociology by Dahrendorf, although it is interpreted more broadly, as the result of "options" and what he calls *Ligaturen* (social bonds): see Dahrendorf (1979).

thinkable. Hans Achinger was the first to point to this problem complex and to make its study the task of sociology.[225] For one, the democratic "state," and even more so "politics," is not a uniform actor; instead, the formation of a socio-political will (politics) occurs in networks of interested parliamentarians, ministerial officials, scientists, scholars, and lobbyists, whereby the representatives of the established institutions themselves also play a not insignificant role.[226] For another, the implementation of socio-political programs (policies) by institutions created for that very purpose (e.g. factory inspection, providers of social services), which in turn develop their own interests and procedures. Finally, all these political measures meet with a sphere preformed by social structures and divergent life conditions, they exert their effect *as interventions* with uncertain consequences. (Kaufmann 1982a). This perspective opens up a broad research field, which in Germany was subsequently taken up especially by Sociology.[227] Political science, as well, after some initial hesitation, has devoted itself especially to labor and labor market policy (Hartwich 1983; Abromeit and Blanke 1987). By contrast, economics as a discipline has increasingly marginalized research on social policy.[228] This seems to have been a result of the drifting apart of economics and social sciences, which – under Anglo-American influence – characterized the

---

[225] Achinger (1966). Already in *Sozialpolitik als Gesellschaftspolitik* (1979, first 1958, pp. 84–114), had pointed to the "effect of the institutes." Based on this, he developed a research program, much of which was implemented – with funds from the Deutsche Forschungsgemeinschaft, by the "Commission for urgent social-political questions" which he headed. See Achinger (1963, pp. 87–96, esp. 94f.). This was the first larger research initiative on social policy since the Second World War, one to which many up-and-coming scholars owed their path into social policy, including this author.

[226] See especially the analysis of the "conditions of the socio-political process of decision-making" by von Bethusy-Huc (1965, pp. 220–256), a study that arose from the above-mentioned research program.

[227] The beginning of an intensive debate over sociology's engagement with social policy was marked by the 18th Conference of German Sociologists at Bielefeld. See von Ferber and Kaufmann (1977), Kaufmann (1978). – The subsequently founded "Section for Social Policy" within the German Sociological Association has published the series *Soziologie und Sozialpolitik* (Munich and Vienna) since 1981 and *Sozialpolitik und Sozialstaat* (Opladen) since 2002. Since 1987, its meetings have been published in the *Zeitschrift für Sozialreform*. For surveys of social-scientific research on social policy see Tennstedt (1977), Krüger (1979), Kaufmann (1982b), Kohl (1984), Behrens and Leibfried (1987).

[228] This is evident, for example, in the declining importance of the Seminar for Social Policy at the University of Cologne, which in its heyday it was made up of four professors, and from which important impulses have come for social policy theory. See Herder-Dorneich et al. (1992). – The Committee for Social Policy within the *Verein für Socialpolitik* (*Gesellschaft für Wirtschafts- und Sozialwissenschaften*) had a checkered history. After "not having met for years because of internal disagreements," it was reactivated in 1968. Sanmann (1993, p. 21). Among the minutes of the meetings of the committee published in the *Schriften des Vereins für Sozialpolitik N.F.*, the following are especially relevant to the present context: Thiemeyer (1990/1991).

post-war development in Germany and was further accentuated by the politicization of the social sciences after 1966.[229]

5.3 Social Policy Between "Quality of Life" and "Crisis of the Social State" (1967–1999)

5.3.1 Active Social Policy

The sixties provided no strong impulses to either practical or scientific social policy. Still, a new perspective was already in the making under the Grand Coalition, one that understood social policy not only as a reactive-compensatory balancing of economic or social weakness, but as *active, society-shaping social policy.*[230] Relative to the previously dominant form of social policy, this expressed itself in the cabinet decision of 19 March 1970 about the "codification of a social law code," in which, "on the basis of the social value-decisions of the Basic Law . . . the goal is pursued of making social law comprehensible to the population and simplifying its implementation for the administration" (Brackmann 1987, p. 592). Most of all, however, under the social-liberal coalition, the social-political interest shifted from the policy of social protection to *social planning*. Under the leitmotif of *more quality of life*, the goal was to devise "social infrastructures" and to develop the education, health care, and social systems. Social scientists called this the transition *from an income to a personal social service strategy* in social policy.[231] However, this described only a partial aspect of the new orientation. The real novelty was a revived faith in the ability of states to plan and guide, thanks to Keynesianism and new methods in politics and administration. The state, as a *social or welfare state* (both terms came into fashion in competition) was believed to have greater capacity to shape society than in the preceding period (e.g. Luhmann 1971; Scharpf 1973; Mayntz and Scharpf 1973; Naschold and Väth 1974). Active social policy therefore also meant forward-looking, *preventive social policy.*[232] The assertion to be acting preventively, however, meant at the same time an

[229] It is symptomatic that the new edition of the valuable *Handwörterbuch der Sozialwissenschaften* (Stuttgart, 1956–1965) appeared under the title *Handwörterbuch der Wirtschaftswissenschaft* (Stuttgart, 1977–1983) and strongly curtailed the cross-references to other social sciences.

[230] This was first put into words by Hans Peter Widmaier (1970), see also Zapf (1973), Krupp (1974).

[231] Badura and Gross (1976), Gross and Badura (1977). From an economic perspective see Pfaff (1978b).

[232] See, for example, the special thematic issue "*Präventive Sozialpolitik*": Wirtschafts- und Sozialwissenschaftliches Institut des Deutschen Gewerkschaftsbundes: WSI-Mitteilungen 31, no.10 (October, 1978); Standfest (1979).

uncontrolled increase in the possibilities and risks of intervention (Grimm 1991; Luhmann 1981).

It was this shift in the political horizon of attention that gave a boost to sociological and political science research on social policy, and at the same time prompted economic research on social policy to turn more strongly toward the social sciences.[233] The government, for its part, undertook large research programs such as "Humanization of Working Life"[234] and "Citizen-friendly Configuration of the Social Environment" (Kaufmann 1977a; Kaufmann 1979). The unions sought to revive the self-governance of social insurance.[235] A wide variety of theoretical discussions on "social planning" (Keim and Vascovics 1985), the relationship of (social scientific) theory and (political) practice,[236] and on "Quality of life" (Zapf 1972; Glatzer and Zapf 1984) accompanied the conceptual turnaround. The concept of socio-political intervention was now employed in a more differentiated form to link together dimensions of *Lebenslage* (rights, resources, opportunities, abilities) and the relevant political strategies (Kaufmann 1982a).

Alongside the "constructive" approaches to social policy research there also developed "critical" ones (first von Ferber 1967). Achinger had already pointed out that the unfolding social policy leads to a change in social realities that did not reflect only the original intentions (Achinger 1979, pp. 78–89). This criticism was now elaborated and focused on the four catchwords of *juridification, bureaucratization, economization, and professionalization of social policy*. These four critical terms relate to different aspects of socio-political action, but what they share is that they all address the autonomization of social policy vis-à-vis the social problems, the amelioration or resolution of which legitimizes socio-political measures (Hegner 1979). As already during the Weimar period, the *problem of state-centrism* in social policy once again entered the discussion. While economists were demanding correction through market mechanisms, sociologists opted more for intermediate institutions and the promotion of lay competencies, especially within the framework of self-help groups.[237] However, the scientific discussion soon led to the view that the activation of the potential for self-help and of volunteerism can be seen only as a supplement to, but not a replacement of publicly financed, professional services. Moreover, the criticism of the juridification and

[233] The most important joint initiative by economics and sociologists became the SPES project at the University of Frankfurt and the Special Research Sect. 3 "Microanalytical Foundations of Societal Policy" that grew out of it. It brought a sustained advance especially in social statistics and social reporting in the Federal Republic and promoted the founding of the Section "Social Indicators" in the German Sociological Association. For an introduction see Zapf (1977). A historical account is given by Geyer (2008).

[234] See Böhle (1977), Böhle and Standfest (1981), summary by Kreikebaum and Herbert (1988).

[235] Wirtschafts- und Sozialwissenschaftliches Institut des Deutschen Gewerkschaftsbundes (1977), von Ferber (1977b).

[236] Schäfers 1969, Borner 1975, Wissenschaftszentrum Berlin (1977).

[237] Von Ferber (1976), Badura et al. (1981), as well as other essays in this volume; Becher and Pankoke (1981), Becher (1982), Kaufmann (1987).

bureaucratization of social policy was essentially limited to services focused on individuals; legal regulations remain the necessary scaffolding of every social policy (Mayntz 1979; Kaufmann 1988b).

The 1980s brought advances in the analysis of political processes in the area where sociology and political science overlapped. Research on intervention and implementation (Mayntz 1977, 1980, 1983) gave rise to a guidance-theoretical perspective that became applied also to the subject matter of social policy (Ulrich 1994). For it was here that the *mediation problems between state and society*, already articulated around the middle of the nineteenth century, became especially apparent. The goal was twofold: first, to break open the state's monopolistic position as uniformly behaving actor; second, to move into public awareness, alongside markets and hierarchies, other modes of coordination, such as corporatist, solidaristic, or expertise-based forms of guidance.[238] The program of an active social policy thus provoked a critical reflection about the ability of the political system to act in socio-political terms against the backdrop of the theory of a functional-structural differentiation of society (see Sect. 2.1.2).

5.3.2 The German Social State and the Welfare State

The shift in the horizons of political attention, however, would not have been sufficient all by itself to mobilize a sustained engagement with socio-political questions on the part of the social sciences. The added factor – which gave the social sciences resonance in the first place – was a growing *discontent with social conditions*, which clashed noticeably with the contentment of the fifties. The public debates were no longer dominated by the diagnosis of the equalized middle-class society, but by a renaissance of Marxism-inspired analyses of the existing problems and conflicts, analyses that were confirmed by the student revolts themselves.[239] But like the subsequent debate about "new poverty" and the renewed interest it sparked in poverty research, the social criticism was not restricted to the Marxist left (Geißler 1976; Widmaier 1978; Leibfried and Tennstedt 1985; Leibfried and Voges 1992).

In the Marxist theories, the state – and even more so social policy – played only a subordinated role. Instead, Marxist analysts around 1970 were confronted with the results of a secular economic upswing, which – thanks to the power of the unions and to developments in social policy – had also benefited the workers on a broad front. If one wanted to make the persistence of a latent revolutionary situation plausible, one could not do without a *Marxist theory of the state*. And so many debates revolved around precisely this, although they are of interest here only to the

[238] Centers of these discussions developed at the University of Bielefeld and at the Max-Planck-Institute für Gesellschaftsforschung in Cologne. See Kaufmann (1983, 1991), Kaufmann et al. (1985), Glagow (1987), Leisering (1992a), Mayntz and Scharpf (1995), Mayntz (1997).

[239] See Krüger (1979); less useful, by contrast, Ehling (1982).

extent that they paid central attention to social policy. The point under discussion was the degree of the state's autonomy in capitalism. The verdicts ranged from a "social state illusion," which – it was argued – did not substantially alter the fact of class conflict and the tendencies of capitalism toward crises (Müller and Neusüss 1970), all the way to more subtle arguments, which maintained that the conflict between capital and labor, as a result of the development of the welfare state, was shifting into the area of the conditions of reproduction and the inner workings of the state apparatus. Through its continued intervention to pacify class warfare and to stabilize the economic cycle, the state was increasingly relinquishing its autonomy, and as its budgets tightened and political conflicts intensified, it was itself caught in the maelstrom of antagonistic class interests (Offe 1972; Lenhardt and Offe 1977).

Such diagnoses of crisis took on a certain plausibility through the end of the "brief dream of everlasting prosperity" (Lutz 1984) as a result of the currency and oil crisis at the beginning of the 1970s, as well as the influential report by the Club of Rome on "The Limits to Growth" (Meadows et al. 1972). The "welfare state project" seemed to have reached its limits and to lose its "utopian energy," to which, according to Jürgen Habermas, it owed its legitimacy (Habermas 1973, 1985). Or was the end of the phase of expansion of the welfare state and the loss of the effectiveness of Keynesian policies that became evident with the trend toward growing unemployment after 1975 merely a process of adjustment within a fundamentally stable "welfare capitalism"? (Alber 1980, 1983; Flora 1986/1987).

As we have seen, the public discussion moved away from problems of an incremental social policy in various problem areas and toward a view that encompassed society as a whole. It was no longer this or that socio-political reform that was up for debate, but *the welfare state itself.*[240] It was especially the developments in the labor market, in particular the growing structural unemployment[241] and the demographic trends,[242] which constituted a challenge not only for individual socio-political institutions, but for the entire setup of the welfare state.

Accordingly, during the phase described here, the term "social policy" lost all of its structural significance to the term *Sozialstaat* ["social state"]. At the same time, in the 1980s, socio-political research became differentiated into political fields, and there emerged autonomous research and political networks, for example for the spheres of health care, the labor market, or family policy. However, their subject matter cannot be the topic of this account, which focuses on the construction of the *coherence* of social policy. From the middle of the 1970s, this coherence has been increasingly symbolized by the term "social state," and this linguistic usage was

[240] Pathbreaking for the following discussion was Scharpf (1977). For the results of a research program implementing this perspective at the Max-Planck-Institut für Gesellschaftsforschung (Cologne) see Scharpf and Schmidt (2000).

[241] For various facets of the discussion see the volume edited by Matthes (1983), especially the essays by Ralf Dahrendorf, Claus Offe, Jonathan I. Gershuny, Johannes Berger, Günther Schmid, and Friedhart Hegner.

[242] Fundamental Leisering (1992b); on the basic, social-integrative aspects see Kohli (1989).

stabilized by the international debate about the "welfare state" that has emerged since that time.[243]

As I have noted in the introduction, *Sozialstaat* was initially a term of constitutional law that only slowly gained in importance (Grimm 1983; Benda 1966; Tomandl 1967; Hartwich 1970; Zacher 1968b, 1977). The dominant interpretation today speaks of a *social goal dimension of the state*:

> The most important goals of the 'social state' are: help against misery and poverty and a dignified minimum existence for everyone; greater equality through the dismantling of differences in prosperity and the control of dependency conditions; more security against the 'vicissitudes of life;' and, finally, lifting and spreading prosperity ... The most important premise of 'the social,' however, is this: the juxtaposition of state and society is maintained; the state has no monopoly of the 'social' and no title to unmake society in order to guarantee its 'social' character (Zacher 1987, p. 18f.; 2000, 2012).

Even if this catalog of goals is largely congruent with the tradition of socio-political thinking and action, it would be wrong to speak of a mere formula for legitimizing social policy. Rather, the social goal of the state is one of the criteria for evaluating *all* activities of the state and can develop its specific meaning only within the framework of an interpretation that essentially encompasses all constitutional norms. This also turns the often-invoked opposition of *Rechtsstaat* and *Sozialstaat* into a sham fight:

> *Rechtsstaat* and democracy must see themselves as the medium of the social state process. And the social state as process must see itself within the medium of the permanent, complex tension and decision of individuals and collectives ... It is time to back away from the expectation that constitutional interpretation will produce the social state. Defining the social state is the business of politics (Zacher 1977, pp. 260, 266).

The reception of the concept of the social state into the social scientific discussion was then also oriented less toward arguments based on state law and social law; instead, it followed the international discussion about the "welfare state," and it was in this way, especially, that it took on socio-political connotations in the narrower sense (Talos 1979; Spieker 1986). What became particularly influential in the international context was the thesis formulated by T. H. Marshall in the wake of passage of the Universal Declaration of Human Rights: it spoke of the gradual evolution of the status of the citizen through the development of civic personal rights, the rights of political participation, and rights of social participation (Marshall 1964). Based on Marshall's ideas, Talcott Parsons and Niklas Luhmann coined the concept of "inclusion" to illustrate the characteristic of the responsibility of the social state:

> Every person must have access to all functional circles. Everyone must possess legal capacity, must be able to establish a family, participate in the exercise of political power or at least be able to participate in controlling it; everyone must be taught in schools,

[243] There is little literature that provides an overview over this very multi-layered debate, especially since it is still in full swing. Some beginning attempts: M. G. Schmidt (1998), Lessenich and Ostner (1998), Scharpf and Schmidt (2000, vol. 1).

> provided with medical care if needed, and enabled to participate in economic transactions. The principle of inclusion replaces that form of solidarity that is based on the notion that one belongs to one, and only one, group (Luhmann 1993a, p. 30f.).[244]

This last sentence points to a central presupposition of contemporary social theory: like Hegel before it (see Sect. 2.1.2), it provides evidence for the assumption that a structural autonomization of functional contexts takes place in the wake of modernization, that is, the formation of social subsystems that develop their own "inherent logic," economic, political, scientific, religious, familial and so on (Luhmann 1983). In connection with the simultaneously emerging principle of "formal organization" – this means that individuals receive access to the benefit structures that are vital to them only on the basis of special provisions. Such provisions are especially membership rights and social entitlements.[245]

The English and (derived from it) the international notion of the "welfare state" means essentially the totality of the socio-political institutions of a country, though excluding labor law. Although this notion systematically includes also the public services of education health care, personal social services, and housing, the international discussion restricts itself largely to the area of monetary benefits of social security or social protection. This restriction emerges essentially from the data set, since only here the costs and benefits are grasped in a way that is more or less comparable (OECD 1985; 1996).

Comparative welfare state research brought a crucial impulse into the scientific engagement with social policy in the eighties. It came out of the United States, but soon made its way also into German social science.[246] However, the comparison was usually made without an explicit theoretical concept. What makes a social or welfare state often remains unclear, or only some of its aspects are explicated.[247] The difficulties of an all-encompassing comparison of entire "welfare states" become only gradually apparent, and research has shifted increasingly to a comparison with reference to individual institutional complexes or specific problem areas (Zacher 1991; Alber and Bernardi-Schenkluhn 1992; Schmid 1996a; Reinhard et al. 1998). The by now substantial findings of this research have also led to textbook-like summary accounts (Schmidt 1998; Schmid 1996b).

---

[244] See already Parsons (1971); deepening discussion in Luhmann (1995).

[245] This idea had now been generalized by Rifkin (2000).

[246] See Flora and Heidenheimer 1981, Alber (1982), Flora (1986/1987), Ritter (1991), Lessenich and Ostner (1998), Lessenich (2000), Kaufmann (2013).

[247] As examples of conceptual theoretical work I shall mention: Widmaier (1976), Matzner (1982), Rieger (1992), Prisching (1996), Huf (1998), Nullmeier (2000), Kaufmann (2001), Zacher (2001). – For a questioning of theories of the social state see Kreissl (1987).

5.3.3 Social Policy and the "Crisis of the Welfare State"

Although the crisis metaphor with reference to the social state is derived from Marxist theory, it has now been widely adopted.[248] It should not be overlooked, though, that the development of modern society is "constitutionally" crisis-ridden. A social formation for which continued innovation and the resultant, unforeseen changes are constitutive constantly produces threats to what exists and direction-changing decisions (Koselleck 1959). Although the evolution of the welfare state was almost constantly commented upon critically especially from the economic perspective (Külp and Haas 1977), this criticism did not break through politically until the socialist economic systems had collapsed after 1989 and the competition over where to invest within the European Union intensified as a result of the complete liberalization of the movement of capital within Europe around the same time. While the results of social policy had been judged as overwhelmingly positive in the political public until then, the "excessive" social costs now emerged as a risk to a country's place for doing business. In the case of Germany, the rise in the social share had been caused largely by reunification, which means that the struggle over the allocation of resources that erupted can also be interpreted as a conflict over how to distribute the costs of unification.[249]

This narrowing of social policy to the aspect of allocation makes it easy to construe a *conflict between economic policy and social policy* (e.g. Berthold and Külp 1987). This has the tendency to lead to a new polarization between economists and social scientists, even though the prevailing understanding in both camps is that the foreseeable shifts in the generational structure and the changes in the labor market will give rise to a substantial need for reform in the area of social policy, and that this reform will not be possible without cuts in benefits and services in certain areas.[250] In the German case, observers have addressed especially contributions to social security – which are high by international standards – as non-wage labor costs, and have raised questions about the limits to social security benefits and the need for supplementation.[251] Occasionally, however, the very legitimacy of the social state in its current form is questioned (Necker et al. 1983); Spieker (1986); Habermann (1994).

---

[248] The first with reference to the welfare state was probably O'Connor (1970), quoted in Offe (1972, p. 56); see Strasser (1979), Flora (1979).

[249] Kaufmann (1997a, pp. 14–17); see also the compelling analysis by Czada (1998).

[250] The writings with general or practical reform proposals fill entire shelves. See for example Herder-Dorneich et al. (1984), Zacher (1984), Kleinewefers (1985), Opielka and Ostner (1987), Bermbach et al. (1990), Döring and Hauser (1995), Siebert (1996), Schönig and L'Hoest (1996), Walter-Raymond-Stiftung (1960), Lampert (1997b), Giersch (1997), *Sonderheft 'Sozialstaat.' Jahrbuch für Nationalökonomie und Statistik* 216 (1997), Hauser (1998, 2000).

[251] See Rolf et al. (1988), Vobruba (1990), Nullmeier and Rüb (1993), Riedmüller and Olk (1994), Leisering (1995).

Against the economic recommendation that the current difficulties should be essentially overcome by strengthening market forces, including the area of social security and social services,[252] social scientists preferred the approach of generalizing the problematic of economic and social policy from the perspective of *welfare production* and advocated a *pluralistic* strategy of the selective use of instruments of guidance from public law, the free market, associations, and solidarity, taking into account their specific suitability for solving particular problems.[253]

To adequately investigate the effects of different welfare state arrangements on the living conditions of those concerned, the kind of cross-sectional comparisons at a particular point in time that have long been carried out by the study of social inequality from various theoretical perspectives are not adequate.[254] Social situations can change over the course of a life, and the moral provocation of social inequality becomes particularly evident where gradual, cumulative processes of social discrimination must be expected. The way in which sociopolitical measures work in interrelationship with labor market, household, and network support, that is, the individualized effects of the interplay of institutional arrangements of welfare production and its historical change, become clearest if one examines the course of individual lives (Mayer and Müller 1989; Mayer 1990). This basic idea, too, has given rise to a broad research current.[255]

It might be possible to reverse the irrelevance of the term "social policy" to the discussion of the social state if a sharper distinction were drawn between a *social policy of the first order and a social policy of the second order* (Kaufmann 1998). Social policy of the first order, as the programmatic focus on solutions to social problems, is still at the forefront of how social policy thinks of itself, even though the political debates over social policy have for quite some time revolved in practice around very different issues, for example, consolidating the funding for the statutory pension insurance, or boosting the efficiency in the health care system. The greater the panoply of socio-political measures, the more urgent are the problems of their coordination, efficiency, and financing. Today these problems of the second order pose the greatest practical and scientific challenge.

In the 1990s, talk of the crisis of the social state reached a new dimension with the so-called *globalization debate* (Seeleib-Kaiser 2001; Schwengel 1999). International challenges now joined the risks of the demographic trend and of structural unemployment discussed since the late seventies, and the interconnections

[252] See Engels (1985); more moderate, Molitor (1986). For a critical view of the neoliberal position: Berger and Offe (1982).

[253] Fundamental on the concept of welfare production: Zapf (1981); see also Hegner (1987), Heinze (1986), Kaufmann (1994), Evers and Olk (1996).

[254] A good survey of theory is provided by H.-P. Müller (1992); on the more recent discussion see Berger and Hradil (1990).

[255] The centers of this research are the Max Planck Institut für Bildungsforschung in Berlin and the Collaborative Research Centre 186 "Statuspassagen und Risikolagen im Lebensverlauf" at the University of Bremen; for an example see Leibfried and Leisering (1995).

discovered in the eighties between household production, the change in women's living conditions, and social policy (Mayer et al. 1991; Langan and Ostner 1991; Kulawik 1996; Kaufmann 1997a, pp. 58–62, 69–113), which alone would offer plenty of incendiary material for a scientific and practical debate about the future of the social state in its current form. These challenges have three very distinct dimensions: first, the questions about European unification and the emergence of a European social policy (Leibfried and Pierson 1995; Schmähl and Rische 1997; Streeck 1998; Schulte 1999); second, the questions arising from the emergence of transnational companies that seek to maximize their decisions of where to locate through strategies independent of national considerations; and, third, questions that arise from the growth and increasing interdependence of the financial markets, which are exerting pressures to boost the profitability of companies ("shareholders value"), but also a pull of capital flight from states that have so far looked upon capital as a rich basis for taxation (Kaufmann 1997a, pp. 114–140; Leibfried and Rieger 1997; Manow and Plümper 1998; Rieger 1998).

The globalization debate also revived a classic discourse of social policy, namely the question about the conditions of social solidarity and the integrative function of the social state (Kaufmann 1997b, 2002; Tragl 2000). In addition to weakening nation state integration, globalization is above all expected to intensify the competitive situation also in the area of work (Heinze et al. 1999). So far, empirical studies have not shown an erosion of the acceptance of social state solidarity, at least in Germany (Roller 1992, 1996; Ullrich 2000; Andreß et al. 2001).

The debates are still in full swing and cannot be summarized at this time.[256] Three questions, in particular, are still waiting for clarification within the context of the present discussion:

1. To what extent it is actually true that the magnitude of a country's social services constitute a disadvantage in international competition, and if so, in what way?[257]
2. To what extent is the growing interdependence of states weakening their ability to form an orbit for the formation of social policy measures?[258]
3. Which criteria should be used to assess proposals for a "restructuring of the social state"? Are there scientifically justifiable criteria, or does this restructuring remain a purely political matter?

It must be noted that in these debates, as well, the participating writers rarely depart from the argumentative space of their own discipline. Only a few of the theorems put forth in the debates can be regarded as sufficiently substantiated at this

[256] For overviews see Ritter (1996a), Leibfried (2000).

[257] Against the thesis of a dismantling of national welfare states as a consequence of international competition, it has been argued that national social policy is precisely a condition of the opening of national economies of the global market. See Rieger and Leibfried (2001).

[258] In this respect European integration is proving more influential than globalization. See Scharpf (1999, pp. 111–139).

time (Schmidt 1998, pp. 291–295). If it is true, however, that social policy deals with the *mediation between state and civic society,* or to put it in more modern terms: with the processing of the problems consequent upon a function-oriented structural differentiation of modernizing societies, it cannot be enough to look at matters *either* from the perspective of the state (i.e. legally or in terms of political science), *or* from the perspective of the free market or from a broader concept of provisioning and welfare production (i.e. either economically or sociologically). Instead, the point is precisely to interweave the disciplinary perspectives so as to grasp the hybrid entity of "social policy" or "welfare state" in its characteristic nature. Likewise, it is inadequate to discuss social policy only with regard to its immediate effects on the life conditions and developmental opportunities of individuals. As was demonstrated not least by the conceptual discussions, social policy always has systems-functional aspects alongside personnel-functional ones. Raising these aspects is difficult in a culture fixated on the values of individualist self-development. As a rule, however, individual utilities alone cannot mobilize political majorities. Social policy, including social redistribution policy, is one way in which a polity guarantees its basic solidarity. And it does so for the sake of collective utility such as human capital formation, domestic pacification, or the realization of accepted values. In this, cultural ideals, institutional traditions, and political orientations continue to play a motivating role. And these differ from country to country: in Germany, for example, the concept of justice seems to take on renewed influence in the social scientific and social policy discourse (Leisering 1999, 2004). Not least for that reason, cultural ideals deserve more scientific attention.

6 Concluding Remarks

For reasons of economy, this study, wich spans a period of more than 150 years, had to adhere closely to the conceptual history of '*Sozialpolitik*.' In conclusion, I will briefly point to supplements to this perspective to illustrate where it is situated in reference to the international social scientific discussion.

The fact that Germany, which was economically backward compared to England and France around the middle of the nineteenth century, became the pioneer in socio-political thinking, and to a more limited degree also of state actions in terms of social policy, was due to the continuities of German state and administrative theory. The traditions of the paternalistic princely state persisted in the nineteenth century: "The pronounced Christian understanding of office and service, the expectation toward authority that it would ensure the realization of 'happiness' and 'good order,' the penchant, finally, to reform the administrative apparatus rather than overthrow the state – all this did not really change even in the age of liberalism. If we look at the history of public law, we can see, also after the transition to the nineteenth century, as well, the history of public law revealed the dominance of the administrative theorist over the state theorist, the continuation of *Policeywissenschaften* [science of public policy] as part of legal education, and the combination – so typical for Germany – of state administration and self-governance, federal structures, and a pronounced sense of social responsibility" (Stolleis 2013, p. 59). The thinking about social policy thus arose within the context of a specific state tradition, which, on the one hand, set the sphere of public responsibility broadly, while, on the other hand, when it came to the fulfillment of public tasks, did not rely on centralized structures (as in France, for example), but on decentralized and in part "social" providers. That was precisely the reason why the dialectic of "state" and "society" seemed so very plausible within the German context.

The German tradition of thinking about social policy differs from the Anglo-American tradition in its stronger emphasis on collective functions of social policy, while Anglo-American justifications derive their legitimacy primarily from arguments of individual welfare in the sense of the prevailing utilitarianism (Pinker 1971). George Wilhelm Friedrich Hegel and Lorenz von Stein on the German, and Jeremy Bentham and John Stuart Mill on the British side can be regarded as the representative pioneering thinkers of their respective social policy discourse in the nineteenth century. Moreover, characteristic for the German tradition of social policy is the focus on the *workers' question*, while the *poverty question* was the central issue for British social policy. In Scandinavia, meanwhile, the "passion for equality" (Graubard 1988) dominated the discourse, and in France it was the invocation of "solidarité" (Bode 1999). A more detailed description of the national differences in how societies deal with the social repercussions of liberalization and industrialization would have to start from the divergent conceptions of state and society.[259]

The term *Sozialpolitik* not only has the advantage of holding a central place in the German discourses on the "social question" and related themes during nearly the entire period under discussion. It has also more or less retained its original function of addressing social scientific problem diagnoses and political measures in an overarching "socio-political" context, and it has reemerged precisely in this function within the context of the more recent discussions about the crisis of the social state. Still, there is no denying that the concept of "social policy" was not adequate for providing an exhaustive account of the 'socio-political' problem area. The relationships between "state" and "society," or in more modern terms: between the "political system" and the other social subsectors are, of course, much more varied than their portrayal from the perspective of social policy. Especially over the last few decades, the sphere of domestic politics has become enormously differentiated – one need recall only environmental, research, and technology policy. Moreover, the boundaries between domestic and foreign policies have flattened out. Political fields have also emerged within the sphere of social policy: for example, people currently speak more often of labor market policy, family and youth policy, health policy, and pension policy than of social policy. These areas are also being increasingly put on their own scientific foundations. This has blurred

[259] See Kaufmann (2013, German Social Policy, vol. 5), especially the sections on "State and Society" of the country studies.

the unifying conceptual bracket of social policy, which is probably one of the chief reasons why the semantic of the social state or welfare state has recently all but displaced that of "social policy."

The terms "*sozialer Staat*" (first in Lorenz von Stein) and "*Wohlfahrtsstaat*" (first in Adolph Wagner) arose within the context of the German tradition presented here, and they embarked upon their international conceptual career only after the Second World War in the form of the "welfare state," a term that came out of Great Britain. This development was triggered by the programmatic goal of a society "free of fear and want," which the American President F. D. Roosevelt and the British Prime Minister Winston Churchill, in the face of the military successes of the Axis powers, proclaimed as the guiding model of a post-war order in the so-called Atlantic Charter on 14 August 1941. A fairly straight line leads from the Atlantic Charter to the General Declaration of Human and Civic Rights by the United Nations (1948), which for the first time placed "economic, social, and cultural rights" (Articles 22–27) alongside the classic civic rights and freedoms (Kaufmann 2012, ch. 5). This created the international model of a polity that granted also social rights, a model that subsequently merged with the international concept of the welfare state. In Germany, however, the term *Wohlfahrtsstaat* was given a largely polemical reception and linked to the idea of state-centered system of protection and provision, of the kind that existed in Great Britain and Scandinavia, while the German system of independent social insurances structured according to occupational groups was associated with the model of the "social state" or the "social market economy." An international social-scientific comparison, however, depicts "social state" and "social market economy" as the German variant of "welfare state semantics" (Lessenich 2003).

It is important, though, to draw a more precise distinction: in the Anglo-American world, "welfare state" describes "the *institutional outcome* of the assumption by a society of legal and therefore formal and explicit responsibility for the basic well-being of all of its members."[260] Thus, in contrast to the German "social state," "welfare state" does not refer to a characteristic of the concept of the state or a goal of the state, but to the institutional realization of the state goal in the form of various "social services." This has to do with the substantially weaker concept of the state in the Anglo-American tradition compared to its continental European counterpart (Dyson 1980). In the German tradition, "social policy" always addressed the state itself as the origin of "social policy," and since the social-scientific tradition of the Bismarck period, in particular, social scientists have shown a penchant to project themselves into the position of the state as a uniform actor responsible for national cohesion and try to do the thinking for the state which is considered a unitary actor. To be sure, with the advance of systems-theoretical notions of society, this monolithic understanding of the state is dissolving. However, the concept of the state remains the underpinning of the self-description of the political system in the German

[260] Girvetz (1968, p. 512), emphasis mine.

self-understanding, while a self-description oriented more strongly toward the democratic process dominates the Anglo-American world. However, while the welfare institutions (more analytically: the "welfare sector") in the British and Scandinavian system are largely under state administration and are financed by tax revenues, whereas in the German case they are largely administrated by formally independent bodies of public law (e.g. social insurance funds) and are financed mainly by insurance contributions, the semantic difference between "welfare state" and "social state" becomes plausible also from this perspective: in the international concept of "welfare state," "state" refers to the institutions which are designed to provide "welfare," whereas the German concept of the "social state" refers primarily to governmental responsibility for "the social" on the constitutional level.

These observations remain still semantic and thus oriented toward the topic of this study. At the same time however they open a window onto the broader perspective of the institutional interconnections, which could not be the subject of this analysis. Social state and social policy imply cultural orientations that legitimate the equal dignity of all humans and thus accord them the same fundamental rights. These cultural orientations have old roots in Judaism, antiquity, and Christianity, but they attained their political form only in the wake of the Enlightenment and with the help of various social movements. But the political form of the state that guarantees rights of liberty and rights of participation acquires its social quality only on the basis of an efficient economic system. The greatest possible synergy of economic and social policy is therefore the prerequisite for the success of the policies of the welfare state. Exploring the conditions of such synergies would be one task of a theory of the welfare state. The fact that social policy has today been put on the defensive in Germany must be understood as the result of a decline of this synergy.

References*

Abelshauser W (1957) Die Weimarer Republik – Ein Wohlfahrtsstaat? In: Abelshauser W (ed) Die Weimarer Republik als Wohlfahrtsstaat. Stuttgart, pp 9–31

Abelshauser W (1991) Die ordnungspolitische Epochenbedeutung der Weltwirtschaftskrise in Deutschland: Ein Beitrag zur Entstehungsgeschichte der sozialen Marktwirtschaft. In: Petzina D (ed) Ordnungspolitische Weichenstellungen nach dem Zweiten Weltkrieg. Berlin, pp 11–29

---

* Note on changes in the name of the Federal Ministry of Labour in the Federal Republic of Germany: The *Bundesministerium für Arbeit und Sozialordnung* (Federal Ministry of Labour and Social Order) was split into the *Bundesministerium für Gesundheit und soziale Sicherung* (Federal Ministry of Health and Social Security) and a section of the *Bundesministerium für Wirtschaft und Arbeit* (Federal Ministry of the Economy and Labour) in October 2002, to be merged again in November 2005 under the name *Bundesministerium für Arbeit und Soziales* (Federal Ministry of Labour and Social Affairs).

Abromeit H, Blanke B (eds) (1987) Arbeitsmarkt, Arbeitsbeziehungen und Politik in den 80er Jahren. Leviathan special issue no. 8

Acham K (1994) Der 'Kollektivismus' als Problem der Soziologie im deutschen Sprach-Kulturraum. In: Nörr KW, Schefold B, Tenbruck F (eds) Geisteswissenschaften zwischen Kaiserreich und Republik. Zur Entwicklung von Nationalökonomie, Rechtswissenschaft und Sozialwissenschaft im 20. Jahrhundert. Stuttgart, pp 317–334

Achinger H (1939) Sozialpolitik und Fürsorge. Ein Abgrenzungsversuch, begründet aus den Ursachen der Notstände. Berlin

Achinger H (1966) Soziologie und Sozialreform. In: Soziologie und moderne Gesellschaft. Verhandlungen des vierzehnten Deutschen Soziologentages vom 20. bis 24. Mai 1959 in Berlin, 2nd edn. Stuttgart, pp 39–52

Achinger H (1979 [first published 1958]) Sozialpolitik als Gesellschaftspolitik. Von der Arbeiterfrage zum Wohlfahrtsstaat, 3rd edn. Frankfurt am Main

Achinger H et al (eds) (1955) Neuordnung der sozialen Leistungen. Köln

Achinger H, Preller L, Wallraff HJ (eds) (1965) Normen der Gesellschaft. Festgabe für Oswald von Nell-Breuning SJ zu seinem 75. Geburtstag. Mannheim

Adler M (1927) Über den Begriff der Sozialpolitik. Der Kampf 20:379–386

Adorno TW et al (1972) Der Positivismusstreit in der deutschen Soziologie, 2nd edn. Neuwied

Alber J (1980) Der Wohlfahrtsstaat in der Krise? Zeitschrift für Soziologie 9:313–342

Alber J (1982) Vom Armenhaus zum Wohlfahrtsstaat. Frankfurt am Main New York

Alber J (1983) Der Sozialstaat in der Bundesrepublik 1950–1983. Frankfurt am Main New York

Alber J, Bernardi-Schenkluhn B (1992) Westeuropäische Gesundheitssysteme im Vergleich. Frankfurt am Main New York

Albrecht G (1928) Wandlungen in Wesen und Aufgaben der Sozialpolitik. Jahrbücher für Nationalökonomie und Statistik 128/I:181–206

Albrecht G (1930) Sozialpolitik gestern und heute. Soziale Praxis 39:886–889

Albrecht G (1955) Sozialpolitik. Göttingen

Albrecht G (1959) Bemerkungen zu einer neuen Theorie der Sozialpolitik. Jahrbücher für Nationalökonomie und Statistik 171:352–371

Albrecht S (1983) Hermann Hellers Staats- und Demokratieauffassung. Frankfurt am Main New York

Albrecht G, Arndt H (eds) (1948) Verhandlungen auf der Tagung der Volks- und Betriebswirte in Marburg/Lahn, 15. und 16. September 1948. Berlin München

Althaus H (1939) Nationalsozialistische Volkswohlfahrt. Wesen, Aufgaben und Aufbau, 4th edn. Berlin

Amonn A (1924) Der Begriff der 'Sozialpolitik'. Schmollers Jahrbuch für Wirtschafts.- und Sozialwissenschaften 48:159–199

Amonn A (1926) Sozialpolitik als Wissenschaft. Schmollers Jahrbuch für Wirtschafts- und Sozialwissenschaften 50 I:417–458

Amonn A (1927) Objekt und Grundbegriffe der Theoretischen Nationalökonomie, 2nd edn. Leipzig Wien

Andreß J, Heien T, Hofäcker D (2001) Wozu brauchen wir noch den Sozialstaat? Der deutsche Sozialstaat im Urteil seiner Bürger. Wiesbaden

Auerbach W (1955) Mut zur sozialen Sicherheit. Köln

Auerbach W (1968) Zusammenhänge, Illusion und Wirklichkeit der sozialen Sicherheit. Frankfurt am Main

Bäcker G et al (2000) Sozialpolitik und soziale Lage in der Bundesrepublik Deutschland, 3rd edn, 2 vols. Köln

Backhaus J (1994) Wirtschaftsverfassung und ordnungspolitische Grundvorstellungen im nationalökonomischen Denken der zwanziger Jahre. In: Nörr KW, Schefold B, Tenbruck F (eds) Geisteswissenschaften zwischen Kaiserreich und Republik. Zur Entwicklung von Nationalökonomie, Rechtswissenschaft und Sozialwissenschaft im 20. Jahrhundert. Stuttgart, pp 403–421

Badura B, von Ferber C (eds) (1981) Selbsthilfe und Selbstorganisation im Gesundheitswesen. München Wien

Badura B, Gross P (1976) Sozialpolitische Perspektiven. Eine Einführung in Grundlagen und Probleme sozialer Dienstleistungen. München

Badura B et al (1981) Einleitung: Sozialpolitische Perspektiven. In: Badura B, von Ferber C (eds) Selbsthilfe und Selbstorganisation im Gesundheitswesen. München Wien, pp 1–38

Bartmann H (1981) Verteilungstheorie. München

Bauer C (1931) Wandlungen der sozialpolitischen Ideenwelt im deutschen Katholizismus des 19. Jahrhunderts. In: Görres-Gesellschaft zur Pflege der Wissenschaft im katholischen Deutschland, Veröffentlichungen der Sektion für Wirtschafts- und Sozialwissenschaft, 2, pp 11–46

Bauer C (1974) Georg von Hertling als Sozialpolitiker und Sozialethiker. In: Carlen L, Steinberger F (eds) Festschrift für Nikolaus Grass zum 60. Geburtstag. Innsbruck München, pp 187–203

Bauer-Mengelberg K (1925) Thema 'Soziologie und Sozialpolitik'. Soziale Praxis 34:701–704

Becher B (1982) Gesellschaftlicher Wandel und neue Funktionsbedingungen kommunaler Sozialpolitik. Sociologia Internationalis 20:87–115

Becher P (1965) Vergleich und Kritik der sozialpolitischen Auffassungen von Lujo Brentano, Adolph Wagner, Georg von Hertling und Franz Hitze. Dissertation. München

Becher B, Pankoke E (1981) Sozialadministration und selbstaktive Felder. Archiv für Wissenschaft und Praxis der sozialen Arbeit 12:219–239

Beck U (1974) Objektivität und Normativität. Die Theorie-Praxis-Debatte in der modernen deutschen und amerikanischen Soziologie. Reinbek bei Hamburg

Becker HP (1965) Die soziale Frage im Neoliberalismus – Analyse und Kritik. Löwen

Becker U et al (2007) Alterssicherung in Deutschland. Festschrift für Franz Ruland zum 65. Geburtstag. Baden-Baden

Behrens J, Leibfried S (1987) Sozialpolitische Forschung – Eine Übersicht zu universitären und universitätsnahen Arbeiten. Zeitschrift für Sozialreform 33:1–19

Benda E (1966) Industrielle Herrschaft und sozialer Staat. Wirtschaftsmacht von Großunternehmen als gesellschaftspolitisches Problem. Göttingen

Berger J, Offe C (1982) Die Zukunft des Arbeitsmarktes. Zur Ergänzungsbedürftigkeit eines versagenden Allokationsprinzips. In: Schmidt G et al (eds) Materialien zur Industriesoziologie. Kölner Zeitschrift für Soziologie und Sozialpsychologie, special issue no. 24:348–371

Berger PA, Hradil S (eds) (1990) Lebenslagen, Lebensläufe, Lebensstile. Soziale Welt. Special issue no. 7. Göttingen

Berlin W (ed) (1977) Interaktion von Wissenschaft und Politik. Theoretische und praktische Probleme der anwendungsorientierten Sozialwissenschaften. Frankfurt am Main New York

Bermbach U, Blanke B, Böhret C (eds) (1990) Spaltungen der Gesellschaft und die Zukunft des Sozialstaates. Opladen

Bernhard L (1912) Unerwünschte Folgen der deutschen Sozialpolitik. Berlin

Bernstein E (1890) Die Voraussetzungen des Sozialismus und die Aufgaben der Sozialdemokratie. Repr.1973. Berlin

Berthold N, Külp B (1987) Rückwirkungen ausgewählter Systeme der Sozialen Sicherung auf die Funktionsfähigkeit der Marktwirtschaft. Berlin

Blanke S (2005) Soziales Recht oder kollektive Privatautonomie? Hugo Sinzheimer im Kontext nach 1900. Tübingen

Blasius D (1971) Lorenz von Steins Lehre vom Königtum der sozialen Reform und ihre verfassungspolitischen Grundlagen. Der Staat 10:33–51

Blau J (1980) Sozialdemokratische Staatslehre in der Weimarer Republik. Darstellung und Untersuchung der staatstheoretischen Konzeptionen von Hermann Heller, Ernst Fraenkel, Otto Kirchheimer. Marburg

Bloch K (1932) Über den Standort der Sozialpolitik. Dissertation. München

Blum R (1969) Soziale Marktwirtschaft – Wirtschaftspolitik zwischen Neoliberalismus und Ordoliberalismus. Tübingen

Blüm N, Zacher HF (eds) (1989) Vierzig Jahre Sozialstaat Bundesrepublik Deutschland. Baden-Baden
Böckenförde E-W (1976a [first published 1963]) Lorenz von Stein als Theoretiker der Bewegung von Staat und Gesellschaft zum Sozialstaat. In: Böckenförde EW (ed) Staat, Gesellschaft, Freiheit. Studien zur Staatstheorie und zum Verfassungsrecht. Frankfurt am Main, pp 146–184
Böckenförde E-W (1976b) Die politische Funktion wirtschaftlich-sozialer Verbände und Interessenträger in der sozialstaatlichen Demokratie. Ein Beitrag zum Problem der 'Regierbarkeit'. Der Staat 15:457–483
Bode I (1999) Solidarität im Vorsorgestaat. Der französische Weg sozialer Sicherung und Gesundheitsversorgung. Frankfurt am Main New York
Boese F (1939) Geschichte des Vereins für Sozialpolitik 1872–1932. Berlin
Boettcher E (ed) (1957) Sozialpolitik und Sozialreform. Tübingen
Bogs W (1955) Grundfragen des Rechts der sozialen Sicherheit und seiner Reform. Berlin
Bogs W (1981) Die Sozialversicherung in der Weimarer Demokratie. Supplement 2 der Vierteljahresschrift für Sozialrecht. München
Böhle F (1977) Humanisierung der Arbeit und Sozialpolitik. In: Von Ferber C, Kaufmann F-X (eds) Soziologie und Sozialpolitik. Kölner Zeitschrift für Soziologie und Sozialpsychologie, special issue no. 19:290–324
Böhle F, Standfest E (1981) Einleitung zu: Detlef Perner und Gerhard Bäcker: Sozialpolitik und Produktionsprozeß. Beiträge praxisorientierter Forschung für eine präventive, arbeitsprozess-bezogene Sozialpolitik. Köln, pp 1–14
Bohnstedt W (1934) Sozialpolitik im neuen Reich. Soziale Praxis 43:1–7
Bonz H-J (1991) Für Staatsfeinde keine Rente. Das Ruhen der Renten bei staatsfeindlicher Betätigung im nationalsozialistischen Deutschland. Zeitschrift für Sozialreform 37:517–531
Borchert J (1994) Prolegomena zu einer familienpolitischen Strukturreform des Sozialstaates. Zeitschrift für Sozialreform 40:440–462
Born KE (1957) Staat und Sozialpolitik seit Bismarcks Sturz. Wiesbaden
Born KE (1959) Sozialpolitische Probleme und Bestrebungen in Deutschland von 1848 bis zur Bismarckschen Sozialgesetzgebung. Vierteljahresschrift für Sozial- und Wirtschaftsgeschichte 46:29–44
Born KE (1966) Zur Verwendung des Begriffes 'Sozialpolitik'. In: Quellensammlung zur Geschichte der deutschen Sozialpolitik 1867 bis 1914. Einführungsband. Wiesbaden, pp 11–14
Borner S (1975) Wissenschaftliche Ökonomik und politische Aktion. Bern Stuttgart
Brackmann K (1987) Das Sozialgesetzbuch: die Arbeiten der Sachverständigenkommission und die Vorstellungen für eine Fortsetzung der Kodifikation. Zeitschrift für Sozialreform 33:592–600
Brandt K (1993) Geschichte der deutschen Volkswirtschaftslehre. Vol. 2: Vom Historismus bis zur Neoklassik. Freiburg im Breisgau
Brauer T (1931) Sozialpolitik und Sozialreform. Jena
Braun H (1978) Das Streben nach 'Sicherheit' in den 50er Jahren. Archiv für Sozialgeschichte 18:279–306
Braun H (1892) Unser Programm. Sozialpolitisches Centralblatt 1:1f
Bredendiek W (1953) Christliche Sozialreformer des 19. Jahrhunderts. Leipzig
Bremme G (1961) Freiheit und soziale Sicherheit. Motive und Prinzipien sozialer Sicherung, dargestellt an England und Frankreich. Stuttgart
Brentano L (1923 [first published 1897]) Zum Jubiläum des Vereins für Sozialpolitik. In: Schriften des Vereins für Sozialpolitik, vol 163. München Leipzig, pp 1–22
Briefs G (1923) Zur Krisis in der Sozialpolitik. Kölner Sozialpolitische Vierteljahresschrift 3:1–16
Briefs G (1925) Die wirtschafts- und sozialpolitischen Ideen des Katholizismus. In: Bonn MJ, Palyi M (eds) Die Wirtschaftswissenschaft nach dem Kriege. Festgabe für Lujo Brentano zum 80. Geburtstag, vol 1. München Leipzig, pp 195–226
Briefs G (1929) Rezension von Eduard Heimann: Soziale Theorie des Kapitalismus – Theorie der Sozialpolitik. Soziale Praxis 38:columns 1041–1049

Briefs G (1930a) Der wirtschaftliche Wert der Sozialpolitik. Schriften der Gesellschaft für soziale Reform. Issue no. 83. Jena

Briefs G (ed) (1930b) Probleme der sozialen Betriebspolitik. Berlin

Briefs G (1931) Der wirtschaftliche Wert der Sozialpolitik – Eine Sammelschrift. Schriften der Gesellschaft für soziale Reform. Issue no. 84/85. Jena

Briefs G (1952) Zwischen Kapitalismus und Syndikalismus. Die Gewerkschaften am Scheidewege. München

Brockhaus-Enzyklopädie (diverse Titel): 10th edn, 15 vols. (1851–1855); 11th edn, 15 vols. (1864–1868); 12th edn, 15 vols. (1875–1879) ; 13th edn, 16 vols. (1882–1887); 14th edn, 16 vols. (1892–1895). Leipzig

Brück GW (1981) Allgemeine Sozialpolitik: Grundlagen – Leistungen -Zusammenhänge, 2nd edn. Köln

Brüll A (1897) Socialpolitik. In: Staatslexikon, 1st edn, vol 5. Columns 140–151

Bundesministerium für Arbeit und Soziales, Bundesarchiv (eds) (2001–2008) Geschichte der Sozialpolitik in Deutschland seit 1945, vols 1–11. Baden-Baden. (See footnote on p. 125).

Bundesministerium für Arbeit und Sozialordnung (ed) (1962–1977) Übersicht über die soziale Sicherung. Bonn. Since (1994) Übersicht über das Sozialrecht. Bonn

Bundesministerium für Arbeit und Sozialordnung (ed) (1994–2000) Übersicht über das Arbeitsrecht. Bonn

Burghardt A (1979 [first published 1966]) Lehrbuch der allgemeinen Sozialpolitik. Berlin. New Edition under the title: Kompendium der Sozialpolitik. Berlin

Cahnman WJ, Schmitt CM (1979) The concept of social policy (Sozialpolitik). Journal of Social Policy 8:47–59

Castel R (2000 [französisch 1995]) Metamorphosen der sozialen Frage. Eine Chronik der Lohnarbeit. Konstanz

Cathrein V (1899) Sociale Frage. In: Wetzer und Welte's Kirchenlexikon, 2nd edn. Freiburg im Breisgau: columns 431–465

Christmann A, Hesselbach W, Jahn M (eds) (1974) Sozialpolitik – Ziele und Wege. Köln

Clemens W (1994) 'Lebenslage' als Konzept sozialer Ungleichheit – Zur Thematisierung sozialer Differenzierung in Soziologie, Sozialpolitik und Sozialarbeit. Zeitschrift für Sozialreform 40:141–165

Conrad E (1906) Der Verein für Sozialpolitik und seine Wirksamkeit auf dem Gebiet der gewerblichen Arbeiterfrage. Jena

Contzen H (1877) Geschichte der socialen Frage von den ältesten Zeiten bis zur Gegenwart. Berlin

Czada R (1998) Vereinigungskrise und Standortdebatte: Der Beitrag der Wiedervereinigung zur Krise des westdeutschen Modells. Leviathan 26:24–59

Dahrendorf R (1965) Das Mitbestimmungsproblem in der deutschen Sozialforschung. Eine Kritik. München

Dahrendorf R (1979) Lebenschancen: Aufsätze zur sozialen und politischen Theorie. Frankfurt am Main

Dipper C (1992) Sozialreform – Geschichte eines umstrittenen Begriffs. Archiv für Sozialgeschichte 32:323–351

Donzelot J (1984) L'invention du social. Essai sur le déclin des passions politiques. Paris

Döring D, Hauser R (eds) (1995) Soziale Sicherheit in Gefahr. Zur Zukunft der Sozialpolitik. Frankfurt am Main

Dürig G (1953) Verfassung und Verwaltung im Wohlfahrtsstaat. Juristenzeitung 8:193–199

Dyson K (1980) The state tradition in Western Europe. Oxford

Ehling M (1982) Theoretische Ansätze in der Sozialpolitik. Untersuchungen zum geschichtlichen und aktuellen Einfluß der Soziologie auf die Sozialpolitik. Frankfurt am Main

Eickhoff AF (1932) Georg von Hertling als Sozialpolitiker. Köln

Engelhardt WW (1991) Einleitung in eine 'Entwicklungstheorie' der Sozialpolitik. Institutionelle und Lebenslage-Analysen als Grundlagen der Sozialpolitik und Sozialpolitiklehre. In: Thiemeyer T (ed) Theoretische Grundlagen der Sozialpolitik II. Berlin, pp 9–122

Engels W (1985) Über Freiheit. Gleichheit und Brüderlichkeit. Bad Homburg
Erdmann G (1957) Die Entwicklung der deutschen Sozialgesetzgebung, 2nd edn. Berlin Frankfurt am Main
Eucken W (1949) Die soziale Frage. In: Salin E (ed) Synopsis. Festschrift für Alfred Weber. Heidelberg, pp 113–131
Eucken W (1950 [first published 1940]) Die Grundlagen der Nationalökonomie, 6th edn. Berlin
Eucken W (1952) Grundsätze der Wirtschaftspolitik. Bern Tübingen
Evers A, Olk T (1996) Wohlfahrtspluralismus. Vom Wohlfahrtsstaat zur Wohlfahrtsgesellschaft. Opladen
Feldman GD (1984) Vom Weltkrieg zur Weltwirtschaftskrise. Göttingen
Feldman GD, Steinisch I (1978) Die Weimarer Republik zwischen Sozial- und Wirtschaftsstaat – Die Entscheidung gegen den Achtstundentag. Archiv für Sozialgeschichte 18:353–439
Feldman GD, Steinisch I (1980) Notwendigkeit und Grenzen sozialstaatlicher Intervention. Eine vergleichende Fallstudie des Ruhreisenstreits in Deutschland und des Generalstreiks in England. Archiv für Sozialgeschichte 20:57–117
Flora P (1979) Krisenbewältigung oder Krisenerzeugung? Der Wohlfahrtsstaat in historischer Perspektive. In: Matthes J (ed) Sozialer Wandel in Westeuropa. Frankfurt am Main New York, pp 92–136
Flora P (ed) (1986/1987) Growth to limits. The Western European welfare states since World War II, vols 1,2,4. Berlin New York
Flora P, Heidenheimer A (eds) (1981) The development of welfare states in Europe and America. New Brunswick London
Forsthoff E (ed) (1968) Rechtsstaatlichkeit und Sozialstaatlichkeit. Darmstadt
Fraenkel E (1972) Rätemythos und soziale Selbstbestimmung. Ein Beitrag zur Verfassungsgeschichte der deutschen Revolution. In: Saladin P, Wildhaber L (eds) Der Staat als Aufgabe. Gedenkschrift für Max Imboden. Basel Stuttgart, pp 75–114
Fraenkel E (1973 [first published 1958]) Hugo Sinzheimer. In: Fraenkel E (ed) Reformismus und Pluralismus. Materialien zu einer ungeschriebenen politischen Autobiographie. Zusammengestellt von Falk Esche und Frank Grube. Hamburg, pp 131–142
Frerich J (1996) Sozialpolitik. Das Sozialleistungssystem der Bundesrepublik Deutschland, 3rd edn. München Wien
Frerich J, Frey M (1996) Handbuch der Geschichte der Sozialpolitik in Deutschland, 2nd edn, 3 vols. München
Frese M (1993) Sozial- und Arbeitspolitik im "Dritten Reich". Ein Literaturbericht. Neue politische Literatur 38:403–446
Fröbel J (1848) Monarchie oder Republik. Aus der Deutschen Volkszeitung besonders abgedruckt. Mannheim
Fröbel J (1850) System der socialen Politik. Leipzig
Fröbel J (1975 [first published 1847]) System der socialen Politik. Mannheim. Reprint. Aalen
Gadamer H-G (1971) Die Begriffsgeschichte und die Sprache der Philosophie. Opladen
Geck LHA (1931) Staatliche Sozialpolitik – Gesellschaftspolitik – Betriebliche Sozialpolitik. Soziale Praxis 40:46–51, 82–87
Geck LHA (1950) Sozialpolitische Aufgaben. Tübingen
Geck LHA (1952/1953) Sozialpolitik eine Wirtschaftswissenschaft? Soziale Welt 4:23–37
Geck LHA (1961) Das Aufkommen des Wortes 'sozial' im Deutschen. Die Muttersprache. Zeitschrift zur Pflege und Erforschung der deutschen Sprache, Jahrgang 1961: 294–308
Geck LHA (1963) Über das Eindringen des Wortes "sozial" in die deutsche Sprache. Göttingen
Gehrig H (1909) Die sozialpolitischen Anschauungen der deutschen Freihandelsschule. Jena
Gehrig H (1914) Die Begründung des Prinzips der Sozialreform. Eine literar-historische Untersuchung über Manchestertum und Kathedersozialismus. Jena
Geißler H (1976) Die Neue soziale Frage. Freiburg im Breisgau
Gerhardt J (1930) Liberalismus und Wirtschaftsdemokratie. Berlin
Gerhardt J (1939) Deutsche Arbeits- und Sozialpolitik. Berlin

Geyer MH (ed.) (2008) Bundesrepublik Deutschland 1974–1982. Der 'vermessene' Sozialstat (Geschichte der Sozialpolitik in Deutschland seit 1945, vol. 6, edited by Bundesministerium für Arbeit und Soziales, Bundesarchiv. Baden-Baden. (See footnote on p. 125).

Giersch H (ed) (1997) Reforming the welfare state. Berlin

Girvetz HK (1968) Welfare state. In: Sills DL (ed) International encyclopedia of the social sciences, vol 16, pp 512–521

Gladen A (1974) Geschichte der Sozialpolitik in Deutschland. Wiesbaden

Glagow M (ed) (1987) Dezentrale Gesellschaftssteuerung. Probleme der Integration polyzentrischer Gesellschaft. Pfaffenweiler

Glatzer W, Zapf W (eds) (1984) Lebensqualität in der Bundesrepublik Deutschland. Objektive Lebensbedingungen und subjektives Wohlbefinden. Frankfurt am Main New York

Goldscheid R (1908) Entwicklungswerttheorie, Entwicklungsökonomie. Menschenökonomie. Leipzig

Goldscheid R (1911) Höherentwicklung und Menschenökonomie. Grundlegung der Sozialbiologie. Leipzig

Gorges I (1980) Sozialforschung in Deutschland 1872 bis 1914. Königstein im Taunus

Graubard SR (ed) (1988) Die Leidenschaft für Gleichheit und Gerechtigkeit. Essays über den nordischen Wohlfahrtsstaat. Baden-Baden

Grewe W (1951) Der Begriff des 'sozialen Staates' in der deutschen Verfassungsentwicklung. Der Arbeitgeber 2:39–42

Grimm D (1983) Die sozialgeschichtliche und verfassungsrechtliche Entwicklung zum Sozialstaat. In: Koslowski P, Kreuzer P, Löw R (eds) Chancen und Grenzen des Sozialstaats: Staatstheorie – Politische Ökonomie – Politik. Tübingen, pp 41–65

Grimm D (1991) Verfassungsrechtliche Anmerkungen zum Thema Prävention. In: Grimm D (ed) Die Zukunft der Verfassung. Frankfurt am Main, pp 197–220

Grimmer-Solem E (2003) The rise of historical economics and social reform in Germany, 1864–1894. Oxford

Gross P, Badura B (1977) Sozialpolitik und soziale Dienste: Entwurf einer Theorie personenbezogener Dienstleistungen. In: Von Ferber C, Kaufmann F-X (eds) Soziologie und Sozialpolitik. Kölner Zeitschrift für Soziologie und Sozialpsychologie, special issue no. 19:361–385

Große Kracht H-J (ed) (2006) Joseph Höffner (1906–1987) Soziallehre und Sozialpolitik. Paderborn

Grosser D et al (1988) Soziale Marktwirtschaft: Geschichte – Konzept – Leistung. Stuttgart

Grün K (1845) Die soziale Bewegung in Frankreich und Belgien. Reprint 1974. Hildesheim

Grüske K-D et al (1991) Adolph Wagners "Grundlegung der politischen Ökonomie" Vademecum zu einem Klassiker der Finanzwissenschaft. Düsseldorf

Guillebaud CW (1941) The social policy of Nazi Germany. Cambridge

Günther A (1922) Sozialpolitik. First Part: Theorie der Sozialpolitik. Berlin Leipzig

Günther E (1930) Sozialpolitik. Berlin Wien

Günther A, Heyde L (1924) Soziologie und Sozialpolitik. In: Verhandlungen des Vierten Deutschen Soziologentages am 29. und 30. September 1924 in Heidelberg. New edition 1969. Frankfurt am Main, pp 8–117

Gurvitch G (1972 [first published 1932]) L'idée du droit social. New edition. Aalen

Gutowski A, Merklein R (1985) Arbeit und Soziales im Rahmen einer marktwirtschaftlichen Ordnung. Hamburger Jahrbuch für Wirtschafts- und Gesellschaftspolitik 30:49–67

Habermann G (1994) Der Wohlfahrtsstaat – Die Geschichte eines Irrwegs. Frankfurt am Main Berlin

Habermas J (1973) Legitimationsprobleme im Spätkapitalismus. Frankfurt am Main

Habermas J (1985) Die Krise des Wohlfahrtsstaates und die Erschöpfung utopischer Energien. In: Habermas J (ed) Die neue Unübersichtlichkeit. Frankfurt am Main, pp 141–163

Hammerschmidt P (1999) Die Wohlfahrtsverbände im NS-Staat. Die NSV und die konfessionellen Verbände Caritas und Innere Mission im Gefüge der Wohlfahrtspflege des Nationalsozialismus. Opladen

Handwörterbuch der Sozialwissenschaften (1956–1965) 12 vols. Stuttgart. New edition under the title: Handwörterbuch der Wirtschaftswissenschaft, 1977–1983. Stuttgart

Handwörterbuch der Staatswissenschaften (1898–1929) 2nd edn, 7 vols. (1898–1907); 3rd edn, 8 vols. (1909–1911); 4th edn, 8 vols. (1923–1929). Jena

Harnisch H (1994) Gustav von Schmoller und der gesellschaftliche Wandel seiner Zeit. In: Kocka J et al (eds) Von der Arbeiterbewegung zum modernen Sozialstaat. Festschrift für Gerhard A. Ritter. München, pp 560–581

Hartwich H-H (1967) Arbeitsmarkt, Verbände und Staat 1918–1933. Berlin

Hartwich H-H (1970) Sozialstaatspostulat und gesellschaftlicher status quo. Köln Opladen

Hartwich H-H (ed) (1983) Gesellschaftliche Probleme als Anstoß und Folge von Politik. Wissenschaftlicher Kongreß der Deutschen Vereinigung für politische Wissenschaft (DVPW) 4.-7. Oktober 1982 in der Freien Universität Berlin. Opladen

Häuser K (1994) Das Ende der historischen Schule und die Ambiguität der deutschen Nationalökonomie in den Zwanziger Jahren. In: Nörr KW, Schefold B, Tenbruck F (eds) Geisteswissenschaften zwischen Kaiserreich und Republik. Zur Entwicklung von Nationalökonomie, Rechtswissenschaft und Sozialwissenschaft im 20. Jahrhundert. Stuttgart, pp 47–74

Hauser R (ed) (1998) Reform des Sozialstaats, 2 vols. Berlin

Hauser R (ed) (2000) Die Zukunft des Sozialstaats. Berlin

Hebeisen MW (1995) Souveränität in Frage gestellt. Die Souveränitätslehren von Hans Kelsen, Carl Schmitt und Hermann Heller im Vergleich. Baden-Baden

Hegel GWF (1821) Grundlinien der Philosophie des Rechts oder Naturrecht und Staatswissenschaft im Grundrisse. English edition: Stephen H (ed) (2008) Outlines of the philosophy of right. (trans) Knox: Oxford World's Classics

Hegel GWF (Georg Wilhelm Friedrich) (1983) Die Philosophie des Rechts: Die Vorlesung von 1819/1820 in einer Nachschrift. Edited by Dieter H. Frankfurt am Main

Hegner F (1976) Die Entwicklung des sozialwissenschaftlichen Klassenbegriffs bei den Frühsozialisten und bei Lorenz von Stein. Archiv für Rechts- und Sozialphilosophie, LXII TM: 401–422

Hegner F (1979) Bürgernähe. Staatsbürgerrolle und soziale Aktion. Praxisbezogene Orientierungspunkte für notwendige Änderungen im System der Sozialen Sicherung. Bielefeld

Hegner F (1987) Zur Entwicklung von erwerbsgebundener und erwerbsfreier Zeit. In: Hesse J, Zöpel C (eds) Neuorganisation der Zeit. Baden-Baden, pp 33–81

Heimann E (1924) Marktwirtschaft, Klassengesellschaft und Sozialpolitik. Über die wissenschaftliche Grundlegung der Sozialpolitik und ihr Schrifttum. Kölner Sozialpolitische Vierteljahresschrift 3:45–71

Heimann E (1929) Soziale Theorie des Kapitalismus – Theorie der Sozialpolitik. Tübingen. Unchanged reprint with a foreword by Bernhard B. 1980. Frankfurt am Main

Heimann E (1930) Über Begriff und Wesen der Sozialpolitik. Eine Erwiderung. Soziale Praxis 39(585–588):609–613

Heimann E (1931a) Kapitalismus, Organwirtschaft, Sozialpolitik und ihre theoretische Erfassung. Weltwirtschaftliches Archiv 34:250–264

Heimann E (1931b) Sozialpolitik. In: Gunkel H, Zschernack L (eds) Die Religion in Geschichte und Gegenwart, 2nd edn, vol 5. Tübingen, pp 651–654

Heimann E (1954) Wirtschaftssysteme und Gesellschaftssysteme. Tübingen

Heimann E (1964) Der entfremdete Sozialismus und die Konsumgesellschaft. Hamburger Jahrbuch für Wirtschafts- und Gesellschaftspolitik 9:160–174

Heimann E (1961) Soziale Ideologien und soziale Reform (1961). Hamburger Jahrbuch für Wirtschafts- und Gesellschaftspolitik 16:334–342

Heimann E, Weber A (1931) Grundlagen und Grenzen der Sozialpolitik. In: Verhandlungen des Vereins für Sozialpolitik in Königsberg 1930. München Leipzig, pp 23–82

Heimann H, Meyer T (eds) (1982) Reformsozialismus und Sozialdemokratie. Zur Theoriediskussion des Demokratischen Sozialismus in der Weimarer Republik. Berlin Bonn

Heinze RG (ed) (1986) Neue Subsidiarität. Leitidee für eine zukünftige Sozialpolitik. Opladen

Heinze RG, Schmid J, Strünck C (1999) Vom Wohlfahrtsstaat zum Wettbewerbsstaat: Arbeitsmarkt- und Sozialpolitik in den 90er Jahren. Opladen

Held A (1878) Sozialismus. Sozialdemokratie und Sozialpolitik. Leipzig

Heller H (1926) Die Krisis der Staatslehre. Reprint in: Drath M, Niemeyer G, Stammer O, Borinski F (eds) Gesammelte Schriften vol 2. Leiden (1971), pp 3–30

Heller H (1930a) Rechtsstaat oder Diktatur? Reprint in: Drath M, Niemeyer G, Stammer O, Borinski F (eds) Gesammelte Schriften, vol 2. Leiden (1971), pp 443–462

Heller H (1930b) Grundrechte und Grundpflichten. Reprint in: Drath M, Niemeyer G, Stammer O, Borinski F (eds) Gesammelte Schriften, vol 2. Leiden (1971), pp 281–317

Heller H (1934) Staatslehre. Reprint in: Drath M, Niemeyer G, Stammer O, Borinski F (eds) Gesammelte Schriften, vol 3. Leiden (1971), pp 79–406

Heller H (1971) Gesammelte Schriften, 3 vols. Edited by Drath M, Niemeyer G, Stammer O, Borinski F. Leiden

Helmstädter E (1989) Die Wirtschaftsordnung in der Bundesrepublik Deutschland: Soziale Marktwirtschaft. In: Weidenfeld W, Zimmermann H (eds) Deutschland-Handbuch. Eine doppelte Bilanz. Bonn, pp 241–257

Henkel HA et al (eds) (1998) Gegen den gesellschaftspolitischen Imperialismus der reinen Ökonomie. Gedächtnisschrift für Gerhard Weisser. Marburg

Hentschel V (1983) Geschichte der deutschen Sozialpolitik (1880–1980) – Soziale Sicherung und Kollektives Arbeitsrecht. Frankfurt am Main

Herder-Dorneich P et al (eds) (1984) Überwindung der Sozialstaatskrise – Ordnungspolitische Ansätze. Baden-Baden

Herder-Dorneich P et al (eds) (1992) Sozialpolitiklehre als Prozeß. Baden-Baden

Herders Conversations-Lexikon (1902–1907) 1st edn, 4 vols. (1854–1857); 2nd edn, 4 vols. (1876–1879); 3rd edn, 8 vols. (1902–1907). Freiburg im Breisgau

Herkner H (1895) Sozialreform und Politik. Zeitschrift für die gesamte Staatswissenschaft 51:575–596

Herkner H (1922 [first published 1894]) Die Arbeiterfrage, 8th edn, 2 vols. Berlin Leipzig

Herkner H (1923a) Der Verein für Sozialpolitik in Vergangenheit, Gegenwart und Zukunft. In: Die Zukunft der Sozialpolitik – Die Not der geistigen Arbeiter. Jubiläumstagung des Vereins für Sozialpolitik in Eisenach 1922. München Leipzig, pp 83–99

Herkner H (1923b) Sozialpolitische Wandlungen in der wissenschaftlichen Nationalökonomie. Der Arbeitgeber 13:34–38

Herkner H (1924) Unbestrittene und bestrittene Sozialpolitik. Schmollers Jahrbuch für Wirtschafts- und Sozialwissenschaften 48:201–218

Herkner H (1925) Sozialpolitischer Liberalismus. In: Bonn MJ, Palyi M (eds) Die Wirtschaftswissenschaft nach dem Kriege. Festgabe für Lujo Brentano zum 80. Geburtstag, vol 1. München Leipzig, pp 31–52

Hermans BHA (1972) Das Problem der Sozialpolitik und Sozialreform auf den deutschen Katholikentagen von 1848 bis 1891. Ein Beitrag zur Geschichte der katholisch-sozialen Bewegung. Bonn

Heyde L (1966 [first published 1920]) Abriß der Sozialpolitik. Leipzig, 12th edn. Heidelberg

Heyder U (1977) Der sozialwissenschaftliche Systemversuch Eduard Heimanns. Frankfurt am Main

Heyder U (1982) Reformtheorie und Gesellschaftswandel im Werk Eduard Heimanns. In: Heimann H, Meyer T (eds) Reformsozialismus und Sozialdemokratie. Berlin Bonn, pp 75–94

Hickel R (ed) (1976) Die Finanzkrise des Steuerstaats. Beiträge zur politischen Ökonomie der Staatsfinanzen: Rudolf Goldscheid, Joseph A. Schumpeter. Frankfurt am Main

Hilberath L (1930) Neuere Definitionen des Begriffs der 'Sozialpolitik'. Kölner Sozialpolitische Vierteljahresschrift 9:278–291

Hilferding R (1910) Das Finanzkapital. New edition 1973. Frankfurt am Main

Hitze F (1877) Die sociale Frage. Paderborn

Hitze F (1880) Kapital und Arbeit und die Reorganisation der Gesellschaft. Paderborn
Hockerts HG (1980) Sozialpolitische Entscheidungen im Nachkriegsdeutschland. Alliierte und deutsche Sozialversicherungspolitik 1945 bis 1957. Stuttgart
Hockerts HG (1998a) Einführung. In: Hockerts HG (ed) Drei Wege deutscher Sozialstaatlichkeit: NS-Diktatur, Bundesrepublik und DDR im Vergleich. München, pp 7–25
Hockerts HG (ed) (1998b) Drei Wege deutscher Sozialstaatlichkeit: NS-Diktatur. Bundesrepublik und DDR im Vergleich. München
Hoffmann M (1948) Über den Begriff und die Grenzen der Sozialpolitik. Dissertation Erlangen
Höffner J (1953) Soziale Sicherheit und Eigenverantwortung: Der personale Faktor in der Sozialpolitik. Paderborn
Höffner J (1960) Eigentumsstreuung als Ziel der Sozialpolitik. In: Walter-Raymond-Stiftung (ed) Eigentum und Eigentümer in unserer Gesellschaftsordnung. Köln Opladen, pp 34–50
Höffner J (1962a) Sozialpolitik. In: Staatslexikon, 6th edn, vol 7. pp 347–360
Höffner J (1962b) Sozialreform. In: Staatslexikon, 6th edn, vol 7. pp 387–393
Höffner J (1962c) Christliche Gesellschaftslehre. New edition 1997. Edited by Lothar R. Kevelaer
Höffner J (1966) Gesellschaftspolitik aus christlicher Verantwortung. Münster
Hofmann E (1848) Woher und Wohin? Eine populaire Schrift zur Aufklärung über die social-politische Bewegung der Neuzeit. Königsberg
Hofmann W (1961) Gesellschaftslehre als Ordnungsmacht. Berlin
Holleis E (1978) Die sozialpolitische Partei. München
Hollerbach A (1993) Heinrich Rosin (1855–1927), Pionier des allgemeinen Verwaltungsrechts und des Sozialversicherungsrechts. In: Heinrichs H (ed) Deutsche Juristen jüdischer Herkunft. München, pp 369–384
Honecker M (1971) Konzept einer sozialethischen Theorie. Grundfragen evangelischer Sozialethik. Tübingen
Horstmann R-P (1997) Hegels Theorie der bürgerlichen Gesellschaft. In: Siep L (ed) Hegel, G.W.F. (Georg Wilhelm Friedrich) – Grundlinien der Philosophie des Rechts. Berlin, pp 193–216
Huber ER (1972) Vorsorge für das Dasein: Ein Grundbegriff der Staatslehre Hegels und Lorenz von Steins. In: Schnur R (ed) Festschrift für Ernst Forsthoff zum 70. Geburtstag. München, pp 139–163
Huf S (1998) Sozialstaat und Moderne – Modernisierungseffekte staatlicher Sozialpolitik. Berlin
Internationales Jahrbuch der Sozialpolitik, ab 1931. Edited by International Labour Office. Genf
Iwersen A, Tuchfeldt E (eds) (1993) Sozialpolitik vor neuen Aufgaben. Horst Sanmann zum 65. Geburtstag. Bern
Jahrbuch für Sozialpolitik, 1930, 1931. Edited by Staatssekretär des Reichsarbeitsministeriums Dr. Geib, Hermann. Berlin
Jastrow J (1902) Sozialpolitik und Verwaltungswissenschaft, vol I: Arbeitsmarkt und Arbeitsnachweis, Gewerbegerichte und Einigungsämter. Berlin
Joerg JE (1867) Geschichte der social-politischen Parteien in Deutschland. Freiburg im Breisgau
Jonas F (1976) Geschichte der Soziologie, vol 1. Reinbek bei Hamburg
Jostock P (1946) Grundzüge der Soziallehre und der Sozialreform. Freiburg im Breisgau
Junius C (=Julius Fröbel) (1847) Neue Politik. In zwei Theilen. Mannheim
Kahlenberg FP, Hoffmann D (2001) Sozialpolitik als Aufgabe zentraler Verwaltungen in Deutschland – Ein verwaltungsgeschichtlicher Überblick 1945–1994. In: Bundesministerium für Arbeit und Sozialordnung Bundesarchiv (eds) Geschichte der Sozialpolitik in Deutschland seit 1945, vol 1: Grundlagen der Sozialpolitik. Baden-Baden, pp 103–182. (See footnote on p. 125).
Kahn-Freund O (1976) Hugo Sinzheimer (1875–1945). In: Kahn-Freund O, Ramm T (eds) Hugo Sinzheimer: Arbeitsrecht und Rechtssoziologie. Gesammelte Aufsätze und Reden, 2 vols, Vol. 1. Frankfurt am Main Köln, pp 1–31
Kaiser J-C, Loth W (eds) (1997) Soziale Reform im Kaiserreich: Protestantismus, Katholizismus und Sozialpolitik. Stuttgart

Karrenberg F (1965) Katholische Soziallehre und evangelische Sozialethik. In: Achinger H, Preller L, Wallraff HJ (eds) Normen der Gesellschaft. Festgabe für Oswald von Nell-Breuning SJ zu seinem 75. Geburtstag. Mannheim, pp 49–71

Kaskel W (1920) Das neue Arbeitsrecht. Berlin

Kath D (1995) Sozialpolitik. In: Vahlens Kompendium der Wirtschaftstheorie und Wirtschaftspolitik, 6th edn, vol 2. München, pp 405–459

Kaufmann F-X (1973) Sicherheit als soziologisches und sozialpolitisches Problem. Untersuchungen zu einer Wertidee hochdifferenzierter Gesellschaften, 2nd edn. Stuttgart

Kaufmann F-X (ed) (1977a) Bürgernahe Gestaltung der sozialen Umwelt: Probleme und theoretische Perspektiven eines Forschungsverbundes. Meisenheim am Glan

Kaufmann F-X (1977b) Sozialpolitisches Erkenntnisinteresse und Soziologie. Ein Beitrag zur Pragmatik der Sozialwissenschaften. In: Von Ferber C, Kaufmann F-X (eds) Soziologie und Sozialpolitik. Kölner Zeitschrift für Soziologie und Sozialpsychologie, special issue no. 19:35–75 Überarbeitete Fassung In: Kaufmann F-X (2009) Sozialpolitik und Sozialstaat, pp 33–70

Kaufmann F-X (1978) Bericht über den Themenbereich 'Sozialpolitik'. In: Bolte KM (ed) Materialien aus der soziologischen Forschung. Verhandlungen des 18. Deutschen Soziologentages vom 28.9. bis 1.10.1976 in Bielefeld. Neuwied, pp 196–204

Kaufmann F-X (1979) Bürgernahe Sozialpolitik. Planung, Organisation und Vermittlung sozialer Leistungen auf örtlicher Ebene. Frankfurt am Main New York

Kaufmann F-X (1982a) Elemente einer soziologischen Theorie sozialpolitischer Intervention. In: Kaufmann F-X (ed) Staatliche Sozialpolitik und Familie. München Wien, pp 49–86 English translation: Socio-political intervention: elements of a sociological theory. In: Kaufmann F-X (2012) European foundations of the welfare state. Bergholm New York Oxford, chapter 7

Kaufmann F-X (1982b) Stand und Entwicklung der Forschung zur Sozialpolitik in der Bundesrepublik Deutschland. In: Hesse JJ (ed) Politik und Verwaltungswissenschaft. Politische Vierteljahrsschrift, special issue no. 13:344–365

Kaufmann F-X (1983) Steuerungsprobleme im Wohlfahrtsstaat. In: Matthes J (ed) Krise der Arbeitsgesellschaft? Verhandlungen des 21. Deutschen Soziologentages in Bamberg 1982. Frankfurt am Main New York, pp 474–490 Erweiterte Fassung. In: Kaufmann F-X (2009) Sozialpolitik und Sozialstaat. Wiesbaden, pp 229–262

Kaufmann F-X (ed) (1987) Staat, intermediäre Instanzen und Selbsthilfe. Bedingungsanalysen sozialpolitischer Intervention. München Wien

Kaufmann F-X (1988a) Christentum und Wohlfahrtsstaat. In: Zeitschrift für Sozialreform 34, pp 65–89 English translation: Christianity and social reform. In: Kaufmann F-X (ed) (2012) European foundations of the welfare state. Bergholm New York Oxford, chapter 4 (in print)

Kaufmann F-X (1988b) Steuerung wohlfahrtsstaatlicher Abläufe durch Recht. Gesetzgebungstheorie und Rechtspolitik Jahrbuch für Rechtssoziologie und Rechtstheorie 13:65–108

Kaufmann F-X (1989) Sozialwissenschaften. In: Staatslexikon, 7th edn, vol 5. Freiburg im Breisgau, pp 46–50

Kaufmann F-X (1991) The relationship between guidance, control, and evaluation. In: Kaufmann F-X (ed) The public sector – challenge for coordination and learning. Berlin New York, pp 213–234

Kaufmann F-X (1994) Staat und Wohlfahrtsproduktion. In: Derlien HU et al (eds) Systemrationalität und Partialinteresse. Festschrift für Renate Mayntz. Baden-Baden, pp 357–380 English translation: The state and the production of welfare. In: Kaufmann F-X (2012) European foundations of the European welfare state. Bergholm New York Oxford, chapter 9

Kaufmann F-X (1997a) Herausforderungen des Sozialstaates, 6th edn. 2004. Frankfurt am Main

Kaufmann F-X (1997b) Schwindet die integrative Funktion des Sozialstaates? Berliner Journal für Soziologie 7:5–19. See also: Kaufmann F-X (2009) Sozialpolitik und Sozialstaat. Wiesbaden, pp 287–306

Kaufmann F-X (1998) Der Sozialstaat als Prozeß – für eine Sozialpolitik zweiter Ordnung. In: Ruland F (ed) Verfassung, Theorie und Praxis des Sozialstaats. Festschrift für Hans F. Zacher. Heidelberg, pp 307–322. English translation: First order and second order social policies. In: Kaufmann F-X (2012) European foundations of the welfare state. Bergholm New York Oxford, chapter 8

Kaufmann F-X (2001) Towards a theory of the welfare state. In: Leibfried S (ed) Welfare state futures. Cambridge, pp 15–36

Kaufmann F-X (2002) Sozialpolitik zwischen Gemeinwohl und Solidarität. In: Münkler H, Fischer K (eds) Gemeinwohl und Gemeinsinn – Rhetoriken und Perspektiven sozial-moralischer Orientierung. Berlin, pp 19–54

Kaufmann F-X (2003) Die Entstehung sozialer Grundrechte und die wohlfahrtsstaatliche Entwicklung. Vortrag G 456 der Nordrhein-Westfälischen Akademie der Wissenschaften. Paderborn. English translation: Welfare internationalism before the welfare state: the emergence of social rights. In: Kaufmann F-X (2012) European foundations of the welfare state. Bergholm New York Oxford, chapter 5

Kaufmann F-X (2006) Joseph Höffner als Sozialpolitiker. In: Große Kracht H-J (ed) Joseph Höffner (1906–1987): Soziallehre und Sozialpolitik. Paderborn, pp 37–50

Kaufmann F-X (2007a) Gemeinsame Fragen der Organisation und des Rechts der sozialen Leistungen. In: Bundesministerium für Arbeit und Soziales Bundesarchiv (eds) Geschichte der Sozialpolitik in Deutschland seit 1945, vol 4: Bundesrepublik Deutschland 1957–1966 Sozialpolitik im Zeichen des erreichten Wohlstands. Edited by Ruck M, Boldorf M. Baden-Baden, pp 285–296. (See footnote on p. 125).

Kaufmann F-X (2007b) Alterssicherung und Nachwuchssicherung. In: Becker U et al (eds) Alterssicherung in Deutschland. Festschrift für Franz Ruland zum 65. Geburtstag. Baden-Baden, pp 245–270

Kaufmann F-X (2009) Sozialpolitik und Sozialstaat. Sozialpolitische Analysen, 3rd edn. Wiesbaden

Kaufmann F-X (2012) European foundations of the welfare state. Bergholm New York Oxford

Kaufmann F-X (2013) Variations of the welfare state. Great Britain, Sweden, France and Germany between capitalism and socialism. In: Leisering L (ed) German social policy, vol. 5. Berlin Heidelberg

Kaufmann F-X, Majone G, Ostrom V (eds) (1985) Guidance, control, and evaluation in the public sector. The Bielefeld interdisciplinary project. Berlin New York

Keim KD, Vascovics L (eds) (1985) Wege zur Sozialplanung. Erfahrungen und Chancen in der Bundesrepublik Deutschland. Opladen

Keller P (1955) Dogmengeschichte des wohlstandspolitischen Interventionismus. Winterthur

Keynes JM (1935) The general theory of employment, interest and money. New York

Klein W (ed) (1994) Soziale Marktwirtschaft: ein Modell für Europa. Festschrift für Gernot Gutmann. Berlin

Kleinewefers H (1985) Reformen für Wirtschaft und Gesellschaft: Utopien, Konzepte, Realitäten. Frankfurt am Main New York

Kleinhenz G (1970) Probleme wissenschaftlicher Beschäftigung mit der Sozialpolitik. Dogmengeschichtlicher Überblick und Entwurf eines Wissenschaftsprogramms für die Theorie der Sozialpolitik. Berlin

Kleinhenz G (ed) (1995) Soziale Ausgestaltung der Marktwirtschaft. Festschrift für Heinz Lampert. Berlin

Kleinhenz G, Lampert H (1971) Zwei Jahrzehnte Sozialpolitik in der BRD – Eine kritische Analyse. Ordo – Jahrbuch für die Ordnung von Wirtschaft und Gesellschaft 22:103–158

Klotz W (1927) Zur Begriffsbestimmung der Sozialpolitik. Ein Beitrag zur Grundlegung der Sozialpolitik als Wissenschaft, Dissertation. Frankfurt am Main Leipzig

Koch R (1978) Demokratie und Staat bei Julius Fröbel 1805–1893. Liberales Denken zwischen Naturrecht und Sozialdarwinismus. Wiesbaden

Kohl J (1984) Sociological research in social policy, the case of Germany. In: Sociological research and social security. Proceedings of the European Institute of Social Security. EISS Yearbook 1982–83, Part II. Deventer, pp 105–123

Kohli M (1989) Moralökonomie und 'Generationenvertrag'. In: Haller M, Hoffmann-Nowottny HJ, Zapf W (eds) Kultur und Gesellschaft. Verhandlungen des 24. Deutschen Soziologentags, des 111. Österreichischen Soziologentags und des 8. Kongresses der Schweizerischen Gesellschaft für Soziologie in Zürich 1988. Frankfurt am Main New York, pp 532–555

Koselleck R (1959) Kritik und Krise. Eine Studie zur Pathogenese der bürgerlichen Welt. New edition 1973. Frankfurt am Main

Koselleck R (ed) (1978) Historische Semantik und Begriffsgeschichte. Stuttgart

Koselleck R (1986) Sozialgeschichte und Begriffsgeschichte. In: Schieder W, Selling V (eds) Sozialgeschichte in Deutschland, vol I: Die Sozialgeschichte innerhalb der Geschichtswissenschaft. Göttingen, pp 89–109

Koslowski P (ed) (1995) The theory of ethical economy in the historical school. Heidelberg

Koslowski S (1989) Die Geburt des Sozialstaats aus dem Geist des Deutschen Idealismus. Person und Gemeinschaft bei Lorenz von Stein. Weinheim

Kowalski W (1967) Vom kleinbürgerlichen Demokratismus zum Kommunismus. Zeitschriften aus der Frühzeit der deutschen Arbeiterbewegung (1834–1847)

Kraus O (1964) Grundfragen der Gesellschaftspolitik. Berlin

Kreikebaum H, Herbert K-J (1988) Humanisierung der Arbeit: Arbeitsgestaltung im Spannungsfeld ökonomischer, technologischer und humanitärer Ziele. Wiesbaden

Kreissl R (1987) Die Krise der Theorie des Wohlfahrtsstaates – Konsequenzen für die Verrechtlichungsdebatte. Kritische Vierteljahresschrift für Gesetzgebung und Rechtswissenschaft 2:89–111

Kretschmar G (1972) Der Evangelisch-Soziale Kongreß. Der deutsche Protestantismus und die soziale Frage. Stuttgart

Krohn C-D (1985) Die Krise der Wirtschaftswissenschaft in Deutschland im Vorfeld des Nationalsozialismus. Leviathan 13:311–333

Krüger J (1975) Wissenschaftliche Beratung und sozialpolitische Praxis. Stuttgart

Krüger J (1979) Anmerkungen zur sozialwissenschaftlichen Wiederentdeckung der Sozialpolitik. Archiv für Wissenschaft und Praxis der sozialen Arbeit 10:241–255

Krüger J, Pankoke E (eds) (1985) Kommunale Sozialpolitik. München Wien

Krupp H-J (1974) Perspektiven der Sozialpolitik. In: Christmann A, Hesselbach W, Jahn M (eds) Sozialpolitik, Ziele und Wege. Köln, pp 525–544

Kuczynski J (1960) Bürgerliche und halbfeudale Literatur aus den Jahren 1840–1847 zur Lage der Arbeiter. Eine Chrestomathie. Berlin

Kulawik T (1996) Modern bis maternalistisch: Theorien des Wohlfahrtsstaates. In: Kulawik T, Sauer B (eds) Der halbierte Staat. Grundlagen feministischer Politikwissenschaft. Frankfurt am Main New York, pp 47–81

Külp B, Haas H-D (eds) (1977) Soziale Probleme der modernen Industriegesellschaft. Verhandlungen auf der Arbeitstagung der Gesellschaft für Wirtschafts- und Sozialwissenschaften – Verein für Sozialpolitik – in Augsburg vom 13–15. September 1976. 2 vols. Berlin

Külp B, Schreiber W (eds) (1971) Soziale Sicherheit. Köln Berlin

Kurz HD (1989) Die deutsche theoretische Nationalökonomie zu Beginn des 20. Jahrhunderts zwischen Klassik und Neoklassik. In: Schefold B (ed) Studien zur Entwicklung der ökonomischen Theorie VIII. Berlin, pp 11–61

Lampert H (1985) Die Wirtschafts- und Sozialpolitik im Dritten Reich. Jahrbücher für Nationalökonomie und Statistik 200(2):101–135

Lampert H (1989) 'Denken in Ordnungen' als ungelöste Aufgabe. Jahrbücher für Nationalökonomie und Statistik 206:446–456

Lampert H (1992) Leistungen und Grenzen der 'Ökonomischen Theorie der Sozialpolitik'. In: Herder-Dorneich P et al (eds) Sozialpolitiklehre als Prozeß. Baden-Baden, pp 115–130

Lampert H (1997a) Die Wirtschafts- und Sozialordnung der Bundesrepublik Deutschland, 13th edn. München

Lampert H (1997b) Krise und Reform des Sozialstaates. Frankfurt am Main

Lampert H (1998) Lehrbuch der Sozialpolitik, 5th edn. Berlin [first published 1980]
Lampert H (2001) Walter Eucken als Sozialpolitiker. In: Schulz-Nieswandt F (ed) Einzelwirtschaften und Sozialpolitik zwischen Markt und Staat in Industrie- und Entwicklungsländern. Festschrift für Werner Wilhelm Engelhardt. Marburg, pp 181–192
Lampert H, Bossert A (1987) Die Soziale Marktwirtschaft – eine theoretisch unzulänglich fundierte ordnungspolitische Konzeption? Hamburger Jahrbuch für Wirtschafts- und Gesellschaftspolitik 32:109–130
Lampert H, Schubert F (1977) Sozialpolitik V: In der Deutschen Demokratischen Republik. Handwörterbuch der Wirtschaftswissenschaft, vol. 7, pp. 130–152
Langan M, Ostner I (1991) Geschlechterpolitik im Wohlfahrtsstaat. Aspekte im internationalen Vergleich. Kritische Justiz 24:302–312
Lange FA (1865) Die Arbeiterfrage in ihrer Bedeutung für Gegenwart und Zukunft. Duisburg. Reprint 1979. Hildesheim New York
Langner A (ed) (1980) Katholizismus, Wirtschaftsordnung und Sozialpolitik 1945–1963. Paderborn
Lechevalier J (1833) Question sociale. De la réforme industrielle, considérée comme problème fondamentale de la politique positive. Paris
Leenen WR (1978) Tausendundeine Definition: Was ist Sozialpolitik? Sozialer Fortschritt 27:1–6
Leibfried S (2000) Nationaler Wohlfahrtsstaat, Europäische Union und 'Globalisierung': Erste Annäherungen. In: Allmendinger J, Ludwig-Mayerhofer W (eds) Soziologie des Sozialstaats. Gesellschaftliche Grundlagen, historische Zusammenhänge und aktuelle Entwicklungstendenzen. München, pp 79–108
Leibfried S, Leisering L (1995) Zeit der Armut. Frankfurt am Main
Leibfried S, Pierson P (eds) (1995) European social policy: between fragmentation and integration. Washington D.C.
Leibfried S, Rieger E (1997) Die sozialpolitischen Grenzen der Globalisierung. Politische Vierteljahresschrift 38:771–796
Leibfried S, Tennstedt F (eds) (1985) Politik der Armut und die Spaltung des Sozialstaats. Frankfurt am Main
Leibfried S, Voges W (eds) (1992) Armut im modernen Wohlfahrtsstaat. Kölner Zeitschrift für Soziologie und Sozialpsychologie, special issue no. 32
Leisering L (1992a) Selbststeuerung im Sozialstaat – zur Verortung der Rentenreform in der Sozialpolitik der 80er Jahre. Zeitschrift für Sozialreform 38:3–39
Leisering L (1992b) Sozialstaat und demographischer Wandel. Wechselwirkungen, Generationenverhältnisse, politisch-institutionelle Steuerung. Frankfurt am Main New York
Leisering L (1995) Grenzen des Sozialversicherungsstaats? Sozialer Wandel als Herausforderung staatlicher Einkommenssicherung. Zeitschrift für Sozialreform 41:860–880
Leisering L (1999) Eine Frage der Gerechtigkeit: Armut und Reichtum in Deutschland. Aus Politik und Zeitgeschichte B 18:9–17
Leisering L (2004) Paradigmen sozialer Gerechtigkeit. Normative Diskurse im Umbau des Sozialstaats. In: Liebig S, Lengfeld H, Mau S (eds) Verteilungsprobleme und Gerechtigkeit in modernen Gesellschaften. Frankfurt am Main New York, pp 29–68
Lenel HO (1986) Alexander Rüstows wirtschafts- und sozialpolitische Konzeption. Ordo – Jahrbuch für die Ordnung von Wirtschaft und Gesellschaft 37:45–58
Lenhardt G, Offe C (1977) Staatstheorie und Sozialpolitik. Politisch-soziologische Erklärungsansätze für Funktionen und Innovationsprozesse der Sozialpolitik. In: Von Ferber C, Kaufmann F-X (eds) Soziologie und Sozialpolitik. Kölner Zeitschrift für Soziologie und Sozialpsychologie, special issue no. 19:98–127
Lepsius MR (1955) Beitrag zur soziologischen Theorie der Sozialpolitik. Dissertation. München
Lepsius MR (1979) Soziale Ungleichheit und Klassenstrukturen in der Bundesrepublik Deutschland: Lebenslagen, Interessenvermittlung und Wertorientierungen. In: Wehler H-U (ed) Klassen in der europäischen Sozialgeschichte. Göttingen, pp 166–209

Lessenich S (2000) Soziologische Erklärungsansätze zur Entstehung und Funktion des Sozialstaats. In: Allmendinger J, Ludwig-Mayerhofer W (eds) Soziologie des Sozialstaats. Gesellschaftliche Grundlagen, historische Zusammenhänge und aktuelle Entwicklungstendenzen. München, pp 39–78

Lessenich S (2003) Wohlfahrtsstaatliche Grundbegriffe – Semantiken des Wohlfahrtsstaats. In: Lessenich S (ed) Wohlfahrtsstaatliche Grundbegriffe. Historische und aktuelle Diskurse. Frankfurt am Main New York, pp 9–19

Lessenich S, Ostner I (eds) (1998) Welten des Wohlfahrtskapitalismus. Der Sozialstaat in vergleichender Perspektive. Frankfurt am Main New York

Leubuscher C (1923) Die Krise der Sozialpolitik. Soziale Praxis 32:339–343, 363–366, 387–390

Liebersohn H (1980) Religion and industrial society. The Protestant Congress in Wilhelmine Germany. Philadelphia

Liefmann-Keil E (1949) Intervention und Rahmenplanung. Bemerkungen zu Lord Beveridge: Vollbeschäftigung in einer freien Gesellschaft. Jahrbücher für Nationalökonomie und Statistik 161:112–136

Liefmann-Keil E (1961) Ökonomische Theorie der Sozialpolitik. Berlin

Lindenlaub D (1967) Richtungskämpfe im Verein für Sozialpolitik, 2 vols. Wiesbaden

Lindgens G (1987) Die politischen Implikationen der katholischen Soziallehre. In: Fetscher I, Münkler H (eds) Pipers Handbuch der politischen Ideen, vol 5. München, pp 83–104

Louis M (1969) Der Begriff der 'Wirtschaftsdemokratie'. eine problemgeschichtliche Untersuchung zum deutschen Wirtschaftsverfassungsrecht. Dissertation. Münster

Luhmann N (1971) Politische Planung. Opladen

Luhmann N (1981) Politische Theorie im Wohlfahrtsstaat. München Wien

Luhmann N (1982) The Differentiation of Society. New York

Luhmann N (1983) Der Wohlfahrtsstaat zwischen Evolution und Rationalität. In: Koslowski P, Kreuzer P, Löw R (eds) Chancen und Grenzen des Sozialstaats: Staatstheorie – Politische Ökonomie – Politik. Tübingen, pp 26–40

Luhmann N (1993a) Gesellschaftliche Struktur und semantische Tradition. In: Luhmann N (ed) Gesellschaftsstruktur und Semantik, vol 1. Frankfurt am Main, pp 9–71

Luhmann N (1993b) Wie ist soziale Ordnung möglich? In: Luhmann N (ed) Gesellschaftsstruktur und Semantik, vol 2. Frankfurt am Main, pp 195–285

Luhmann N (1995) Inklusion und Exklusion. In: Luhmann N (ed) Soziologische Aufklärung 6. Opladen, pp 237–264

Lütge F (1932) Der Begriff Sozialpolitik. Ein neuer Versuch. Jahrbücher für Nationalökonomie und Statistik 137:481–514

Lutz B (1984) Der kurze Traum immerwährender Prosperität: Eine Neuinterpretation der industriell-kapitalistischen Entwicklung im Europa des 20. Jahrhunderts. Frankfurt am Main New York

Machtan L (1988) Adolph Wagner und die Gründung des Vereins für Socialpolitik – Zwei unveröffentlichte Briefe aus dem Jahre 1872. Zeitschrift für Sozialreform 34:510–523

Mackenroth G (1957 [first published 1952]) Die Reform der Sozialpolitik durch einen deutschen Sozialplan. Berlin. Gekürzter Wiederabdruck. In: Boettcher E (ed) Sozialpolitik und Sozialreform. Tübingen, pp 43–74

Mann FK (1978) Steuerpolitische Ideale. Vergleichende Studien zur Geschichte der ökonomischen und politischen Ideen und ihres Wirkens in der öffentlichen Meinung 1600–1935. Darmstadt

Manow P (2001) Ordoliberalismus als ökonomische Ordnungstheologie. Leviathan 29:179–198

Manow P, Plümper T (1998) Die Erkenntnisgrenzen der Diskursanalyse. Politische Vierteljahresschrift 39:590–601

Marlo K (= Winkelblech K-G) (1850) Untersuchungen über die Organisation der Arbeit oder System der Weltökonomie, vol. I, 1. Abteilung: Historischer Teil. Kassel

Marr H (1923) Zur Krise der Sozialpolitik. Rückblick und Ausblick. Soziale Praxis 23:547–551, 563–571, 648–651, 666–668, 696–698, 710–713, 727–730, 757–760

Marshall TH (1964 [first published 1950]) Social class and citizenship. In: class, citizenship, and social development. Essays by T. H. Marshall with an introduction by Seymour Martin Lipset. Garden City, pp 65–122

Mason TW (1977) Sozialpolitik im Dritten Reich. Arbeiterklasse und Volksgemeinschaft. Opladen

Matthes J (ed) (1983) Krise der Arbeitsgesellschaft? Verhandlungen des 21. Deutschen Soziologentages in Bamberg 1982. Frankfurt am Main New York

Matzner E (1982) Der Wohlfahrtsstaat von morgen. Entwurf eines zeitgemäßen Musters staatlicher Interventionen. Frankfurt am Main New York

Maurer I (1973) Reichsfinanzen und große Koalition. Zur Geschichte des Reichskabinetts Müller (1928–1930). Frankfurt am Main

Mayer KU (1990) Soziale Ungleichheit und die Differenzierung von Lebensverläufen. In: Zapf W (ed) Die Modernisierung moderner Gesellschaften. Verhandlungen des 25. Deutschen Soziologentages in Frankfurt am Main 1990. Frankfurt am Main New York, pp 667–687

Mayer KU, Müller W (1989) Lebensverläufe im Wohlfahrtsstaat. In: Weymann A (ed) Handlungsspielräume. Untersuchungen zur Individualisierung und Institutionalisierung von Lebensverläufen in der Moderne. Stuttgart, pp 41–60

Mayer KU, Allmendinger J, Huinink J (eds) (1991) Vom Regen in die Traufe: Frauen zwischen Beruf und Familie. Frankfurt am Main New York

Mayntz R (1977) Die Implementation politischer Programme. Theoretische Überlegungen zu einem neuen Forschungsgebiet. Die Verwaltung 10:51–66

Mayntz R (1979) Regulative Politik in der Krise? In: Matthes J (ed) Sozialer Wandel in Westeuropa. Verhandlungen des 19. Deutschen Soziologentages Berlin 1979. Frankfurt am Main New York, pp 55–82

Mayntz R (ed) (1980) Implementation politischer Programme: Empirische Forschungsberichte. Königstein im Taunus

Mayntz R (ed) (1983) Implementation politischer Programme 2: Ansätze zur Theoriebildung. Opladen

Mayntz R (1997) Soziale Dynamik und politische Steuerung. Theoretische und methodologische Überlegungen. Frankfurt am Main New York

Mayntz R, Scharpf FW (eds) (1973) Planungsorganisation. München

Mayntz R, Scharpf FW (eds) (1995) Gesellschaftliche Selbstregelung und politische Steuerung. Frankfurt am Main New York

Meadows D et al (1972) Grenzen des Wachstums. Bericht des Club of Rome zur Lage der Menschheit. Stuttgart

Meier HG (1971) Begriffsgeschichte. In: Ritter J, Gründer K (eds) Historisches Wörterbuch der Philosophie, vol 1. Basel, columns 788–808

Messner J (1930) Um die katholisch-soziale Einheitslinie. Innsbruck Wien

Messner J (1956 [first published 1934]) Die soziale Frage, 6th edn. Innsbruck

Metz KH (1985) Liberalismus und soziale Frage. Liberales Denken und die Auswirkungen der Industrialisierung in Großbritannien des 19. Jahrhunderts. Zeitschrift für Politik 32:375–392

Meyer A (1864) Zum Begriffe der Socialpolitik. Preußische Jahrbücher 14:315–330

Meyer R (1873) Die neueste Literatur zur socialen Frage. Erste und zweite Abteilung. Berlin

Meyers Konversations-Lexikon 1874–1890, 3rd edn, 15 vols. (1874–1878); 4th edn, 16 vols. (1885–1890). Leipzig

Mitscherlich W (1927) Moderne Arbeitersozialpolitik. Leipzig

Mockenhaupt H (1977) Weg und Wirken des geistlichen Sozialpolitikers Heinrich Brauns. Paderborn

Moenning M (1927) Die Stellung der deutschen katholischen Sozialpolitiker des 19. Jahrhunderts zur "Staatsintervention" in der sozialen Frage. Dissertation. Münster

Molitor B (1957) Bausteine einer Theorie der Sozialpolitik. Hamburger Jahrbuch für Wirtschafts- und Gesellschaftspolitik 2:152–163

Molitor B (1986) Sozialpolitik in der Marktwirtschaft. Ordo – Jahrbuch für die Ordnung von Wirtschaft und Gesellschaft 37:59–71

Molitor B (1987/1988) Theorie der Sozialpolitik, 2 vols. München

Molitor B (1990) Sozialpolitikgeschichte in theoretischer Sicht. Hamburger Jahrbuch für Wirtschafts- und Gesellschaftspolitik 35:149–170
Möller R (1978) 'Lebenslage' als Ziel der Politik. Edited by Wirtschafts- und Sozialwissenschaftliches Institut des Deutschen Gewerkschaftsbundes (WSI). WSI-Mitteilungen 31:553–565
Mönch H (1949) Die historischen und strukturellen Grundbedingungen der klassischen theoretischen Sozialpolitik. Schmollers Jahrbuch für Wirtschafts- und Sozialwissenschaften 69 I:129–161
Montesquieu, Charles de Secondat (1745) De l'esprit des lois. Geneva
Müller C (1984) Kritische Bemerkungen zur Kelsen-Rezeption Hermann Hellers. In: Müller C, Staff I (eds) Der soziale Rechtsstaat. Gedächtnisschrift für Hermann Heller 1891–1933. Baden-Baden, pp 693–722
Müller H (1967) Ursprung und Geschichte des Wortes Sozialismus und seiner Verwandten. Hannover
Müller H-P (1992) Sozialstruktur und Lebensstile. Der neuere theoretische Diskurs über soziale Ungleichheit. Frankfurt am Main
Müller C, Staff I (eds) (1984) Der soziale Rechtsstaat. Gedächtnisschrift für Hermann Heller 1891–1933. Baden-Baden
Müller W, Neusüss C (1970) Die Sozialstaatsillusion und der Widerspruch von Lohnarbeit und Kapital. Sozialistische Politik 2:4–67
Müller-Armack A (1947) Wirtschaftslenkung und Marktwirtschaft. Hamburg
Müller-Armack A (1952) Stil und Ordnung der sozialen Marktwirtschaft. In: Lagler E, Messner J (eds) Wirtschaftliche Entwicklung und soziale Ordnung. Festschrift für Ferdinand Degenfeld-Schonburg. Wien, pp 27–38
Müller-Heine K (1977) Zur Definition von Sozialpolitik. Sozialer Fortschritt 26:171–175
Münch U (1997) Sozialpolitik und Föderalismus. Zur Dynamik der Aufgabenverteilung im sozialen Bundesstaat. Opladen
Mundt JW (ed) (1983) Grundlagen lokaler Sozialpolitik. Weinheim Basel
Myrdal G (1939) Monetary equilibrium. London
Myrdal G (1958) Das Wertproblem in den Sozialwissenschaften. Hannover
Myrdal G, Myrdal A (1935) Kris i befolkningsfragan. Stockholm
Nahnsen I (1961) Der systematische Ort der Sozialpolitik in den Sozialwissenschaften. In: Gesellschaft in Geschichte und Gegenwart. Festschrift für Siegfried Lenz. Berlin, pp 115–132
Naphtali F (1928) Wirtschaftsdemokratie – Ihr Wesen, Weg und Ziel. New edition with a foreword by Ludwig Rosenberg and an introduction by Otto Brenner, 1966. Frankfurt am Main
Naschold F, Väth W (eds) (1974) Politische Planungssysteme. Opladen
Nau HH (1996) "Zwei Ökonomien". Die Vorgeschichte des Werturteilsstreits in der deutschsprachigen Ökonomik. In: Nau HH (ed) Der Werturteilsstreit. Marburg, pp 9–64
Nau HH (1997) Eine "Wissenschaft vom Menschen". Max Weber und die Begründung der Sozialökonomik in der deutschsprachigen Ökonomie 1871bis 1914. Berlin
Nau HH (1998) Politisches Ethos und sozialökonomisches Telos. In: Gustav Schmoller: Historisch-ethische Nationalökonomie als Kulturwissenschaft. Ausgewählte methodologische Schriften. Edited by Nau HH. Marburg, pp 13–65
Necker T et al (1983) Sozialstaat – Die Krise seiner Ethik. Köln
Nelson L (1924) Philosophische Vorfragen der Sozialpolitik. In: Wirtschaft und Gesellschaft. Festschrift für Franz Oppenheimer. Frankfurt am Main, pp 23–78
Neuloh O (1950/1951) Die geistigen Wandlungen der deutschen Sozialpolitik. In: Der Arbeitgeber, 15.12.1950/1.1.(1951): 34
Neuloh O (1961) Mensch und Gesellschaft im Leben und Denken von Zwiedineck-Südenhorst. In: Neuloh O (ed) Zwiedineck-Südenhorst, Otto von. Mensch und Gesellschaft. Beiträge zur Sozialpolitik und zu sozialen Fragen. Berlin, pp 21–87
Nipperdey K, Seifert R (1990) Arbeitsrecht, 3rd edn. Wiesbaden
Nolte P (1998) Der Verlust der Utopie und die wiedergefundene Mitte. Vorstellungen sozialer Ordnung in der westdeutschen Gesellschaft (1945–1965). Mitteilungsblatt des Instituts zur Erforschung der europäischen Arbeiterbewegung 20:298–332

Nullmeier F (2000) Politische Theorie des Sozialstaates. Frankfurt am Main New York
Nullmeier F, Rüb FW (1993) Die Transformation der Sozialpolitik: Vom Sozialstaat zum Sicherungsstaat. Frankfurt am Main New York
O'Connor J (1970) The Fiscal Crisis of the State. In: Socialist Revolution no. 1 und 2
OECD (Organization for Economic Cooperation and Development) (1985) Social expenditure 1960–1990. Problems of growth and control. Paris
OECD (1996) Social expenditure statistics of OECD member countries. Paris
Oeter F (1952a) Reproduktion und Amortisation der menschlichen Arbeitskraft. Sozialer Fortschritt 1:61f.
Oeter F (1952b) Familiengerechte Sozialpolitik. Sozialer Fortschritt 1:288–290
Offe C (1972) Strukturprobleme des kapitalistischen Staates. Frankfurt am Main. English: The contraditions of the welfare state. 1984. London
Offermann T (1979) Arbeiterbewegung und liberales Bürgertum in Deutschland 1850–1863. Bonn
Olson M (1968) Die Logik kollektiven Handelns. Tübingen
Opielka M, Ostner I (eds) (1987) Umbau des Sozialstaats. Essen
Oppenheim HB (1872 [first published 1871]) Manchesterschule und Katheder-Sozialismus. In: Oppenheim HB Der Katheder-Sozialismus. Berlin, pp 33–41
Oppenheimer F (1912) Die soziale Frage und der Sozialismus. Jena
Ortlieb H-D (1975) Eduard Heimann: Sozialökonom, Sozialist und Christ – Ein Nachruf. In: Ortlieb H-D (ed) Heimann, Eduard – Sozialismus im Wandel der modernen Gesellschaft. Aufsätze zur Theorie und Praxis des Sozialismus. Ein Erinnerungsband. Berlin Bonn-Bad Godesberg, pp 1–20
Pankoke E (1970) Sociale Bewegung – Sociale Frage – Sociale Politik. Grundfragen der deutschen "Socialwissenschaft" im 19. Jahrhundert. Stuttgart
Pankoke E (ed) (1991) Gesellschaftslehre. Frankfurt am Main
Pankoke E (1995a) Soziale Frage. In: Ritter J, Gründer K (eds) Historisches Wörterbuch der Philosophie, vol 9. Basel, columns 1129–1134
Pankoke E (1995b) Sozialpolitik. In: Ritter J, Gründer K (eds) Historisches Wörterbuch der Philosophie, vol 9. Basel, columns 1227–1236
Parsons T (1971) The system of modern societies. Englewood-Cliffs
Penski U (1982) Staat als soziale Demokratie – Zur staatstheoretischen Position Hermann Hellers. In: Heimann H, Meyer T (eds) Reformsozialismus und Sozialdemokratie. Zur Theoriediskussion des Demokratischen Sozialismus in der Weimarer Republik. Berlin Bonn, pp 167–185
Pesch H (1924) Lehrbuch der Nationalökonomie, 2nd edn, 5 vols. Freiburg im Breisgau
Pfaff M (ed) (1978a) Grenzen der Umverteilung. Berlin
Pfaff M (1978b) Grundlagen einer integrierten Sozialpolitik. In: Pfaff M, Voigtländer H (eds) Sozialpolitik im Wandel. Bonn, pp 147–186
Pfaff M (ed) (1983) Effizienz und Effektivität staatlicher Transferpolitik in der Wirtschaftskrise. Berlin
Pieper J (1947 [first published 1933]) Thesen zur sozialen Politik. Frankfurt am Main
Pinker R (1971) Social theory and social policy. London
Pirker T et al (1955) Arbeiter, Management, Mitbestimmung. Stuttgart
Plessen M-L (1975) Die Wirksamkeit des Vereins für Sozialpolitik von 1872–1890. Studien zum Katheder- und Staatssozialismus. Berlin
Preller L (1947) Sozialpolitik – Kernfrage des Aufbaues, 2nd edn. Stuttgart
Preller L (1949) Sozialpolitik in der Weimarer Republik. New edition 1978. Düsseldorf
Preller L (1962) Sozialpolitik – Theoretische Ortung. Tübingen Zürich
Preller L (1970) Praxis und Probleme der Sozialpolitik, 2 vols. Tübingen Zürich
Pribram K (1924) Diskussionsvotum. Verhandlungen des Vierten Deutschen Soziologentages am 29. und 30. September 1924. Reprint 1969. Heidelberg
Pribram K (1925a) Begriff und Aufgaben der Sozialpolitik und die Soziologie. Soziale Praxis 34:2–4, 36–37, 53–56, 80–81, 95–96

Pribram K (1925b) Die Wandlungen des Begriffs Sozialpolitik. In: Bonn MJ, Palyi M (eds) Die Wirtschaftswissenschaft nach dem Kriege. Festgabe für Lujo Brentano zum 80. Geburtstag, vol 2. München Leipzig, pp 223–267

Pribram K (1925c) Zum Thema 'Soziologie und Sozialpolitik'. Soziale Praxis 34:957–960

Pribram K (1926) Die Sozialpolitik als theoretische Disziplin. Archiv für Sozialwissenschaft und Sozialpolitik 55:577–629

Pribram K (1932) Deutungen der Sozialpolitik. Schmollers Jahrbuch für Wirtschafts- und Sozialwissenschaften 56 I:177–210

Pribram K (1992) Geschichte des ökonomischen Denkens, 2 vols. Frankfurt am Main

Priddat BP (1990) Hegel als Ökonom. Berlin

Priddat BP (1995) Die andere Ökonomie. Eine neue Einschätzung von Gustav Schmollers Versuch einer 'ethisch-historischen' Nationalökonomie im 19. Jahrhundert. Marburg

Prisching M (1996) Bilder des Wohlfahrtsstaates. Marburg

Pütz T (1954) Neue Wege und Ziele der Sozialpolitik. Wien

Pütz T (1967) Bemerkungen zum Erkenntnisobjekt der Sozialpolitik als wissenschaftlicher Disziplin. In: Mayer-Maly T et al (eds) Festschrift für Hans Schmitz zum 70. Geburtstag, vol II. Wien, pp 176–193

Quesel C (1989) Soziologie und Soziale Frage. Lorenz von Stein und die Entstehung der Gesellschaftswissenschaft in Deutschland. Wiesbaden

Raphael L (1996) Die Verwissenschaftlichung des Sozialen als methodische und konzeptionelle Herausforderung für eine Sozialgeschichte des 20. Jahrhunderts. Geschichte und Gesellschaft 22:165–193

Rassem M (1992) Wohlfahrt, Wohltat, Wohltätigkeit, Caritas. In: Brunner O, Conze W, Koselleck R (eds) Geschichtliche Grundbegriffe. Historisches Lexikon zur politisch-sozialen Sprache in Deutschland, vol 7. Stuttgart, pp 637–677

Rathmann A (1988) Eduard Heimann (1889–1967) – Von Marx und seiner "überwältigend großartigen" Lehre zum religiös-freiheitlichen Sozialismus. In: Lösche P et al (eds) Vor dem Vergessen bewahren. Lebenswege Weimarer Sozialdemokraten. Berlin, pp 121–144

Ratz U (1980) Sozialreform und Arbeiterschaft. Die 'Gesellschaft für soziale Reform' und die sozialistische Arbeiterbewegung von der Jahrhundertwende bis zum Ausbruch des Ersten Weltkrieges. Berlin

Rauecker B (1926) Einführung in die Sozialpolitik. Berlin

Recker M-L (1985) Nationalsozialistische Sozialpolitik im Zweiten Weltkrieg. München

Reichwein R (1965) Funktionswandlungen der betrieblichen Sozialpolitik. Köln Opladen

Reidegeld E (1996) Staatliche Sozialpolitik in Deutschland. Historische Entwicklung und theoretische Analyse von den Ursprüngen bis 1918. Opladen

Reinhard HJ, Kruse J, von Maydell BB (eds) (1998) Invaliditätssicherung im Rechtsvergleich. Baden-Baden

Reulecke J (1983) Sozialer Frieden durch soziale Reform. Der Centralverein für das Wohl der arbeitenden Klassen in der Frühindustrialisierung. Wuppertal

Richter L (1932) Zur staatstheoretischen Bedeutung der sozialpolitischen Schlichtung. Leipzig

Richter M (1955) (ed) Die Sozialreform. Dokumente und Stellungnahmen. Loseblattsammlung. Bad Godesberg

Riedel M (1979a) Gesellschaft, bürgerliche. In: Brunner O, Conze W, Koselleck R (eds) Geschichtliche Grundbegriffe. Historisches Lexikon zur politisch-sozialen Sprache in Deutschland, vol 2. Stuttgart, pp 719–800

Riedel M (1979b) Gesellschaft, Gemeinschaft. In: Brunner O, Conze W, Koselleck R (eds) Geschichtliche Grundbegriffe. Historisches Lexikon zur politisch-sozialen Sprache in Deutschland, vol 2. Stuttgart, pp 801–862

Riedmüller B, Olk T (eds) (1994) Grenzen des Sozialversicherungsstaates. Leviathan special issue no. 14

Rieger E (1992) Die Institutionalisierung des Wohlfahrtsstaats. Opladen

Rieger E (1998) Wohlfahrtsstaat und Globalisierung. Antikritisches zu Erklärungsproblemen und Interpretationsversuchen. Politische Vierteljahreszeitschrift 39:819–828

Rieger E (1999) Zur 'Theorie der Sozialpolitik und des Wohlfahrtsstaates: Der Beitrag Max Webers. Zentrum für Sozialpolitik der Universität Bremen (ZeS). ZeS-Arbeitspapier 14/99
Rieger E, Leibfried S (2001) Grundlagen der Globalisierung: Perspektiven des Wohlfahrtsstaates. Frankfurt am Main
Riehl WH (1851) Die bürgerliche Gesellschaft. Stuttgart Tübingen
Riehl WH (1854) Die Naturgeschichte des Volkes als Grundlage einer deutschen Social-Politik. Vol. 1: Land und Leute. Stuttgart Tübingen
Rifkin J (2000) The age of access : how the shift from ownership to access is transforming modern life. London
Ritter E (1954) Die katholisch-soziale Bewegung Deutschlands im neunzehnten Jahrhundert und der Volksverein. Köln
Ritter GA (1991) Der Sozialstaat. Entstehung und Entwicklung im internationalen Vergleich, 2nd edn. München
Ritter GA (1994) Die Entstehung des Räteartikels 165 der Weimarer Reichsverfassung. Historische Zeitschrift 258:73–112
Ritter GA (1996a) Probleme und Tendenzen des Sozialstaates in den 1990er Jahren. Geschichte und Gesellschaft 22:393–408
Ritter GA (1996b) Zur Geschichte der sozialen Ideen im 19. und frühen 20. Jahrhundert. In: Ritter GA (ed) Arbeiter, Arbeiterbewegungen und soziale Ideen in Deutschland. München, pp 11–66
Ritter GA (1996c) Arbeiter, Arbeiterbewegungen und soziale Ideen in Deutschland. München
Robbers G (1983) Hermann Heller: Staat und Kultur. Baden-Baden
Rolf G, Spahn P, Bernd WG (eds) (1988) Sozialvertrag und Sicherung. Zur ökonomischen Theorie staatlicher Versicherungs- und Umverteilungssysteme. Frankfurt am Main New York
Roller E (1992) Einstellungen der Bürger zum Wohlfahrtsstaat der Bundesrepublik Deutschland. Wiesbaden
Roller E (1996) Kürzungen von Sozialleistungen aus der Sicht der Bundesbürger. Zeitschrift für Sozialreform 42:777–788
Röpke W (1949) Civitas Humana – Grundfragen der Gesellschafts- und Wirtschaftsreform. 3rd edn. Erlenbach Zürich
Rosin H (1893) Das Recht der Arbeiterversicherung. Berlin
Roth G (1968) Stein, Lorenz von. In: Sills DL (ed) International encyclopedia of the social sciences, vol 15, pp 257–259
Rothfels H (1929) Prinzipienfragen der Bismarckschen Sozialpolitik. Königsberg
Rudloff W (1998) Die Wohlfahrtsstadt: Kommunale Ernährungs-, Fürsorge- und Wohnungspolitik am Beispiel Münchens 1910–1933, 2 vols. Göttingen
Rüstow A (1959) Sozialpolitik diesseits und jenseits des Klassenkampfes. In: Aktionsgemeinschaft soziale Marktwirtschaft (ed) Sinnvolle und sinnwidrige Sozialpolitik. Ludwigsburg, pp 11–21
Sachße C, Tennstedt F (1988) Geschichte der Armenfürsorge in Deutschland, vol 2: Fürsorge und Wohlfahrtspflege 1871–1929. Stuttgart
Sachße C, Tennstedt F (1992) Geschichte der Armenfürsorge in Deutschland, vol 3: Der Wohlfahrtsstaat im Nationalsozialismus. Stuttgart
Salz A (1914) Die Rechtfertigung der Sozialpolitik (Ein Bekenntnis). Heidelberg
Sanmann H (1972) Sozialpolitik. In: Ehrlicher W et al (eds) Kompendium der Volkswirtschaftslehre, 3rd edn, vol 2. Göttingen
Sanmann H (ed) (1973) Leitbilder und Zielsysteme der Sozialpolitik. Berlin
Sanmann H (1993) Forschung, Lehre, Management – Rückblick auf mehr als 40 Berufsjahre. In: Iwersen A, Tuchfeldt E (eds) Sozialpolitik vor neuen Aufgaben. Bern, pp 17–39
Schachtschabel HG (1952) Ziele und Grenzen sozialer Sicherung. Sozialer Fortschritt 1:57f.
Schäfers B (1967) Ein Rundschreiben Max Webers zur Sozialpolitik. Soziale Welt 18:261–271
Schäfers B (1969) Thesen zur Kritik der Soziologie. Frankfurt am Main
Scharpf FW (1973) Planung als politischer Prozeß. Frankfurt am Main

Scharpf FW (1977) Public organization and the waning of the welfare state: a research perspective. European Journal of Political Research 5:339–362

Scharpf FW (1999) Regieren in Europa: Effektiv und demokratisch? Frankfurt am Main New York

Scharpf FW, Schmidt VA (eds) (2000) From vulnerability to competitiveness: welfare and work in the open economy. Oxford

Scheer C (1975) Sozialstaat und öffentliche Finanzen. Köln

Schelsky H (1965 [first published 1953]) Die Bedeutung des Schichtungsbegriffs für die Analyse der gegenwärtigen deutschen Gesellschaft. In: Schelsky H (ed) Auf der Suche nach Wirklichkeit. Düsseldorf, pp 311–336

Scherner KO (1996) Sozialrechtsgeschichte der Neuzeit. Stand der Forschung und offene Fragen. Zeitschrift für neuere Rechtsgeschichte 18:102–148

Schieckel H (1955) Deutsche Sozialpolitik. München

Schieder W (1984) Sozialismus. In: Brunner O, Conze W, Koselleck R (eds) Geschichtliche Grundbegriffe. Historisches Lexikon zur politisch-sozialen Sprache in Deutschland, vol 5. Stuttgart, pp 923–996

Schluchter W (1968) Entscheidung für den sozialen Rechtsstaat. H. Heller und die staatstheoretische Diskussion in der Weimarer Republik. Köln

Schmähl W, Rische H (eds) (1997) Europäische Sozialpolitik. Baden-Baden

Schmid J (1996a) Wohlfahrtsverbände in modernen Wohlfahrtsstaaten. Soziale Dienste in historisch-vergleichender Perspektive. Opladen

Schmid J (1996b) Wohlfahrtsstaaten im Vergleich. Soziale Sicherungssysteme in Europa: Organisation, Finanzierung, Leistungen und Probleme. Opladen

Schmidt K-H (1997) Gustav Schmoller und die Entwicklung einer sozialpolitischen Schule in Deutschland. In: Streissler EW (ed) Studien zur Entwicklung der ökonomischen Theorie XVI: Die Umsetzung wirtschaftspolitischer Grundkonzeptionen in die kontinentaleuropäische Praxis des 19. und 20. Jahrhunderts. Part I. Berlin, pp 43–80

Schmidt MG (1998) Sozialpolitik in Deutschland: Historische Entwicklung und internationaler Vergleich, 2nd edn. Opladen

Schmidt MG (2013) Social policy in the german democratic republic. In: Leisering L (ed) German social policy, vol 4. Berlin Heidelberg

Schmoller G (1864/1865) Die Arbeiterfrage. Preußische Jahrbücher 14 (1864):393–424 (I); 523–547 (II); 15 (1865):32–63 (III)

Schmoller G (1867) Lorenz von Stein. Preußische Jahrbücher 19:245–270

Schmoller G (1874) Die sociale Frage und der preußische Staat. Preußische Jahrbücher 33:323–342

Schmoller G (1875) Über einige Grundfragen des Rechts und der Volkswirtschaft. Ein offenes Sendschreiben an Herrn Professor Dr. Heinrich von Treitschke. Jena

Schmoller G (1890) Die Gerechtigkeit in der Volkswirtschaft. In: Schmoller G (ed) Zur Sozial- und Gewerbepolitik der Gegenwart. Reden und Aufsätze. Leipzig, pp 204–246

Schmoller G von (1912) Aus der neueren sozialpolitischen Literatur. Jahrbuch für Gesetzgebung, Verwaltung und Volkswirtschaft im Deutschen Reich 36:905–928

Schneider M (1993) Demokratisierungs-Konsens zwischen Unternehmern und Gewerkschaften? Zur Debatte um Wirtschaftsdemokratie und Mitbestimmung. In: Schildt A, Sywottek A (eds) Modernisierung im Wiederaufbau. Die westdeutsche Gesellschaft der 50er Jahre. Bonn, pp 207–222

Schönig W, L'Hoest R (eds) (1996) Sozialstaat wohin? Umbau, Abbau oder Ausbau der sozialen Sicherung. Darmstadt

Schreiber W (1963) Zur Frage des Standorts der Sozialpolitik-Lehre im Ganzen der Sozialwissenschaften. In: Karrenberg F, Albert H (eds) Sozialwissenschaft und Gesellschaftsgestaltung. Festschrift für Gerhard Weisser. Berlin, pp 351–361

Schulte B (1999) The welfare state and European integration. European Journal of Social Security 1:7–61

Schulz A (1978) Oswald von Nell-Breuning – eine soziologische Analyse seines Mitbestimmungs-Engagements. Dissertation. Saarbrücken
Schulz F (1987) Zur Dogmengeschichte der funktionalen Finanzwirtschaftslehre. Berlin
Schulze W (1970) "Sozialistische Bestrebungen in Deutschland". Bemerkungen zu einer Aufsatzfolge von Karl Biedermann (1846). Vierteljahresschrift für Sozial- und Wirtschaftsgeschichte 57:93–104
Schulz-Nieswandt F (1991) Über das Verhältnis von Wirtschaftspolitik und Sozialpolitik. Sozialpolitik im System der Sozialwissenschaften. Zeitschrift für Sozialreform 37:531–548
Schulz-Nieswandt F (1992) Sozialökonomik als politische Theorie. Grundzüge des wissenschaftlichen Schaffens von Theo Thiemeyer. Zeitschrift für Sozialreform 38:625–637
Schumpeter J (1916/1917) Das Grundprinzip der Verteilungstheorie. Archiv für Sozialwissenschaft und Sozialpolitik 42:1–88
Schuster T (1835) Gedanken eines Republikaners. Der Geächtete 2:124
Schwaderlapp W (1980) Eigentum und Arbeit bei Oswald von Nell-Breuning. Düsseldorf
Schwarz G (ed) (1990) Das Soziale der Marktwirtschaft. Zürich
Schwengel H (1999) Globalisierung mit europäischem Gesicht. Der Kampf um die politische Form der Zukunft. Berlin
Seeleib-Kaiser M (2001) Globalisierung und Sozialpolitik. Ein Vergleich der Diskurse und Wohlfahrtssysteme in Deutschland, Japan und den USA. Frankfurt am Main New York
Seldte F (1939) Sozialpolitik im Dritten Reich 1933–1938. München Berlin
Shanahan WO (1962) Der deutsche Protestantismus vor der sozialen Frage 1815–1871. München
Siebert H (ed) (1996) Sozialpolitik auf dem Prüfstand: Leitlinien für Reformen. Tübingen
Siemann W (1989) Zwischen Ordnungs- und Sozialpolitik: Die Anfänge parlamentarischer und administrativer Enquêten in Deutschland. Jahrbuch für Europäische Verwaltungsgeschichte 1:293–311
Siep L (1992) Verfassung, Grundrechte und soziales Wohl in Hegels Philosophie des Rechts. In: Siep L (ed) Praktische Philosophie im Deutschen Idealismus. Frankfurt am Main
Simmel G (1989) Über sociale Differenzierung. Sociologische und psychologische Untersuchungen. In: Simmel G (ed) Gesamtausgabe, vol 2. Frankfurt am Main, pp 109–295
Sinzheimer H (1907/1908) Der korporative Arbeitsnormenvertrag. Eine privatrechtliche Untersuchung. 2 parts. Leipzig
Sinzheimer H (1916) Ein Arbeitstarifgesetz. Die Idee der sozialen Selbstbestimmung. im Recht. München, Leipzig, 2nd edn. Berlin 1977
Sinzheimer H (1919) Das Rätesystem. In: Arbeitsrecht und Rechtssoziologie. Frankfurt am Main, Köln, 1976, vol 1, pp 325–340
Sinzheimer H (1927) Grundzüge des Arbeitsrechts, 2nd edn. Jena
Sinzheimer H (1976a) Arbeitsrecht und Rechtssoziologie. Gesammelte Aufsätze und Reden. Edited by Kahn-Freund O, Ramm T, 2 vols. Frankfurt am Main Köln
Sinzheimer H (Fragment, postum) (1976b) Theorie der Gesetzgebung. In: Arbeitsrecht und Rechtssoziologie, vol 2. Frankfurt am Main Köln, pp 245–309
Social-politische Flugblätter, 1874–1876. Berlin
Sohm R (1897) Die sozialen Aufgaben des modernen Staates. Cosmopolis 8 (Okt.-Dez.): 231–245, 586–602
Sombart W (1897) Ideale der Sozialpolitik. Archiv für Soziale Gesetzgebung und Statistik 10:1–48
Sommer E (1872) Nationalökonomie und Socialpolitik in ihrer Beziehung und Wirkung auf die socialen Fragen der Gegenwart. Dresden
"Sozialstaat". Jahrbuch für Nationalökonomie und Statistik. Special issue, 216 (1997). Issue no. 4 + 5
Spann O (1912) Die Erweiterung von Sozialpolitik durch die Berufsvormundschaft. Archiv für Soziale Gesetzgebung und Statistik 34:505–561
Spann O (1931) Die Krise der Sozialpolitik und ihre Lösung in der ständischen Wirtschaftsverfassung. Ständisches Leben 1:2–16

Spieker M (1986) Legitimitätsprobleme des Sozialstaats. Bern

Spindler L (1922) Zur Begriffsbestimmung der Sozialpolitik und Wohlfahrtspflege. Kölner Vierteljahreshefte für Sozialwissenschaften 1:58–67

Staatslexikon (1889–1993) Edited by Görres-Gesellschaft. 1st edn, 5 vols. (1889–1897); 5th edn, 5 vols. (1926–1932); 6th edn, 11 vols. (1957–1970); 7th edn, 7 vols. (1985–1993). Freiburg im Breisgau

Stammhammer J (ed) (1896/1912) Bibliographie der Social-Politik, 2 vols. Jena

Standfest E (1979) Sozialpolitik als Reformpolitik. Aspekte der sozialpolitischen Entwicklung in der Bundesrepublik Deutschland. Köln

Starbatty J (1982) Alfred Müller-Armacks Beitrag zur Theorie und Politik der Sozialen Marktwirtschaft. In: Soziale Marktwirtschaft im vierten Jahrzehnt ihrer Bewährung. Stuttgart New York, pp 7–26

Stegmann FJ (1965) Von der ständischen Sozialreform zur staatlichen Sozialpolitik. München

Stelzig T (1977) Weissers Konzept einer normativen Sozialwissenschaft. In: Von Ferber C, Kaufmann F-X (eds) Soziologie und Sozialpolitik. Kölner Zeitschrift für Soziologie und Sozialpsychologie, special issue no. 19:260–289

Stier-Somlo F (1906) Deutsche Sozialgesetzgebung. Geschichtliche Grundlagen und Krankenversicherungsrecht. Jena

Stolleis M (1998) Wohlfahrt. In: Handwörterbuch der deutschen Rechtsgeschichte, vol 5. Berlin, pp 1486–1488

Stolleis M (2001) Historische Grundlagen: Sozialpolitik in Deutschland bis 1945. In: Bundesministerium für Arbeit und Sozialordnung Bundesarchiv (eds) Geschichte der Sozialpolitik in Deutschland seit 1945. Vol. 1: Grundlagen der Sozialpolitik. Baden-Baden, pp 199–332. (See footnote on p. 125).

Stolleis M (2013) Origins of the German Welfare State - Social policy in Germany to 1945. In: Leisering L (ed) German social policy, vol 2. Berlin Heidelberg

Strasser J (1979) Grenzen des Sozialstaats? Soziale Sicherung in der Wachstumskrise. Köln Frankfurt am Main

Streeck W (ed) (1998) Internationale Wirtschaft, Nationale Demokratie. Herausforderungen für die Demokratietheorie. Frankfurt am Main New York

Sultan H (1932) Die Staatseinnahmen. Versuch einer soziologischen Finanztheorie als Teil einer Theorie der politischen Ökonomie. Tübingen

Syrup F, Neuloh O (1957) Hundert Jahre staatliche Sozialpolitik 1839–1939. Stuttgart

Talos E (1979) Sozialstaatlichkeit- Entwicklungsverlauf und Funktionen. Österreichische Zeitschrift für Soziologie 4:4–19

Tennstedt F (1977) Sozialwissenschaftliche Forschung in der Sozialversicherung. In: Von Ferber C, Kaufmann F-X (eds) Soziologie und Sozialpolitik. Kölner Zeitschrift für Soziologie und Sozialpsychologie, special issue no. 19:483–523

Tennstedt F (1981) Sozialgeschichte der Sozialpolitik in Deutschland. Vom 18. Jahrhundert bis zum Ersten Weltkrieg. Göttingen

Tennstedt F (1983) Vom Proleten zum Industriearbeiter. Arbeiterbewegung und Sozialpolitik 1800 bis 1914. Köln

Tennstedt F (1988) Geschichte des Sozialrechts. In: Von Maydell BB, Ruland F (eds) Sozialrechtshandbuch. Neuwied, pp 66–133

Tennstedt F (1994) Sozialreform als Mission. Anmerkungen zum politischen Handeln Theodor Lohmanns. In: Kocka J et al (eds) Von der Arbeiterbewegung zum modernen Sozialstaat. Festschrift für Gerhard A. Ritter. München, pp 538–559

Tennstedt F, Leibfried S (1979) Sozialpolitik und Berufsverbote im Jahre 1933. Zeitschrift für Sozialreform 25:129–153, 211–238

Tennstedt F, Winter H (eds) (1993) Von der Haftpflichtgesetzgebung zur ersten Unfallversicherungsvorlage. Quellensammlung zur Geschichte der deutschen Sozialpolitik 1867 bis 1914. Vol. 2, 1. Abteilung. Stuttgart

Tennstedt F, Winter H (eds) (1994) Grundfragen staatlicher Sozialpolitik: Die Diskussion der Arbeiterfrage auf Regierungsseite vom preußischen Verfassungskonflikt bis zur Reichstagswahl von 1881. Quellensammlung zur Geschichte der deutschen Sozialpolitik 1867 bis 1914. Vol. 1, 1. Abteilung. Stuttgart
Teppe K (1977) Zur Sozialpolitik im Dritten Reich am Beispiel der Sozialversicherung. Archiv für soziale Gesetzgebung und Statistik 17:195–250
Thiemeyer T (1963) Die Überwindung des wohlfahrtsökonomischen Formalismus bei Gerhard Weisser. In: Karrenberg F, Albert H (eds) Sozialwissenschaft und Gesellschaftsgestaltung. Festschrift für Gerhard Weisser. Berlin, pp 131–149
Thiemeyer T (1975) Soziale 'Selbstverwaltung' unter ökonomischem Aspekt. Zeitschrift für Sozialreform 21:539–559
Thiemeyer T (1979) Privatwirtschaft und Gemeinwirtschaft. Aufgaben und Grenzen der staatlichen und freigemeinnützigen Betriebe in der Marktwirtschaft. In: Neumann LF (ed) Sozialforschung und soziale Demokratie. Festschrift für Otto Blume. Bonn, pp 303–320
Thiemeyer T (1988) Wirtschaftspolitik als Wissenschaft. Gerhard Weissers System der Politik aus normativen Grundentscheidungen. Sozialer Fortschritt 37:73–78
Thiemeyer T (ed) (1990/1991) Theoretische Grundlagen der Sozialpolitik, 2 vols. Berlin
Thier E (1930) Rodbertus, Lassalle, Adolph Wagner. Ein Beitrag zur Theorie und Geschichte des deutschen Staatssozialismus. Jena
Timm H (1952) Die deutsche Sozialpolitik und der Bruch der großen Koalition im März 1930. Düsseldorf
Tomandl T (1967) Der Einbau sozialer Grundrechte in das positive Recht. Tübingen
Tönnies F (1914/1915) Rechtsstaat und Wohlfahrtsstaat. Archiv für Rechts- und Wirtschaftsphilosophie 8:65–70
Tönnies F (1919) Die Entwicklung der sozialen Frage bis zum Weltkriege, 3rd edn. Berlin Leipzig
Tönnies F (1930) Sozialpolitik als soziale Idee. Weltwirtschaftliches Archiv 31:161–175
Töpfer I (1970) Die Verhandlungen des Vereins für Sozialpolitik und die Rechtspolitik der späten Bismarck- und wilhelminischen Zeit. Dissertation. Frankfurt am Main
Topitsch E (ed) (1965) Logik der Sozialwissenschaften. Köln
Tormin H (1949) Einführung in die Sozialpolitik. Stuttgart
Tragl T (2000) Solidarität und Sozialstaat. Theoretische Grundlagen, Probleme und Perspektiven des modernen sozialpolitischen Solidaritätskonzeptes. München
Ullrich CG (2000) Solidarität im Sozialversicherungsstaat: Die Akzeptanz des Solidarprinzips in der gesetzlichen Krankenkasse. Frankfurt am Main New York
Ulrich G (1994) Politische Steuerung. Staatliche Intervention aus systemtheoretischer Sicht. Opladen
Utz A-F (1961) Die philosophischen Grundlagen der Wirtschafts- und Sozialpolitik. Freiburg (Schweiz)
Valentin V (1998) Geschichte der deutschen Revolution von 1848–1849, vol 1. Weinheim Berlin
van der Borght R (1904) Grundlagen der Sozialpolitik, 2nd edn. under the title: Grundzüge der Sozialpolitik. Leipzig 1923
Vobruba G (ed) (1989) Der wirtschaftliche Wert der Sozialpolitik. Berlin
Vobruba G (ed) (1990) Strukturwandel der Sozialpolitik. Lohnarbeitszentrierte Sozialpolitik und soziale Grundsicherung. Frankfurt am Main
Volkert J (1991) Sozialpolitik und Wettbewerbsordnung: Die Bedeutung der wirtschafts- und sozialpolitischen Konzeption Walter Euckens für ein geordnetes sozialpolitisches System der Gegenwart. Ordo – Jahrbuch für die Ordnung von Wirtschaft und Gesellschaft 42:91–115
von Baader F (1835) Über das dermalige Missverhältnis der Vermögenslosen oder Proletairs zu den Vermögen besitzenden Klassen der Sozietät in Betreff ihres Auskommens, sowohl in materieller, als intellektueller Hinsicht, aus dem Standpunkt des Rechts betrachtet. München
von Balás K (1926) Die Grundlage der Sozialpolitik. Jena
von Beckerath E (1962) Stein – Wagner – Schäffle, das 'Dreigestirn' der deutschen Finanzwissenschaft. In: Von Beckerath E (ed) Lynkeus – Gestalten und Probleme aus Wirtschaft und Politik. Tübingen, pp 75–101

von Beckerath E, Giersch H (eds) (1963) Probleme der normativen Ökonomik und der wirtschaftspolitischen Beratung. Verhandlungen auf der Arbeitstagung des Vereins für Socialpolitik in Bad Homburg 1962. Berlin
von Berlepsch HH (1903) Warum betreiben wir die soziale Reform? Jena
von Berlepsch H-J (1987) 'Neuer Kurs' im Kaiserreich? Die Arbeiterpolitik des Freiherrn von Berlepsch 1890–1896. Bonn
von Bethusy-Huc V (1965) Das Sozialleistungssystem der Bundesrepublik Deutschland. Tübingen
von Bortkiewicz L (1899) Der Begriff 'Sozialpolitik'. Jahrbücher für Nationalökonomie und Statistik 72: III. Folge vol 17:332–349
von Bruch R (1985) Bürgerliche Sozialreform im deutschen Kaiserreich. In: Von Bruch R (ed) "Weder Kommunismus noch Kapitalismus". Bürgerliche Sozialreform in Deutschland vom Vormärz bis zur Ära Adenauer. München
von Ferber C (1967) Sozialpolitik in der Wohlstandsgesellschaft. Was stimmt nicht mit der deutschen Sozialpolitik? Hamburg
von Ferber C (1976) Demokratisierung und Sozialstaat im Verständnis der Soziologie. In: Schulenburg W (ed) Reform in der Demokratie. Hamburg, pp 47–62
von Ferber C (1977a) Soziologie und Sozialpolitik. In: Von Ferber C, Kaufmann F-X (eds) Soziologie und Sozialpolitik. Kölner Zeitschrift für Soziologie und Sozialpsychologie, special issue no. 19:11–34
von Ferber C (1977b) Wird der sozialpolitische Handlungsspielraum der Sozialen Selbstverwaltung ausgeschöpft? In: Borsdorf U (ed) Gewerkschaftliche Politik: Reform aus Solidarität. Köln, pp 373–392
von Ferber C, Kaufmann F-X (eds) (1977) Soziologie und Sozialpolitik. Kölner Zeitschrift für Soziologie und Sozialpsychologie, special issue no. 19
von Hertling G (1884) Aufsätze und Reden socialpolitischen Inhalts. Freiburg im Breisgau
von Hertling G (1893) Naturrecht und Socialpolitik. Köln
von Hippel E (1982) Der Schutz des Schwächeren. Tübingen
von Ketteler WE (1864) Arbeiterfrage und Christentum. Mainz
von Lavergne-Peguilhen M (1838) Grundzüge der Gesellschaftswissenschaft. Vol. 1: Die Bewegungs- und Productionsgesetze. Königsberg
von Lavergne-Peguilhen M (1841) Grundzüge der Gesellschaftswissenschaft. Vol. 2: Die Kulturgesetze, Abtheilung 1. Königsberg
von Lavergne-Peguilhen M (1863) Sozialpolitische Studien. Berlin
von Mayr G (1921) Begriff und Gliederung der Staatswissenschaften, 4th edn. Tübingen
von Mohl R (1835) Über die Nachtheile, welche sowohl den Arbeitern selbst, als dem Wohlstande und der Sicherheit der gesamten bürgerlichen Gesellschaft von dem fabrikmäßigen Betrieb der Industrie zugehen und über die Notwendigkeit gründlicher Vorbeugungsmittel. Archiv der politischen Ökonomie und Polizeiwissenschaft 2:141–185
von Mohl R (1851) Gesellschaftswissenschaften und Staatswissenschaften. Zeitschrift für die gesamte Staatswissenschaft 7:3–71
von Mohl R (1855) Die Geschichte und Literatur der Staatswissenschaften, vol I. New edition 1960. Graz
von Mohl R (1869) Staatsrecht, Völkerrecht und Politik, vol 3: Politik. Part 2. Tübingen
von Nell-Breuning O (1956–1960) Wirtschaft und Gesellschaft heute, vols I–III. Freiburg im Breisgau
von Nell-Breuning O (1957) Solidarität und Subsidiarität im Raume von Sozialpolitik und Sozialreform. In: Boettcher E (ed) Sozialpolitik und Sozialreform. Tübingen, pp 213–226
von Nell-Breuning O (1968a) Streit um Mitbestimmung. Frankfurt am Main
von Nell-Breuning O (1968b) Baugesetze der Gesellschaft: Gegenseitige Verantwortung – Hilfreicher Beistand. Freiburg im Breisgau
von Nell-Breuning O (1970a) Betriebliche Sozialpolitik und soziale Betriebspolitik. In: von Nell-Breuning O (ed) Aktuelle Fragen der Gesellschaftspolitik. Köln, pp 27–34
von Nell-Breuning O (1970b) Aktuelle Fragen der Gesellschaftspolitik. Köln

von Nell-Breuning O (1979) Soziale Sicherheit: Zu Grundfragen der Sozialordnung aus christlicher Verantwortung. Freiburg im Breisgau

von Nell-Breuning O, Sacher H (1949) Zur Sozialen Frage. Freiburg im Breisgau

von Philippovich E (1908) Das Eindringen der sozialpolitischen Ideen in die Literatur. In: Die Entwicklung der Volkswirtschaftslehre im neunzehnten Jahrhundert. Gustav Schmoller zur siebenzigsten Wiederkehr seines Geburtstages. Part II, Kap. XXXI. Leipzig, pp 1–51

von Philippovich E, Heimann E (1924) Entwicklungsgang der wirtschafts- und sozialpolitischen Systeme und Ideale. In: Grundriß der Sozialökonomik I. Abt., I. part: Wirtschaft und Wirtschaftswissenschaft, 2nd edn. Tübingen, pp 125–201

von Scheel H (1878) Unsere socialpolitischen Parteien. Leipzig

von Stein L (1842) Der Socialismus und Communismus des heutigen Frankreich. Leipzig

von Stein L (1850) Geschichte der sozialen Bewegung in Frankreich von 1789 bis auf unsere Tage, 3 vols. Zitiert nach dem Nachdruck der von Gottfried Salomon 1921 herausgegebenen Ausgabe. Darmstadt 1972

von Stein L (1856) System der Staatswissenschaft. Vol. 2: Die Gesellschaftslehre, 1. Abteilung: Der Begriff der Gesellschaft und die Lehre von den Gesellschaftsklassen. Stuttgart Augsburg

von Stein L (1866) Die Verwaltungslehre, Theil 2: Die Lehre von der inneren Verwaltung. Stuttgart. Reprint 1975. Aalen

von Stein L (1888) Handbuch der Verwaltungslehre, 3rd edn. Part 3: Die Verwaltung und das gesellschaftliche Leben. Stuttgart

von Stein L (1964) The history of the social movement in France: 1789–1850, introduced, edited, and translated by Kaethe Mengelberg. Totowa N.J.

von Treitschke H (1859) Die Gesellschaftswissenschaft. Ein kritischer Versuch. Leipzig

von Treitschke H (1875) Die gerechte Vertheilung der Güter. Offener Brief an Gustav Schmoller. Preußische Jahrbücher 35:409–447

von Westphalen FA (1931) Die theoretischen Grundlagen der Sozialpolitik. Jena

von Wiese L (1921 [first published 1910]) Einführung in die Sozialpolitik, 2nd edn. Leipzig

von Wiese L (1926) Sozialpolitik. Handwörterbuch der Staatswissenschaften 7:612–622

von Wiese L (1956) Sozialpolitik III: Sozialpolitik als Wissenschaft. Handwörterbuch der Staatswissenschaften 9:547–554

von Zwiedineck-Südenhorst O (1911) Sozialpolitik. Leipzig Berlin

von Zwiedineck-Südenhorst O (1923) Zum Schicksal der Sozialpolitik in Deutschland. Schmollers Jahrbuch für Wirtschafts- und Sozialwissenschaften 47:77–142

von Zwiedineck-Südenhorst O (1961) Sozialpolitik, Wissenschaft und Symbolik. In: Neuloh O (ed) Zwiedineck-Südenhorst, Otto von: Mensch und Gesellschaft. Beiträge zur Sozialpolitik und zu sozialen Fragen. Berlin, pp 172–185

Voss W (1925) Sozialpolitik als Wissenschaft. Eine Untersuchung über Objekt, Aufgaben und Methoden der Sozialpolitik. Jena

Wagener H (Anonymus) (1878) Die Lösung der sozialen Frage vom Standpunkte der Wirklichkeit und Praxis. Von einem praktischen Staatsmanne. Bielefeld Leipzig

Wagner A (1872a) Rede über die sociale Frage. Gehalten auf der freien kirchlichen Versammlung evangelischer Männer in der K. Garnisonskirche zu Berlin am 12. October 1871. Berlin

Wagner A (1872b) Offener Brief an Herrn H.B. Oppenheim. Eine Abwehr manchesterlicher Angriffe gegen meine Rede über die sociale Frage auf der Octoberversammlung. Berlin

Wagner A (1876) Allgemeine oder theoretische Volkswirtschaftslehre. 1. part: Grundlegung. Leipzig, Heidelberg. Faksimile 1971. Düsseldorf

Wagner A (1891) Über soziale Finanz- und Steuerpolitik. Archiv für soziale Gesetzgebung und Statistik 4:1–81

Wagner A (1912) Die Strömungen in der Sozialpolitik und der Katheder- und Staatssozialismus. Berlin

Walter F (1899) Socialpolitik und Moral. Eine Darstellung ihres Verhältnisses mit besonderer Bezugnahme auf die von Prof. Werner Sombart neuestens geforderte Unabhängigkeit der Sozialpolitik von der Moral. Freiburg im Breisgau

Walter-Raymond-Stiftung (ed) (1960) Eigentum und Eigentümer in unserer Gesellschaftsordnung. Köln Opladen
Wannagat G (1965) Lehrbuch des Sozialversicherungsrechts. Tübingen
Weber A (1931a) Grundlagen und Grenzen der Sozialpolitik. In: Verhandlungen des Vereins für Sozialpolitik in Königsberg 1930. München Leipzig, pp 23–58
Weber A (1931b) Sozialpolitik – Reden und Aufsätze. München Leipzig
Weber M (1904) Die "Objektivität" sozialwissenschaftlicher und sozialpolitischer Erkenntnis. In: Weber M (ed) (1968) Gesammelte Aufsätze zur Wissenschaftslehre, 3rd edn. Tübingen, pp 146–214
Weber M (1924) Debattenreden auf der Tagung des Vereins für Sozialpolitik in Wien 1909 über die Produktivität der Volkswirtschaft. In: Weber M (ed) 1968: Gesammelte Aufsätze zur Soziologie und Sozialpolitik, 3rd edn. Tübingen, pp 416–423
Weber M (1953) Zum Begriff der Sozialpolitik. In: Wagner VF, Marbach F (eds) Wirtschaftstheorie und Wirtschaftspolitik. Festschrift für Alfred Amonn. Bern, pp 167–176
Weber M (ed) (1968) Gesammelte Aufsätze zur Soziologie und Sozialpolitik, 3rd edn. Tübingen
Weddigen W (1930) Sozialpolitik als Wissenschaft. Archiv für Sozialwissenschaft und Sozialpolitik 64:510–546
Weddigen W (1932) Sozialpolitik und Weltwirtschaft. Ein Beitrag zur Theorie der internationalen Sozialpolitik. Weltwirtschaftliches Archiv 35:177–202
Weddigen W (1933) Sozialpolitik. Eine Einführung in Theorie und Praxis. Jena
Weddigen W (ed) (1950) Untersuchungen zur sozialen Gestaltung der Wirtschaftsordnung. Berlin
Weddigen W (1951/1952) Die Aufgaben der Sozialpolitik. Soziale Welt 3:156–163
Weddigen W (1955) Sozialpolitik contra Sozialwissenschaft – Eine Antikritik. Jahrbücher für Nationalökonomie und Statistik 167:70–79
Weddigen W (1956) Sozialpolitik IV: Träger und Methoden. Handwörterbuch der Sozialwissenschaften 9:554–563
Weddigen W (1957) Grundzüge der Sozialpolitik und Wohlfahrtspflege. Stuttgart
Weddigen W (1967) Erdrutsch in der Wissenschaft Sozialpolitik? Schmollers Jahrbuch für Wirtschafts- und Sozialwissenschaften 87:417–440
Wehler H-U (2000) Soziologie und Geschichte als Nachbarwissenschaften. In: Funken C (ed) Soziologischer Eigensinn – Zur "Disziplinierung" der Sozialwissenschaften. Opladen, pp 113–121
Weinzen HW (1982) Gewerkschaften und Sozialismus. Naphtalis Wirtschaftsdemokratie und Agartz' Wirtschaftsneuordnung. Frankfurt am Main
Weippert G (1939) Vom Werturteilsstreit zur politischen Theorie. Weltwirtschaftliches Archiv 49:1–100
Weisser G (1956a) Sozialpolitik. In: Brandt L (ed) Aufgaben deutscher Forschung, 2nd edn, vol 1. Köln Opladen, pp 410–426
Weisser G (1956b) Soziale Sicherheit. Handwörterbuch der Sozialwissenschaften 9:396–412
Weisser G (1959) Distribution (II) Politik. Handwörterbuch der Sozialwissenschaften, vol 2:635–654
Weisser G (1969) Sozialpolitik. In: Bernsdorf W (ed) Wörterbuch der Soziologie, 2nd edn. Stuttgart, pp 1039–1048
Weisser G (1978) Beiträge zur Gesellschaftspolitik. Göttingen
Welsch W (1995) Vernunft: die zeitgenössische Vernunftkritik und das Konzept transversaler Vernunft. Frankfurt am Main
Wenk M (1908) Die Geschichte und Ziele der deutschen Sozialpolitik. Leipzig
Wermert G (1885) Neuere socialpolitische Anschauungen im Katholicismus innerhalb Deutschlands. Jena
Widmaier HP (1970) Aspekte einer aktiven Sozialpolitik. Zur politischen Ökonomie der Sozialinvestitionen. In: Sanmann H (ed) Zur Problematik der Sozialinvesitionen. Berlin, pp 9–44
Widmaier HP (1976) Sozialpolitik im Wohlfahrtsstaat. Zur Theorie politischer Güter. Reinbek bei Hamburg
Widmaier HP (ed) (1978) Zur Neuen Sozialen Frage. Berlin

Wilbrandts R (1926) Zur systematischen Begründung der Sozialpolitik. Kölner Sozialpolitische Vierteljahresschrift 5:5–34
Winkler G (1989) Geschichte der Sozialpolitik der DDR 1945–1985. Berlin (Ost)
Winkler HA (ed) (1974) Organisierter Kapitalismus. Voraussetzungen und Anfänge. Göttingen
Winkler HA (1984) Von der Revolution zur Stabilisierung. Arbeiter und Arbeiterbewegung in der Weimarer Republik 1918 bis 1924. Berlin Bonn
Winkler HA (1985) Der Schein der Normalität. Arbeiter und Arbeiterbewegung in der Weimarer Republik 1924–1930. Berlin Bonn
Winkler HA (1987) Der Weg in die Katastrophe. Arbeiter und Arbeiterbewegung in der Weimarer Republik 1930–1933. Berlin Bonn
Winschuh J (1929) Grenzen der Sozialpolitik. Leipzig
Winterstein H (1969) Sozialpolitik mit anderen Vorzeichen. Berlin
Wirtschafts- und Sozialwissenschaftliches Institut des Deutschen Gewerkschaftsbundes (WSI) (ed) (1977) Sozialpolitik und Selbstverwaltung – Zur Demokratisierung des Sozialstaats. Köln
Wirtschafts- und Sozialwissenschaftliches Institut des Deutschen Gewerkschaftsbundes (WSI) (ed) (1978) Präventive Sozialpolitik. WSI-Mitteilungen 31. Issue no. 10
Wittrock G (1939) Die Kathedersozialisten bis zur Eisenacher Versammlung 1872. Berlin
Wolf J (1892) Sozialismus und kapitalistische Gesellschaftsordnung. Kritische Würdigung beider als Grundlegung einer Sozialpolitik. Stuttgart
Wolf J (1899) Der Kathedersocialismus und die sociale Frage. Berlin
Wunderlich F (1924) Nelsons Sozialpolitik. Soziale Praxis 33:1001–1004, 1037–1040, 1052–1054
Wyott F (1927) Die theoretischen Grundlagen der Sozialpolitik, eine ideengeschichtliche Untersuchung. Dissertation. Gießen
Zacher H (1977) Was können wir über das Sozialstaatsprinzip wissen? In: Stödter R et al (eds) Hamburg, Deutschland, Europa. Festschrift für Hans Peter Ipsen. Tübingen, pp 207–267
Zacher HF (1968a) Soziale Gleichheit. Zur Rechtsprechung des Bundesverfassungsgerichts zu Gleichheitssatz und Sozialstaatsprinzip. Archiv des öffentlichen Rechts 93:341–383
Zacher HF (1968b) Sozialpolitik und Menschenrechte in der Bundesrepublik Deutschland. München
Zacher HF (1980) Sozialpolitik und Verfassung im ersten Jahrzehnt der Bundesrepublik Deutschland. Berlin
Zacher HF (1984) Der gebeutelte Sozialstaat in der wirtschaftlichen Krise. Sozialer Fortschritt 33:1–12
Zacher HF (1987) Das soziale Staatsziel. In: Isensee J, Kirchhof P (eds) Handbuch des Staatsrechts der Bundesrepublik Deutschland, vol 1. Heidelberg, pp 1085–1111. See also Zacher HF (1993) Abhandlungen zum Sozialrecht. Heidelberg, pp 3–72
Zacher HF (ed) (1991) Alterssicherung im Rechtsvergleich. Baden-Baden
Zacher HF (2000) Der Sozialstaat an der Wende zum 21. Jahrhundert. Vierteljahresschrift für Sozialrecht 3(2000):185–206
Zacher HF (2001) Grundlagen der Sozialpolitik in der Bundesrepublik Deutschland. In: Bundesministerium für Arbeit und Sozialordnung Bundesarchiv (eds) Geschichte der Sozialpolitik in Deutschland seit 1945. Vol. 1: Grundlagen der Sozialpolitik. Baden-Baden, pp 333–684. (See footnote on p. 125).
Zacher HF (2013) Social policy in the federal republic of Germany – the constitution of the Social. In: Leisering L (ed) German social policy, vol 3. Berlin Heidelberg
Zapf W (1972) Zur Messung der Lebensqualität. Zeitschrift für Soziologie 2:353–376
Zapf W (1973) Gesellschaftliche Dauerbeobachtung und aktive Politik. Allgemeines Statistisches Archiv 57:143–164
Zapf W (ed) (1977) Lebensbedingungen in der Bundesrepublik Deutschland. Sozialer Wandel und Wohlfahrtsentwicklung. Frankfurt am Main New York

Zapf W (1981) Wohlfahrtsstaat und Wohlfahrtsproduktion. In: Albertin L, Link W (eds) Politische Parteien auf dem Weg zur parlamentarischen Demokratie in Deutschland. Düsseldorf, pp 379–400

Zerche J (1993) Gedanken zu einer Theorie der Sozialpolitik. In: Iwersen A, Tuchfeldt E (eds) Sozialpolitik vor neuen Aufgaben. Horst Sanmann zum 65. Geburtstag. Bern, pp 43–62

Zerche J, Gründger F (1996) Sozialpolitik. Eine Einführung in die ökonomische Theorie der Sozialpolitik, 2nd edn. Düsseldorf

Zöllner W (1977) Arbeitsrecht. München

Index of Persons

This index includes the names of those persons who, in the opinion of the author, have contributed substantially to events or discussions relating to social policy or the welfare state. Biographical data were gathered mainly through the internet but also by personal communication. - The term 'social scientist' refers to professors with a broad expertise ranging from law to political science to political economy and/or sociology; their chairs were often named "Staatswissenschaften" (literally: sciences of the state; the translation "Political Science" would be misleading). The term "social policy" is mentioned only if it is included in the name of the chair held by the respective scholar.

A

Achinger, Hans (1899–1981), professor: social policy and social work 92, 99, 102–103, 108–109, 112, 114

Alber, Jens (1947), professor: sociology 116, 118

Albrecht, Gerhard (1889–1971), professor: political economy 76–77, 82, 84–86, 100, 104, 110

Amonn, Alfred (1883–1962), professor: political economy 62–63, 83, 107

Auerbach, Walter (1905–1975), politician, state secretary of the Federal Ministry of Labour and Social Order (1969–1972) 103

B

Badura, Bernhard (1943), professor: sociology, public health 113–114

Bentham, Jeremy (1778–1831), English philosopher 23, 69, 123

Bernstein, Eduard (1850–1932), English politician, Marxist philosopher 70

Beveridge, William H. (1879–1963), English politician, Director of the London School of Economics and Political Science (1919–1937) 103, 108

Bismarck, Otto Fürst von (1815–1898), Chancellor of the German Reich (1871–1890) 23–24, 35, 44–47, 50, 56–59, 62, 124

Blanke, Bernhard (1941), professor: political science 71, 112

Blüm, Norbert (1935), politician, Federal Minister of Labour and Social Order (1982–1998) 104

Böckenförde, Ernst-Wolfgang (1930), professor: law, legal philosophy 33–34, 106

Böhle, Fritz (1945), sociologist 114

Brauer, Theodor (1880–1942), professor: social ethics 78, 82

Brauns, Heinrich (1868–1939), priest, politician, Minister of Labour of the Weimar Republic (1920–1928) 78

Brentano, Lujo (1844–1931), professor: political economy 48, 52

F.-X. Kaufmann, *Thinking About Social Policy*, German Social Policy 1,
DOI 10.1007/978-3-642-19501-3, © Springer-Verlag Berlin Heidelberg 2013

Briefs, Götz (1889–1974), professor: social science 68–69, 78, 82, 85–87, 102, 108

C

Churchill, Winston (1874–1965), Prime Minister UK (1940–1945) 124

D

Dahrendorf, Ralf (1929–2009), politician, professor: sociology 102, 111, 116

de Saint-Simon, Henri (1760–1825), philosopher, sociologist 28, 36

Dipper, Christoph (1943), professor: history 25, 29, 31, 39, 49, 51, 79

E

Engelhardt, Werner Wilhelm (1926), professor: social policy 104–105, 111

Eucken, Walter (1891–1950), professor: political economy 95–97

F

Flora, Peter (1944), professor: sociology 116, 118–119

Fröbel, C.F. Julius (1805–1897), activist, refugee 36–37

G

Geck, L. H. Adolph (1898–1987), professor: social ethics 26, 28, 30, 36, 39, 82, 84, 102, 104

Geißler, Heiner (1930), general secretary of the Christian Democratic Union (Christlich- Demokratische Union) (1977–1989) 115

Girvetz, Henry K. (1910–1974), professor: philosophy 124

Grimm, Dieter (1937), professor: law, 114, 117

Günther, Adolph (1881–1958), professor: social science 56, 82, 84

Gurvitch, George (1894–1965), professor: sociology 32, 72

H

Habermann, Gerd (1945), philosopher 119

Habermas, Jürgen (1929), professor: philosophy, sociology 116

Hartwich, Hans Hermann (1928), professor: political science 66, 79, 93, 112, 117

Hauser, Richard (1936), professor: political economy 119

Hegel, Georg Wilhelm Friedrich (1770–1831), professor: philosophy 23, 29–34, 37, 40–41, 72, 118, 123

Hegner, Friedhart (1944), management consultant 34, 114, 116, 120

Heimann, Eduard (1889–1967), professor: political economy 25, 65, 70, 82, 86–88

Heller, Hermann (1891–1933), professor: law 70, 75–77

Herder-Dorneich, Philipp (1928), professor: political economy 112, 119

Herkner, Heinrich (1863–1932), professor: social science 43, 63, 66–68, 83

Heyde, Ludwig (1888–1961), professor: social policy 82–84, 88–89, 104

Hilferding, Rudolf (1877–1941), politician, Marxist economist 74

Hitze, Franz (1851–1921), priest, politician, professor: social ethics 46, 59, 82–83

Hockerts, Hans-Günter (1944), professor: history 92–93, 98

Höffner, Joseph (1906–1987), Cardinal (1969–1987), professor: social ethics 79, 99, 102

K

Kaufmann, Franz-Xaver (1932), professor: sociology, social policy 23, 26, 44, 59, 71, 78, 92, 98–103, 106, 108–109, 112, 114–115, 118–121, 123–124

Kelsen, Hans (1881–1973), professor: law, legal philosophy 75, 77

Keynes, John Maynard (1883–1946), professor: political economy 95

Kleinhenz, Gerhard (1940), professor: political economy 81–82, 93, 97, 101

Kohli, Martin (1942), professor: sociology 116

Koselleck, Reinhart (1923–2006), professor: history 25, 119

Krüger, Jürgen (1940), professor: social policy 101, 103, 112, 115

Krupp, Hans-Jürgen, (1933), professor: political economy, politician 113

L

Lampert, Heinz (1930–2007), professor: political economy 24, 43, 92–93, 95–98, 104–105, 111, 119

Lange, Friedrich Albert (1828–1875), philosopher, activist 43

Lassalle, Ferdinand (1825–1864), politician, president of the General German Association of Workers (precursor of the Social-Democratic Party; 1863–1864) 43–44
Le Play, Frédéric (1806–1882), French administrator, social scientist 49
Leibfried, Stephan (1944), professor: political science, social policy 26, 112, 115, 120–121
Leisering, Lutz (1953), professor: social policy 115–116, 119–120, 122
Leo XIII. (1810–1903), Pope (1878–1903) 46
Lessenich, Stephan (1965), professor: sociology 117–118, 124
Liefmann-Keil, Elisabeth (1908–1975), professor: political economy 103, 108
Luhmann, Niklas (1929–1998), professor: sociology 27, 30–31, 113–114, 117–118

M

Mackenroth, Gerhard, (1903–1955), professor: statistics, political economy 95, 97, 109
Manow, Philip (1963), professor: political science 96, 99–100, 121
Marr, Heinz (1876–1914), journalist, professor: sociology 64, 81
Marshall, Thomas Humphrey (1893–1981), professor: sociology 95, 117
Marx, Karl (1818–1883), social scientist, activist 31–32, 34, 44, 59, 70, 87
Mayer, Karl Ulrich (1945), professor: sociology 120–121
Mayntz, Renate (1929), professor: sociology 113, 115
Messner, Johannes (1891–1984), Jesuit, professor: social ethics 78–79, 95
Meyer, Alexander (1832–1908), journalist, politician 41
Mill, John Stuart (1806–1874), philosopher, economist, politician 123
Montesquieu, Charles-Louis de Secondat, Baron de La Brède et de Montesquieu (1689–1755) French philosopher, politican 2, 29
Müller-Armack, Alfred (1901–1978), administrator, social scientist, state secretary of the Federal Ministry of the Economy (1958–1963) 94, 96–97, 102
Myrdal, Gunnar (1901–1978), professor: political economy, politician 95

N

Nahnsen, Ingeborg (1923–1996), professor: social policy 105
Naphtali, Fritz (1888–1961), journalist 70, 73–75
Napoleon III (1808–1873), French Emperor (1852–1870) 44
Nullmeier, Frank (1957), professor: political science 118–119

O

Offe, Claus (1940), professor: political science 116, 119–120
Oppenheim, Heinrich (1819–1880), journalist 48
Ostner, Ilona (1943), professor: sociology 117–119, 121

P

Pankoke, Eckart (1939–2007), professor: sociology 26, 30–31, 43, 103, 114
Parsons, Talcott (1902–1975), professor: sociology 30, 117–118
Pesch, Heinrich (1854–1926), Jesuit, professor: political economy 79
Pfaff, Martin (1939), professor: political economy, politician 108, 113
Pinker, Robert (1931), professor: sociology, social work 27, 123
Preller, Ludwig (1897–1974), politician 66, 100, 104, 110
Pribram, Karl E. (1877–1973), professor: political economy 40, 52, 55–56, 63, 80, 82, 84–86

R

Ricardo, David (1772–1823), broker, political economist, politician 30
Rieger, Elmar, (1959), professor: sociology 53, 118, 121
Riehl, Wilhelm Heinrich (1823–1897), journalist 40–42, 102
Ritter, Gerhard A. (1929), professor: history 25, 70–72, 74, 94, 118, 121
Roosevelt, Franklin D. (1882–1945), 32nd President of the USA (1933–1945) 124
Röpke, Wilhelm (1899–1966), professor: political economy 96–97

Rousseau, Jean Jacques (1712–1778), philosopher 28
Rüstow, Alexander (1885–1963), professor: social science 97

S
Sachße, Christoph (1944), professor: social work 80, 84, 89, 91–92
Sanmann, Horst (1927–2008), social policy 104, 111–112
Say, Jean Paptiste (1767–1832), French political economist 30
Schäffle, Albert (1831–1903), professor: social science 49, 83
Scharpf, Fritz W. (1935), professor: political science 113, 115–117, 121
Schmähl, Winfried (1942), professor: political economy 121
Schmid, Josef (1956), professor: political science 118
Schmidt, Manfred G. (1948), professor: political science 24, 93, 117–118, 122
Schmoller, Gustav (1838–1917; since 1908: von Schmoller), professor: political economy 42–44, 48–50, 53, 59, 64
Schultze-Delitzsch, Hermann (1808–1883), social reformer, politician 43–44
Schulz-Nieswandt, Frank (1958), professor: social policy 97, 101, 110
Schumpeter, Joseph A. (1883–1950), professor: political economy 81, 108
Seeleib-Kaiser, Martin (1964), professor: political science 120
Sinzheimer, Hugo (1875–1945), professor: law, refugee 70–75, 77, 81, 87–88, 95
Smith, Adam (1723–1790), Scottish philosopher and a pioneer of political economy 30
Sombart, Werner (1863–1941), professor: social science 50, 55, 61–62, 82, 84
Spann, Otmar (1878–1950), professor: social science 80, 82–83
Spieker, Manfred (1943), professor: social ethics 117, 119
Stolleis, Michael (1941), professor: public law and legal history 24, 65–66, 89, 103, 123

T
Tennstedt, Florian (1943), professor: social policy 26, 43–47, 65, 80, 84, 89, 91–93, 112, 115
Thiemeyer, Theo (1929–1991), professor: political economy 97, 110–112
Tönnies, Ferdinand (1855–1936), professor: social science 64, 66, 82, 86

U
Utz, Artur Fridolin (1908–2001), dominican, professor: social ethics 99

V
van der Borght, Richard (1861–1926), administrator 60–63
Vobruba, Georg (1948), professor: sociology 85, 119
von Bortkiewicz, Ladislaus (1868–1931), professor: statistics 54, 62–63, 82, 111
von Buß, Franz-Josef, (1803–1878), jurist, politician 29
von Ferber, Christian (1926), professor: sociology, health science 110, 112, 114
von Hertling, Georg (1843–1919), Chancellor of the German Empire (1917–1918), philosopher 58–59
von Ketteler, Wilhelm Emmanuel (1811–1877), Bishop of Mainz (1850–1877), politician 43, 46
von Lavergne-Peguilhen, Moritz (1801–1870), landed proprietor, social scientist 38–39
von Mayr, Georg (1841–1925), statistician 80, 100
von Mohl, Robert (1837–1875), professor: law, political science 32, 39, 52
von Nell-Breuning, Oswald (1890–1991), Jesuit, professor: social ethics 75, 99, 102, 109
von Philippovich, Eugen (1858–1917), professor: political economy 25, 32, 64, 102
von Scheel, Hans (1839–1901), professor: political economy 49
von Stein, Lorenz (1815–1890), professor: social science 31–36, 40–42, 44, 52, 54, 63, 73, 82, 87, 102, 123–124

von Treitschke, Heinrich (1834–1896), professor: history, politican 41–42, 49
von Westphalen, Ferdinand A. (1899–1989), professor: political economy 82–83
von Wiese, Leopold (1876–1969), professor: sociology 46, 63, 81–84, 107
von Zwiedineck-Südenhorst, Otto (1871–1957), professor: social science 63, 68, 81–86

W
Wagner, Adolph (1835–1917), professor: political economy, politican 47–49, 57–59, 62–63, 66, 108, 124
Weber, Max (1864–1920), professor: social science 50, 53–54, 61–62, 73, 81, 101
Weddigen, Walter (1895–1978), professor: political economy 81–83, 86, 94, 104, 106, 110
Weisser, Gerhard (1898–1989), administrator, professor: social policy 101–102, 104–108, 110, 111
Widmaier, Hans Peter (1934), professor: political economy 113, 115, 118
Wilhelm I (1797–1888), German Emperor (1871–1888) 44
Wilhelm II (1859–1941), last German Emperor (1888–1918) 54, 57, 63
Windthorst, Ludwig (1812–1891), politician 45
Wolf, Julius (1862–1935), professor: political economy 53

Z
Zacher, Hans F. (1928), professor: law 32, 55, 60, 93–94 104, 108, 117–119
Zapf, Wolfgang (1937), professor: sociology 113–114, 120

Subject Index

A

Agrarian context 26, 38
Association for Social Policy/*Verein für Socialpolitik* 23, 44, 47–49, 51–55, 66, 68, 100, 112
Association for Social-political Reform/*Verein für sozialpolitische Reform* 38
Association for Social Progress/*Gesellschaft für sozialen Fortschritt* 100
Association for Social Reform/*Gesellschaft für soziale Reform* 51, 64, 85, 100

C

Catholicism 46, 58–59, 78–80, 99–100
Christian Social 26, 78–80, 99–100
Civil rights 28
Class conflict/struggle 33, 34, 59, 82, 95, 107
Codetermination *see* Participation of workers in the economy
Collective bargaining 64–65, 72, 79, 98, 106
Comparative welfare state research 118
Compromise of classes 34, 64, 70, 77
Conceptual history 24–26, 41
Conservatism 25–26, 39
Corporatism 40, 64–65, 72, 79
Crisis of social policy/welfare state 65–69, 119–123
Critics of social policy/welfare state 64, 85, 114, 115, 119

E

Economics 32, 51–52, 54, 80, 82, 101, 112,
Enlightenment 27, 40, 87, 125

F

France 27, 33, 38, 52, 123
Free Association of Catholic Social Politicians/*Freie Vereinigung katholischer Sozialpolitiker* 45
Functional differentiation of society 29–32, 41, 115, 118

G

General Association of German Workers/*Allgemeiner Deutscher Arbeiterverein see* Trade Unions
Globalization 120–121
Great Britain 23, 27, 33, 52, 82, 123–124

H

Human Rights 117, 124–125

I

Inclusion 84, 117
Individual welfare 109–110, 122, 123
Intervention by the state 44, 62, 97, 111–112

K

Kathedersozialisten/Socialists of the Chair 50, 52, 67
Keynesianism 95, 113, 116

L

Labor law 71–72, 108
Liberalism 25–26, 32, 39, 43–44, 59, 67
  Ordoliberalism 95–98
Life circumstances/*Lebenslage* 110–111, 114, 120, 122

F.-X. Kaufmann, *Thinking About Social Policy*, German Social Policy 1,
DOI 10.1007/978-3-642-19501-3, © Springer-Verlag Berlin Heidelberg 2013

M
Marxism/Marxist 70, 88, 107, 115, 119
Middle-Class society 94, 109
Monopolization of economy 75

N
Nazism understanding of social policy 84, 89–92
Normative/ethical orientation in politics 44, 52, 55, 82, 93–100, 121

P
Participation of workers in the economy/Codetermination 71–72, 74–75, 79
Pauperism 27, 33
Person-functional versus system-functional aspects 110, 122
Poverty 43, 115, 123
Politik, different meanings 56
Political rights 28–29, 42
Political science/*Staatswissenschaft* 32, 42, 51, 111–112, 114
Protestantism 46, 80, 96, 99
Provider of services 106–107, 109
Prussia 24, 37, 60–61

Q
Quality of life 113

R
Reformism 25–26, 79
Revisionism 70
Revolution 26, 32

S
Scandinavia 24, 123–124
Science of Society/*Gesellschaftswissenschaft* 28–32, 38, 41
Scientific advice 105, 111
Self-help 39, 43–44, 47–48, 114
Secularization 27
Social administration 34–35
Social Democracy, social-democratic 26, 55, 64, 69–78, 86, 99
Social, economic and cultural rights 59, 118
Social idea 77, 86–87, 122
Social inequality 31, 33, 111,120
Social justice 58, 98, 111, 122
Social law 60, 71, 108, 113,
Social Market Economy/*Soziale Marktwirtschaft* 75, 93–98
Social/workers movement 26, 32, 34, 37–39, 43, 45 49, 53, 63–65, 69–70, 87, 107, 125
Social Planning 113–114
Social Policy *see Sozialpolitik*
Social problems 24, 27, 80
Social question 24, 26, 32–33, 123
Social reform 26, 32–34, 39, 42, 45, 47, 49, 51, 88, 98, 101
  Versus political reform 29, 36–37, 60–61
  Versus revolution 39
Social science, *see also* Science of society 26, 82, 100
Social security 98, 103, 108, 111
Social state/*Sozialstaat* 26, 35–36, 66, 75–77, 93–95, 115–118, 124
Social, Term 26–29
  The social 29–32, 97–98
  Social versus political 37, 40
Socialism 25–26, 32, 63, 69–70, 75
Socialist 27, 35, 37, 50
Sociology 25, 27, 41, 51, 54, 73, 86, 112, 114
Solidarism/Solidarity 59, 78–79, 121
Soviet Union 69
Sozialpolitik/Social Policy or Social Politics
  Term 24, 26, 35–42, 46–47, 50, 81, 92, 101–104
  Active social policy 113–115
  As social science 25, 39, 41, 80–86, 100–113
  As mediation between state and civil society 41, 73, 115, 122
  Methodological problems 53–54, 68, 101, 106
  As production policy 62, 68,106–107
  As distributional policy 57–58, 68, 98
  As influence on class conflicts 58, 62–63, 82–83, 106
  As policy for economic order 61–62, 96,
  As integration of society 83–84, 88, 106, 121
  As transformation of capitalism 86–88,
  As umbrella term 104
  Economic value 85
  On the level of community 101

On the level of enterprise 103
Preventive Social Policy 103
State, theory of 33–35, 75–77, 112, 115–117, 123–124
State and (civil) Society 28, 33, 40–41, 52, 106–107, 114–115, 123
State and economy 71–72, 96, 117, 119, 125
State-Socialism/*Staatssozialismus* 40, 47, 59–60
State under the rule of law/*Rechtsstaat* 66, 77, 117
Stinnes-Legien Agreement 64, 70
Switzerland 23

T
Three-generations-contract 109
Trade Unions 74, 99

U
Unanticipated consequences 64

V
Value debate 53–54, 62–63, 105
Verein für Socialpolitik see Association for Social Policy

W
Weimar Constitution 64, 66, 74–75
Welfare production 120
Welfare state/*Wohlfahrtsstaat* 66, 92, 103, 113, 115–118, 124
Welfare state compromise 70, 71
Workers question/*Arbeiterfrage* 33, 42–43, 80, 103, 107–108, 123

The manufacturer's authorised representative in the EU is Springer
Nature Customer Service Centre GmbH, Europaplatz 3, 69115 Heidelberg,
Germany. If you have any concerns regarding our products, please
contact ProductSafety@springernature.com

Printed and bound by CPI Group (UK) Ltd, Croydon, CR0 4YY
01/10/2026
02225982-0013